## The Book and the Author

IN AN AGE of big bombs on a small planet, this book offers an American way to peace. Professor Etzioni analyses why both the Truman containment and the Eisenhower massive retaliation strategies were discarded, and outlines the probable consequences of the new Kennedy line. He discusses the sources of the cold war, the arms race, and the global clash of East and West, to assess in a hard-headed way various strategies now advocated. Unilateral and multilateral disarmament, the "balance of terror," Herman Kahn's deterrence policy, and the Pentagon's arms control are all critically reviewed.

Drawing on his work as a political sociologist and on his experience in politics, Professor Etzioni offers a new way to peace that has already won many followers: Gradualism, an approach to counter the cold-war hysteria, is combined with an effectively safeguarded arms reduction system, a new policy to accelerate the modernization of underdeveloped countries, and with proposals for the formation of a global community and a New United Nations. The Gradualist way to peace may be hard, but the author points out that there are no easy ones.

Amitai Etzioni, thirty-three, is an associate professor of sociology at Columbia University and a research associate of the Institute of War and Peace Studies. He is the author of three books and has published widely in scholarly journals here and abroad.

# AMITAI ETZIONI

# THE
# WAY

# HARD
# TO PEACE

## A New Strategy

**COLLIER BOOKS**
NEW YORK, N.Y.

A Collier Books Original

First Edition 1962

Collier Books is a division of The Crowell-Collier
Publishing Company

Library of Congress Catalog Card Number: 62–12073

Hecho en los E.E.U.U.
Printed in the United States of America

# Acknowledgment

I AM INDEBTED to Daniel Bell, Leonard D. Cain, Jr., Seymour M. Lipset, Robert Pickus, David Riesman, Arthur L. Stinchbome, and Immanuel Wallerstein for valuable comments on an earlier version of this manuscript. Students, too numerous to be listed, argued with me about practically every point I made in this book; I learned much from these discussions. In particular I benefited from meetings of the Committee of Correspondence at Columbia University and at Berkeley. The names of David E. Armor, Murray Baumgarten, Joan Emerson, Madeleine Kertesz, Ruth Leeds, John Meyer, Ron Milavsky, Sancy Michels, Philip Springer, Martin Wenglinsky, and Barbara Wolff should, however, not go unmentioned. I am particularly grateful for the assistance of Nancy Edelman.

It is hardly necessary in a book of this kind to mention that none of my colleagues or students shares, even in the most indirect way, the responsibility for the positions taken.

# FOR ETHAN, FOR YOUR FOURTH BIRTHDAY

I have walked and prayed for this young child an hour
And heard the sea-wind scream upon the tower,
And under the arches of the bridge, and scream
In the elms above the flooded stream;
Imagining in excited reverie
That the future years had come,
Dancing to a frenzied drum,
Out of the murderous innocence of the sea.

—From W. B. YEATS, *A Prayer for My Daughter*

# Table of Contents

# A Thermonuclear Chance

ON SEPTEMBER 21, 1956, test pilot Thomas Attridge was flying a single-seat jet over the Atlantic Ocean near Long Island. He test-fired his guns; a few minutes later he crashed without warning into some woods about three miles from where he had fired. His jet was hit by three of his own bullets. Flying at a speed faster than that of his shells, although following a different course, test pilot Attridge had entered the bullets' trajectory and shot down his plane and himself. Often it seems that we are set on following his course: clinging to arms that are supposed to give us protection, we ourselves become their target. He who fires the thermonuclear guns might well be hit by their fire, destroying both the ship and those on board. And we are all on board.

Most people, most of the time, wish for peace. But human history can be recounted as a series of interludes between wars. There is no simple remedy for healing such a vast gap between man's sincere desire for peace and his historical experience of frequent war. There is no easy way to peace.

"But the bombs will protect us," say the complacent ones. "There will be no war." A thermonuclear war, they say, would bring the annihilation of us all; therefore nobody will drop these bombs. They feel as safe as did Attridge, placing his trust in guns, as safe as felt their forefathers who said that the cannon, and the machine gun, and the bomber were so deadly that they made war impossible. These weapons only increased the number of casualties in each successive war. The same holds for the new weapons. The number of Americans who were killed or died in World War I was 126,000; in World War II, it was 397,000; estimates of those to die in World War III range between 10 million and 160 million Americans alone.

Every generation believed its war to be just, defending values that could not otherwise be protected, and that its war would be the last. Once the Kaiser, or Hitler, was defeated, peace would reign forever; but there was always another war. World War III, or Nuclear War I, is no different. Bombs might devastate the Soviet Union, or cripple the United States, or both, but they will not end wars. Although World War III might leave more surviving than dead, unless we stop the historical trend toward ever-increasing death and destruction, all will perish in World War IV or V, or whatever the numeral. We either will be gradually blotted out by an atmosphere accumulating deadly radioactive fall-out or come to an abrupt end with the perfection and use of superbombs.

But the large growth in the magnitude of war and the altogether new peril of universal death (if not in the next war, possibly in our lifetime), is the basis of not only danger but also some hope. Throughout the world, ever-increasing numbers of people sense our common fate in the age of the big bombs on a small planet. With new urgency they seek a way to lasting peace. In their desperation some turn to quacks who offer a cure-all that only increases desperation and thus brings our doom closer. There is no magic peace pill.

Peace—if it is ever to be firmly established—will result from a combination of many forces, institutions, and individuals. When history offers us a chance—as it does in the next few years—and this chance is recognized and acted upon, then we have an opportunity to turn the thermonuclear threat into the beginning of the end of wars and to transform the nuclear demon into our obedient Friday. Should the historic opportunity be missed, this might be the beginning of the end.


What is to be done? Are we to hang ourselves on the horns of a dilemma? "Better *Red* than Dead" is the cry of the neo-pacifists; "Give me Liberty or Give me *Death*," chant the armed patriots. But a remedy for international violence can be and has been found: *Neither Red nor Dead* is the minimal requirement that an acceptable strategy has to satisfy.

Five alternative strategies for the West are now in the public domain. *Containment* was tried by Truman; *Massive Retaliation* was Eisenhower's declared policy. Both were given the test of time and were found wanting. The Kennedy administration is introducing a new strategy, adding conventional arms to nuclear arms to build up a *Multideterrence* force. Whatever its virtues, the current plan forces us to race along the edge of a chasm deep enough to swallow us all. On the other hand, *Unilateral Disarmament* substitutes the risk of Communist domination for a threat to survival. Between these two hazards, becoming Dead or Red, lies the *Gradualist* approach. A critical examination of these five strategies constitutes Part I of this book, closing with a presentation of Gradualism, the strategy I advocate.

A Western strategy is needed that will be based upon existing historical trends, forces and opportunities (rather than on an attempt to alter them) and that will be oriented toward a safer and a better world—two goals more intimately related than we frequently assume. Such a strategy cannot be limited to diplomatic maneuvers, military deployments, and formation of bloc alliances; it must treat all the basic elements which compose the international organism now infested with potential violence. It has to concern itself with *psychological-symbolic* forces that affect the public opinion of most nations, with the fate of *armed forces* and arms, and with interbloc *sociopolitical* conflicts. It has to cover more than West Berlin, Communist China, and nuclear tests; have solutions more encompassing than "strengthening the UN" and more feasible than putting the world leaders on the psychoanalytical couch.

The cold war hysteria and the arms race are frequently diagnosed as mere symptoms of a deeper sociopolitical illness—the interbloc power strife. Symptoms they may be, and treating them alone might well be no more than a palliative; but symptoms left uncontrolled might kill the patient, thus preventing the chance to effect a basic treatment and a cure of his real disease. The temperature of the "cold" war must, therefore, be reduced and the arms race checked, both to keep us alive and to give us an opportunity to tackle the deeper issues. Gradualism, the strategy advanced here, is made up of three approaches oriented to the three elements of the problem: a psychological strategy (whose presentation closes the first part of our book), an armament strategy (which concludes the second part), and a sociopolitical orientation (which is presented in the third).

13

Analyzing the cold war, we build on a position advanced by those who advocate unilateral initiative, a position which holds that the interbloc strife involves such a barrier of mutual accusations, incriminations, and counterincriminations, that a solution quite acceptable to both the West and the East might be left lying by the wayside, hidden by a blindfold of suspicion and paranoia. The first phase of Gradualism is, thus, *psychological,* aiming to calm jittery nerves and tone down the interbloc argument, so that the sides can again hear what they are saying to each other. This, however, does not require unilateral disarmament, as some insist; we need not strip ourselves naked to show the other party that we are willing to talk with him. The psychological phase of Gradualism outlines a strategy to restore the interbloc dialogue. An analysis of the historical development of the Communist bloc shows why it might succeed if it is applied now.

Part II of this book concerns itself with three "treatments" for the arms "symptoms." *Arms control,* advocated by the Pentagon and its civilian researchers, will at best reduce the temperature while leaving the disease to plague us; *multilateral disarmament* here and now, advocated by the Communists and recently by the West, hopes to eliminate both the source of trouble and its consequences, but for some "mysterious" reasons, to be explored, it is not carried out. *A new scheme of gradual arms reduction,* closely geared to treatment of the underlying sociopolitical conflict, might prove the feasible middle way between a symptom suppressing palliative and a false cure-all.

Part III deals with the global clash of two major ideological forces and two major global powers, in a world which proves to be small. Peace will not last unless these sources of international violence are uprooted, a test that will require solving some of man's most basic tragedies and removing some of his most pressing miseries. As demanding as this might be, there will not be a safe world unless there is also a better one. Economic development of backward countries, worldwide democratization, and voluntary federation of nations are among the major long-run treatment programs examined.

Chapter 1

## The End of Containment and Massive Retaliation

HISTORY is a graveyard of strategies, for man has not yet learned to master his fate. Strategies come and strategies go, but peace remains as elusive as ever. A brief visit to the strategy graveyard provides a valuable lesson, however: it teaches about attempted "solutions" that did not solve and about the reasons they floundered, and it warns the living of shadows still cast by the past, concealing what might be the much-searched-for way.

Containment was the first American foreign strategy formulated after World War II; a contribution of George F. Kennan and President Harry S. Truman, it never survived the Korean war. John Foster Dulles and President Dwight Eisenhower replaced it with their policy of Massive Retaliation, which did even less well though it reigned longer. It in turn was replaced by a strategy developed by the young Kennedy administration. But both earlier strategies still cast many shadows over our way and our life. The story of their rise and fall should hence be much heeded.

### Soviet Expansion—American Surprise

In the middle of 1945, when Britain, the Soviet Union, and the United States emerged successfully from their joint effort to defeat the Axis powers, the three victorious allies found themselves the world's only remaining superpowers. Although the West seemed unaware of it, the wartime alliance was soon to divide into two hostile camps.

By the end of World War II, the United States still did not accept—in fact, did not even recognize—its inevitable role as

15

a global power and as the leader of the West. It rapidly dismantled its military machinery, and by 1946 its army was reduced to only 400,000 men—less than one twentieth of its World War II strength. The country returned to a peacetime economy and converted its military installations to the production of consumer goods. At that time, the United States still regarded England as a major power, Soviet Russia as a friendly ally, and Joseph Stalin and other Russian leaders as "men of good will." The United Nations was viewed as part of a system of "collective security" in which international disputes would be settled peacefully. With the destruction of the Fascist threat to freedom, America was in a mood to breathe easy; for a short while no other dangers to the Western way of life were recognized.

It rapidly became clear, however, that the Communists were determined to realize their established and long-declared goal of spreading the socialist revolution throughout the world. At the close of World War II, Russia absorbed a number of countries, including Estonia, Latvia, and Lithuania. Other territories were annexed, including parts of Poland, Germany, and Rumania. In Hungary, Poland, Rumania, Bulgaria, and Albania, Communist governments were established through the efforts of local Communist parties backed by the Red Army, which had driven the Nazis out of these areas and was subsequently occupying them.

The United States soon saw that its former ally had become its major challenge and that Britain, as the third superpower, was no more than a weak sister. After a swift succession of crises generated by Communist pressures in Iran, Turkey, and Greece between June, 1945, and March, 1947, the United States concluded that the Communist expansion would cease only if checked by power. It also came to realize that Britain, extremely weakened economically and militarily by World War II, was not only incapable of holding the line, but was itself in dire need of assistance. By 1947 the United States was deeply involved in the new power struggle and had assumed the leadership of the West.

While England and, later, the United States were maintaining the West's position in Greece and the Middle East, it became evident that Western Europe was in urgent need

16

of help. The economies of the Western countries were near collapse, their societies in chaos, and their people demoralized. England had introduced a stringent austerity program, even going so far as to ration bread. On top of this, the severe winter of 1946-1947 virtually halted British transportation; fuel was in critically short supply, and by February, 1947, more than one half of Britain's factories had stopped production. In Germany, wartime devastation was aggravated by an influx of ten million refugees from German areas annexed by Poland after the war. Juvenile delinquency in Germany had increased 400 per cent over the prewar level. Hunger was widespread there as well as in France and Italy. In the Netherlands, 30 per cent of the prewar national wealth had been destroyed, sea-water floods had ruined much of the land, and a quarter of a million people had been killed or were dead of starvation. Conditions elsewhere in Western Europe were similarly dire.

In few situations could Communist ideology have had wider appeal, and the Communist parties in Western Europe made the most of the opportunity. In the first postwar elections, one third of the Italian voters and one fourth of the French electorate supported the Party. Communists held office in a number of postwar governments. In France, even the Vice President and the minister in charge of armaments were Communists; in Italy, the Minister of Justice was a Communist.

In 1947, responding to this emergency, the United States initiated the European Recovery Program, better known as the Marshall Plan. Under the plan, non-Communist European countries were given $12 billion between 1948 and 1952 for economic reconstruction. The Marshall Plan was highly successful, and within a decade these countries were vigorous economic competitors of the United States. In all countries but Italy, moreover, the Communists lost political support; they no longer held office in any Western European government. Following the success of the Marshall Plan, the well-known Point Four Program of technical assistance was instituted to help the development of economically backward countries.

Effective as these nonmilitary measures were, they proved

17

an insufficient means of checking Communist expansion. The United States had, from the outset, to augment its efforts with military means. The assumptions underlying this endeavor had their first test in a clash in Greece.

## Test Number 1: The Greek Civil War

In 1946 the Greek government was under attack by local Communist forces. Native Communist guerrillas were making more and more headway in their endeavor to gain control of the government. The Soviet Union sent no military forces to support the guerrillas, nor did the neighboring Communist countries, Bulgaria and Yugoslavia (the latter at that time still a full-fledged member of the Communist bloc). Bulgaria and Yugoslavia did, however, give the Greek Communists training bases, supply medical and financial aid, and probably provide some weapons. By 1947 it became likely that without external aid the Greek government would fall and the country would become another member of the Communist bloc. After a United Nations investigation showed that the guerrillas had obtained some outside assistance, the United States sent economic and military aid to the Greek government, enabling it to tip the scales and subdue the guerrilla forces.

At the time, almost all observers viewed the Greek civil war as a unique and isolated occurrence; correspondingly, the help given the Greek government seemed to be an emergency stopgap measure and not part of a general strategy. Actually, however, the conflict was typical of many international crises to follow, and the American response to it was the first expression of what was to become known as the doctrine of Containment.

Like later conflicts, the Greek civil war was an instance of pressure by the Communist movement on the border separating West and East. As in many of the subsequent conflicts, the war was initiated not from within the Communist bloc but by native Greek Communists; help from Communist countries was limited, indirect, and difficult to point out to world opinion. The Greek government under attack was, by any standards, corrupt and oligarchic; it was highly unpopular not only with workers, farmers, and intellectuals but also with business and professional people. Support of the threatened government had little appeal either for Western public opinion or for that of other countries. Moreover, United States intervention was far more direct and visible than whatever support the Russians gave. Finally, while the United States was successful in defeating the Communist forces in Greece, it made no attempt to damage the Bulgarian and Yugoslavian bases from which the Communists had been given supplies and to which they retreated at the end of the strife. Nor did the Greek government change its oligarchic ways. All these elements were to be repeated in later conflicts.

In Greece, then, the Communists gained nothing, while the United States developed a new approach to foreign policy. Under pressure of successive crises—smaller ones occurred in those years in Iran, Turkey, and Berlin—the United States formulated its first postwar strategy, reflecting these experiences.

## Strategy Number 1: Containment

A secret memorandum sent to the State Department in 1946 outlined the basic elements of the new policy. It was published the following year in the authoritative journal *Foreign Affairs,* over the signature of "Mr. X." Its author was George F. Kennan, Director of the State Department Policy Planning Unit. In a speech to Congress during the Greek crisis in March, 1947, President Truman adopted the basic elements of Kennan's Containment strategy, adding to it an ideological component and creating what later became known as the Truman Doctrine.

Like any solid exposition of strategy, the basic Containment policy included assumptions about the enemy and his program, an assessment of United States power, suggestions for a course of action, and specification of anticipated results.

A central revelation of the new strategy—which would hardly be considered news today—was that the Russians were a major global power and America's chief adversary. Kennan's analysis of Russia's world outlook pointed out that Russia viewed the West as fundamentally hostile and threatening and as an obstacle to be removed in one way or another in order to assure the spread of Communism. The Russians' strategy, Kennan said, was to probe in every direction, seeking weak spots and power vacuums where they could apply pressure as they had done in Eastern Europe and in China. Kennan emphasized, however, that Russian strategy was highly flexible. The Russians were convinced that the course of history was on their side, yet they had neither a specific timetable to follow nor any dogmatic prescriptions about the means to their ends. This made them quite willing to drop back on one flank or another or even to dispense with an entire policy, if it should prove expedient to do so. In this sense, Russia was far more rational and calculating an adversary than Nazi Germany had been. It was not willing, in its pursuit for still greater gains, to endanger what the Communist revolution had already achieved. Here, Kennan said, was where the Western chance lay.

The strategy of the United States was to be one of "long-term, patient, but firm and vigilant containment." With persistence, flexibility, and resourcefulness, the United States could stop every effort of the Russians to extend their power—wherever and whenever such efforts might take place. A vigorous pursuit of such a policy was expected to accomplish two ends. First, it would check the Communists' expansion and keep them from adding additional countries to their bloc; second, by continually frustrating their efforts, it would force the Communists to give up their course. Kennan pointed out that the Kremlin, like any other leadership, could not afford over the long run to pursue a strategy that yielded only frustration. If it continued to pursue such a course, it would be faced with internal dissatisfaction and conflict—even, possibly, with internal disintegration of the Soviet system. Such total frustration could generate an all-out attack by the Russians, since they would see no gradual way of obtaining their goals; but this possibility was remote. After all, Russia was greatly weakened from World War II and the United States was not; moreover, the United States had atomic bombs, while Russia, at the time, did not.

Truman added one central element to this political-military strategy—he gave it an ideological foundation. While Kennan was essentially concerned with the use of power to check power, Truman saw the same strategy as a defense of liberty. The Communists, he asserted, had taken over one country after another, subordinating the will of the majority to that of a minority. This was not only an inroad on the United States' world position, likely eventually to pose a direct danger to its security, but it was also an attack upon the fundamental values of the United States. Truman said: "I believe that it must be the policy of the United States to support free peoples who are resisting attempted subjugation by armed minorities or by outside pressures."

This change in orientation from a strategy of power-versus-power to a campaign for liberty created a dilemma from which American foreign policy has not yet escaped. It is one thing to clothe a power strategy in an ideological garb; it is quite another when one suddenly realizes that the suit is bigger than the wearer and that nonetheless the wearer has to be made to fill it! Some questions immediately arose: Did the Truman Doctrine imply that the United States would have to defend freedom in countries where it was not in its interest to become militarily involved? Was the United States obligated to defend those areas of the American sphere of influence where people were not free, where they were under a dictator, as in Spain, or under feudal overlords, as in the Middle East? The Truman "addition" to Containment led to its rigid application: every piece of land on this side of the line separating East from West becomes part of the American moral and military commitment. This amendment deprived the United States of much political and military flexibility. Thus, an amplification that was intended to strengthen Containment ended by being one of the causes of its demise.  Turner + Challender

No less fatal was the American policy regarding the *means* of Containment. In 1947 the Soviet Union had an army of four million, comprising 175 combat divisions, and was continuing to conscript about 800,000 men a year. The United States army in the same year numbered about 670,000 men, consisting chiefly of noncombat soldiers. At that time, the United States was relying almost entirely on its monopoly of atomic bombs, for—despite the Greek civil war and Communist efforts at expansion elsewhere—the United States continued to assume that the main danger to its security lay in the possibility of a large-scale Russian attack on the United States mainland. Such an attack, the United States felt, could be stopped before it was started by the threat that Russia itself could be attacked with atomic bombs. It took the Korean war, which was another incident on the pattern of the Greek civil war, to drive the

21

lesson home: The real danger was not a direct attack on the United States. It took the war in Indochina to point out a second lesson: the threat of atomic bombing was not an effective way to "contain" the Russians. But let us take these events up in turn.

### Test Number 2: Korea—The Battle Won, Containment Lost

For a while, the Containment strategy worked. Communist expansion was checked in Greece, Berlin, and the Middle East. Economic assistance to allied West European countries and the creation of NATO, an American-European military alliance, was credited with preventing Russian expansion in West Europe. Thus, in Europe, Containment appeared to be a success. The Russians were being blocked, and Western Europe was steadily gaining in strength and stability.

As Kennan had predicted, however, blocking the Communists on one front merely caused them to put pressure at another—the Far East. Here, Containment was to no avail. The Communists' first gain was a major one; in 1949 they completed the take-over of the huge China mainland. Although this coup actually took place after the Containment formula was well developed, it has often been pointed out that the conditions for successfully applying Containment in China had long since disappeared. The Communists had taken over a good part of the country even before the surrender of Japan in 1945. Because of the inept, corrupt, and dictatorial practices of the Chiang Kai-shek government, it lost the support of practically all elements in China, even that of businessmen and professionals. Although some people still argue that Containment could have been used in China to block the Communists, one thing is generally agreed: Containment's first real test came in Korea.

The Korean war can be seen as a second version, writ large, of the Greek civil war, although there were some important differences. North Korea and South Korea were two zones artificially created out of one country as the result of a postwar agreement between the United States and Russia. The boundary between the two republics was set arbitrarily at the 38th Parallel. South Korea proceeded to develop under the patronage of the United States, North Korea under that of Russia. In June, 1950, the North Korean army crossed the 38th Parallel into South Korea. The United States saw no military significance in the peninsula. However, true to the Truman Doctrine of defending "free" peoples everywhere and considering also the repercussions which a continued series of Communist advances would have on the uncommitted countries, especially in Asia, the United States decided to interfere on behalf of the South Korean government. The rest of the story is only too well known. The United States undertook a strenuous build-up of military forces and machinery. With the help of its allies under the auspices of the United Nations, the United States managed—after a long effort—to subdue the invading forces. In July, 1953, an armistice was signed that fixed the North Korean-South Korean border approximately where it had been before the fighting began. Thus, the Communists were contained; but among the war casualties was Containment.

Of all the military actions ever engaged in by the United States, the Korean war was easily the least popular. It convinced Americans that Containment had two major flaws: high price and low yield. The war cost $22 billion (resulting in higher taxes) and its toll was 157,500 American casualties. Moreover, the Communists might have been blocked, but their strength and determination were left unimpaired. It was possible that they would attack again at the same or at any other place, with the Americans once more sacrificing their sons and resources in an effort to block them—perhaps with a less fortunate outcome. After all, the American forces in Korea had been less than spectacularly effective; their limited victory had not come easily.

Before the Korean war ended, Containment's shortcomings were dramatized by the conflict between President Truman and General Douglas MacArthur, United Nations Supreme Commander in Korea. The argument centered on a strategic-political issue: should the West be content with pushing the North Korean forces back beyond the 38th Parallel, or should they be pursued further, so that all Korea might be unified, under Western influence? Temporary adherence to the second alternative—urged by MacArthur and resisted by Truman—led to the crossing of the 38th Parallel by United Nations forces in

October, 1950. This brought Communist Chinese "volunteers" into the front for the first time. As a consequence, MacArthur demanded the right to bomb China and possibly to use this opportunity to "liberate" the mainland.

MacArthur was expressing the viewpoint of a field general, impatient at having to fight the enemy with one hand while the hand he thought most powerful was tied behind his back. But he was also suggesting a rather far-reaching change in strategy. Truman realized that the Communists were adhering to an implicit "agreement" to keep the war limited. China's involvement was restricted to ground fighting; she did not attack United Nations sea or air forces. Nor did Russia enter into the conflict. Bombardment of China, Truman felt, might precipitate World War III by extending the conflict to China and then—particularly if the Americans were successful in China—bringing Russia into the war as well. The goal in Korea, Truman insisted, was Containment; this would be attained by pushing the Communists back to where they had started. Ultimately MacArthur brought his case to the public and the opposition party, by-passing the Administration, and he disregarded orders limiting the use of non-Korean forces. As a result, Truman relieved him of his duties.

Although Truman's policy generally prevailed over MacArthur's for the duration of the fighting, Containment emerged from Korea gravely wounded. Actually, many of MacArthur's recommendations were not too different from the new strategy to come. For just as the Greek war contributed to the development of the Containment strategy, the Korean war was the crisis out of which the subsequent military policy was born.

## Strategy Number 2: Massive Retaliation

MacArthur received a wildly enthusiastic hero's welcome on returning to the United States after his dismissal. Millions cheered him in each major city he visited, and Broadway greeted him with a ticker-tape parade even bigger than the one General Eisenhower had received when he returned at the end of World War II as the victorious commander of the invasion of Europe. President Truman, meanwhile, was being burned in effigy in towns throughout the United States. Obviously MacArthur's "tougher" line was much more popular than Truman's Containment strategy. The return of the Republican party to office in 1952 after twenty years was, at least partly, a reflection of the widespread public dissatisfaction over the high cost and low yield of the then-unfinished Korean war.

The 1953 inauguration of a Republican administration brought the appointment of John Foster Dulles as Secretary of State. It was Dulles, with the passive support of the President, who formulated the new American strategy. Its basic elements were worked out by John Foster Dulles and Admiral Arthur Radford (then chairman of the Joint Chiefs of Staff) in December, 1952, shortly before the new Administration took office. Eisenhower's approval of the new policy was prompt. The strategy of Massive Retaliation was born out of explicit criticism of the Containment strategy. Containment, Dulles believed, was expensive, ineffective, and immoral.

It was expensive because it would not work unless the United States maintained a 20,000-mile rim encircling the Communists, which would mean keeping in continuous operation an enormous military apparatus spread over half the globe. The United States would have to spend huge sums to bolster its line everywhere, all at once, all the time, while the Communists' cost would be moderate. As attackers, the Communists would be able to focus their efforts on one place at a time—and a place of their own choosing. The cost to the West, Dulles argued, would be so gigantic that the Communists could destroy it without even declaring war, simply by driving it slowly into bankruptcy.

Moreover, Dulles insisted, the fantastic expenditure would purchase nothing. Containment offered no way out of the impasse, but implied simply an endless round of wars. The West could not expect victory over the Communists by way of Containment; the most it could hope for was that by dint of great effort it could maintain the status quo.

Most important of all, the policy was morally bankrupt. It allowed the aggressor to escape without risk, without punishment. If victorious, he would take over; if unsuccessful, he could safely retreat to prepare for the next round, secure in the knowledge that his own territory would suffer no damage. Furthermore, Containment was immoral because it offered no hope to countries already under Communist domination. It

25

made no provision for extending throughout the world the principle of freedom over which, Dulles said, the conflict was being waged.

Massive Retaliation, according to Dulles, would correct all the shortcomings of Containment. It was effective, economical, and morally superior. Its essence, in Dulles' words, was the decision to "depend primarily upon a great capacity to retaliate, instantly, by means and at places of our choosing." In plain English, this meant that if the Communists attacked again, they could expect nuclear bombardment in return. Just which aggressions would be met with bombing and which targets would be bombed would be up to the United States to decide.

The focal point of the Massive Retaliation strategy was *deterrence*. A potential aggressor, it was pointed out, would realize the enormous risk he was running, and, consequently, he would not even attempt an invasion. He would be stopped not by a row of trenches and machine guns but by a psychological barrier. Dulles said: "The only way to stop prospective aggressors is to convince them in advance that if they commit aggression, they will be subjected to retaliatory blows so costly that their aggression will not be a profitable operation." Thus Dulles seemed to feel that in all likelihood the United States would never actually be called upon to make good its threat of retaliation.

Massive Retaliation not only guaranteed that aggression would never be perpetrated, but it also offered great financial savings compared with Containment—"more bang for a buck," as its proponents promised. The new strategy allowed Eisenhower to cut the military budget to about $41 billion by 1955 from a Korean war peak in 1953 of $50 billion. Military forces other than the air force were reduced from 2,700,000 men in 1952 to 1,975,000 in 1955.

An additional advantage of the Massive Retaliation strategy was that if conflict ever erupted again, the United States would be able not merely to defend freedom where it was being threatened, but also to return it to those from whom it had been taken earlier. Once Communist power had been broken through nuclear bombing, countries under Communist rule could be liberated. The Communist bloc would thus not only be contained, it would be pushed back, punished, and possibly destroyed.

One did not have to be an expert to perceive the many and varied advantages of the new strategy. In fact, it had only one disadvantage: it did not work. Massive Retaliation received its major test two years after the new doctrine was formulated, one year after the Korean armistice was signed. Massive Retaliation was found less than inadequate.

## Test Number 3: Massive Retaliation Fails

In assessing the effect of the Indochinese war on American prestige and power, it is often said that the United States was challenged to "put up or shut up." It did "shut up," and thus its bluff was called. The United States turned out to be either unwilling or unable to retaliate, massively or otherwise. Consequently, it gained the reputation of talking loudly but carrying a small stick, and it lost much of its capacity to deter aggression psychologically.

The conflict in Indochina, like that in Greece and later in Laos, was initiated by indigenous Communist forces, which received only indirect and limited assistance from Communist bloc countries. As in the other two conflicts, external Communist aid was difficult to demonstrate to the uncommitted public opinion.

Unlike Greece and Korea, Indochina was under colonial rule; France had dominated the country since late in the nineteenth century. At the end of World War II, there emerged a strong nationalist movement, which was met by a stubborn French refusal to make any real concessions. An anti-French war broke out, and the anticolonial movement became closely identified with the Communists. The French had no popular support in the colony. Forced to fight a guerrilla war in strange jungle territory, the French military resistance deteriorated rapidly.

France's colonial problems in Indochina had originally aroused little sympathy in the United States. By 1953, however, Southeast Asia was far more important in United States foreign policy than it had been before the Communist victory in China and the outbreak of war in Korea. The United States became

27

clearly and firmly committed to supporting the French cause. The United States began by sending military and economic aid to bolster the sagging French campaign, and by 1954 it was paying 75 per cent of the war cost and was furnishing the French with both B-26 bombers and "air technicians." It pressured the French government into continuing the campaign when the latter wanted to negotiate before the French position became hopeless. Then, in 1954, came the crucial battle of Dien Bien Phu. The French stronghold there was besieged; it became clear that its loss would be fatal to the French position in Indochina and that, in fact, its loss was imminent. Three times the French government appealed to the Eisenhower administration to rescue it, but the American planes, which stood nearby armed with atomic bombs, did not take off, nor was a ground force landed. On May 7, 1954, Dien Bien Phu fell. The French were forced to sign a humiliating armistice, and the Communists gained the part of the country north of the 17th Parallel.

The fact that a war was started in Indochina meant that Massive Retaliation had failed to deter, the very thing it was supposed to do best—not to mention rolling back and punishing the aggressor or liberating the people in Communist countries. Instead, the Communists gained a strategic piece of Asia, which later served them as a springboard from which to penetrate Laos and South Vietnam; the United States gained a battered reputation.

Containment, unpopular as it was, had at least the one virtue that it did what it was designed to do. It was one thing to proclaim the limited goal of Containment and attain it with a large measure of success, even after a long and bitter struggle; it was quite another to declare a policy of Massive Retaliation and fire not a single shot, let alone a nuclear bomb, when the United States was challenged. In Indochina the United States seemed unwilling to make good either its threats or its promises. Heavy doubt was cast on its resolve to use nuclear bombs, and hence its capacity to deter became permanently weakened. The threat of retaliation no longer seemed very formidable to the Communists, and this lessening of fear not only encouraged further expansionism but created a danger that World War III might erupt simply from miscalculation. Doubt as to the United

States' real intentions might someday lead the Communists disastrously to underestimate them.

Why did Massive Retaliation fail?

Looking back, it seems clear that several factors were responsible. First of all, Massive Retaliation in Indochina involved a moral ambiguity. The doctrine did not take into account one well-demonstrated feature of Communist expansion—the use of native forces, at least during the first rounds of the campaign. No visible Russian or Chinese aid was given the Indochinese Communists. Superficially, at least, this was a conflict between local forces. Or, as many saw it, it was a struggle by one native faction against the French colonial regime, which was allied with a small, oligarchic, and corrupted group of natives. An American President, it seemed, could hardly justify to his own citizens or to the American allies—much less to neutral countries—the unleashing of a nuclear attack simply because local Communists and nationalists were doing well in Indochina.

Nor did nuclear bombing continue to look like a good military prospect. One can wipe out cities with nuclear bombs and one can even eliminate major military targets. But for tracking down guerrilla fighters in the jungle, the bombs are all but useless. Moreover, to succeed militarily in Indochina—particularly in order to achieve a "roll-back" of the enemy—it would be necessary to gain and hold territory, which would mean landing ground forces on the Asian mainland. This was exactly what Eisenhower and Dulles did not want to do, for it would seem a reversion to the much-maligned Korean strategy. Furthermore, this tactic was something the United States military machinery, with its reduced ground forces, would have been all but incapable of carrying out.

Not least important was the fact that what was supposed to have been *one-sided* deterrence when the doctrine was formulated in 1952 turned out two years later to be *two-way* deterrence. Russia exploded her first hydrogen bomb in 1953; by 1954 it possessed a considerable atomic stockpile. The United States' atomic stockpile was larger—estimates gave the United States a lead of four to one in this period—and the United States still had a head start in development of other nuclear weapons. But certainty in such matters was impossible.

29

Intelligence is never fully reliable and wars are very tricky to predict. Whatever the true situation was, the judgment that Massive Retaliation might lead to Counter—even if less Massive—Retaliation was a significant factor in keeping America's hands off the trigger. Thus, instead of deterring, Massive Retaliation itself was deterred.

Subsequent rounds gave the Russians still more evidence of the weak spots in United States policy and demonstrated the United States' inability to carry out its strategy. In 1956 came a major opportunity for liberation, one of the central goals of Massive Retaliation. Groups of students started a revolt in Budapest, Hungary, which spread so widely that Soviet tanks and infantry divisions had to be sent to subdue the rebellion. There were clear signs that Polish groups might join the uprising; East Germany, where three years before the Soviets had used tanks to suppress workers' strikes, was in a state of ferment. For the first time since 1945 there were real indications that the Soviet bloc, or at least its vital Eastern European wing, might be about to collapse. What did the United States do at this point? It promised the Russians that it would not interfere, would send no troops—much less bombs—to help the rebels. Publicly and privately it informed the rebels that they should expect no military help from the West. After asking and receiving Russian permission to do so, the United States sent food parcels and medical supplies through the Red Cross. Since 1956 there have been no important uprisings within the Communist bloc.

The reason for such Western self-restraint is evident: The Russians were under such great pressure that, in order to neutralize a forthcoming Western attack, they might have struck first with nuclear bombs at Western military bases and cities. The West was not willing to involve its mainland in a nuclear war for the sake of liberation. One can argue for or against such a decision, but one fact seems clear beyond all doubt: it is extremely unwise to declare liberation as one of your central goals, one for which you are willing to "retaliate massively" (in other words, to fight a nuclear war), unless you are willing to do just that. You lose the respect of your allies, of neutral nations, and, worst of all, of your adversary, without whose respect your deterrence power simply ceases to exist. Not least important, anti-Communist undergrounds within the Soviet bloc will conclude that they have been betrayed. It is not an exaggeration to state that, because of its unworkable policy, the United States played the role of accomplice in suppressing the "Freedom Fighters" in Hungary and other East European countries. While the Russians suppressed the uprising physically, the Americans crushed it spiritually, by frustrating the fighters' hopes and expectations.

It took several more years and a protracted and critical dilemma in Berlin (Communist pressure on the Western sector began anew in 1958) before American policy makers fully absorbed the fact that the Massive Retaliation doctrine had been gravely wounded in Indochina and was not going to recover. By 1960 the United States' relative military strength had changed markedly. The status of the United States had declined from one of atomic monopoly (until 1950) to nuclear superiority (through about 1956) to nuclear parity (until about 1959)—until in 1960 the country found itself on the wrong side of a "missile gap," which is a polite way of referring to the Russians' superior capacity to deliver nuclear bombs.

## Conclusion

In the period when the United States commanded great nuclear superiority and Massive Retaliation could actually have been carried out, it adhered to the Truman Doctrine of Containment. The American people rejected this policy as too costly in blood and resources, ineffective, and morally unsatisfactory; a new policy was formulated to meet these objections. Ironically, the United States embarked on this new policy just at the time when Russia's steadily growing nuclear power made Massive Retaliation unfeasible. The United States thus committed itself to a strategy which it could not and did not apply. Containment, in sum, had been workable but unacceptable. Massive Retaliation was thoroughly "acceptable" (there is little doubt that, had Eisenhower been eligible to run, he would have been re-elected by a wide margin in 1960, despite or because of his association with this strategy), but it had little military, political or moral validity. Not only did Massive Retaliation fail to liberate, punish, or roll back; it did not even contain. Thus the time was ripe for a new administration and a new strategy.[1]

# Chapter 2

## Multideterrence—Big Bombs, Small Bombs

WITH THE evident failure of Massive Retaliation and Containment, a new strategy, Multideterrence, began to command an increasing following in political and military circles. The Kennedy administration, in fact, immediately adopted many of the specific programs the new doctrine advocates, in particular the build-up of conventional arms and civil defense; thus this strategy is of more than historical interest. The new strategy has been advocated for years by various experts, especially members of RAND Corporation, a research center subsidized by the Air Force. The most thorough public presentation of this approach is given in *On Thermonuclear War* by Herman Kahn, until recently on the staff of RAND, consultant to various military agencies, sometimes referred to as the semi-official spokesman of the Pentagon. Many of the following comments are based on an analysis of Kahn's position.

### The Diagnosis: Nuclear Blackmail

The two most readily identifiable groups in the present public argument over nuclear war are those who think it will be prevented by both sides' perfecting nuclear bombs ("the balance of terror") and those who think it will be prevented by one side—ours—dropping its arms altogether (unilateralists). The two groups agree on one assumption—that nuclear war would mean the end of civilization. The advocates of Multideterrence deny this. The choice, they insist, need not be between mutual

[1] Of the many discussions of American foreign policy in the period covered in this chapter, there are two of special value: Robert E. Osgood, *Limited War: The Challenge to American Strategy* (Chicago: The University of Chicago Press, 1957), and John W. Spanier, *American Foreign Policy Since World War II* (New York: Praeger, 1960).

suicide and unilateral disarmament, for there is a whole range of other possibilities.

Two main arguments back up the multideterrence viewpoint: one is technical, the other is strategic. Technically, it is pointed out, Doomsday bombs simply do not exist. As yet, no single bomb can wipe out even the whole of a small country. Moreover, bombs must somehow be gotten to their targets. The bomb carriers, or "means of delivery," are only now being perfected; long-range missiles are still few in number and vulnerable to defensive countermeasures. In addition, RAND experts point out, a carefully planned civil defense system would greatly decrease potential death and destruction. We must note, however, that even according to this view it is only a matter of time—and of not much time—before Doomsday bombs can be built; they will almost certainly be available by 1968. Other experts claim that even *today* there are nuclear devices capable of devastating whole continents. According to one report, the West could produce a radioactive cloud over Japan—without the East's even being aware of it—which could be carried by wind to China, killing virtually the entire population of China. (In the process, the report states, most of the Japanese would also be killed.) So much for the technical viewpoint.

From a strategic viewpoint, RAND representatives say, only a completely irrational enemy would employ a Doomsday bomb, even if he had one. He who uses such bombs is quite likely thereby to do away with himself as well as with the object of his attack. The most effective strategy for the enemy, according to Kahn, is to *blackmail* the West by bombing a military installation, a small region, or a city—or, best of all, by merely threatening to bomb such targets. By dealing in blackmail the Communists can gain their objectives with little fear that they will be destroyed by an American nuclear attack, for they will confront the West with this dilemma: either the West meets their demands, or a devastating nuclear bombardment will be launched (in which event the fact that the United States can also bomb Russia will be of small comfort). Any reasonable American president can make only one decision: to make the concession in question. The blackmailer gets what he asks for—especially if he is clever, demanding "insignificant" concessions, one at a time, each ultimatum appearing to be the last one.

As long as the United States relies almost exclusively on Massive Retaliation and nuclear bombs, the RAND analysts argue, it will be faced with a long series of Indochinas, it will be blackmailed constantly and successfully, and it will have no alternative but to make one concession after another. Obviously no sensible American president will unleash a suicidal nuclear holocaust unless the concession demanded is huge. By keeping the stakes relatively low—a part of Southeast Asia, rights of access to East Berlin, two islands off China—the Communists will devour the West by inches.

Equally ominous, as Communist power grows relative to that of the United States, the line between issues regarded as minor and those regarded as major will move upward; in a few years issues that now seem crucial will come to seem less and less important. Berlin, Formosa—ultimately even Western Europe?—will no longer seem indispensable when the price of holding onto them grows perilously high. Eventually the Communists may scarcely need to use blackmail; more and more neutral nations, fearing that they can no longer depend on the United States to defend them, will ally themselves with the Soviet Union. Already there are widespread fears about the weakness of American resolve, even among the allies to which the United States is culturally, historically, economically, and militarily most committed—the Western Europeans. With mounting Communist pressure, Asians, Africans, and Latin Americans will feel even less assured than the Europeans about United States willingness to fight a nuclear war to save their skins.

## The Prognosis: A Multilevel Deterrent

The only way out of this dilemma, RAND experts say, is to develop more means of deterrence, so that the United States can deter not only an all-out attack on the American mainland but also nuclear blackmail, limited provocations by conventional troops, and the challenge of local Communist rebel forces. *The essence of multideterrence, therefore, is the possession of a force to counter every sort of threat the enemy might make.* If the West will be so armed, the enemy's threats will be neutralized and his blackmail will not pay off.

The list of the necessary types of deterrents, which follows, is a long one. But Kahn and his colleagues persuasively insist that every one of the items is of vital importance. The effectiveness of each is contingent on the presence of the others. If one is eliminated, it leaves a gap in the Western defenses which the enemy can readily exploit.

1. *Nuclear bombs*. Nuclear weapons have to be built and constantly improved, in order to prevent an enemy who also has such bombs from using them or threatening with them. Only the knowledge that homicide means suicide can stop an enemy from using these bombs to gain his objectives.

2. *Limited war capabilities*. This means that conventional arms must be greatly expanded, so that "minor" provocations can be countered without resort to nuclear bombardment on the one hand or continuous "accommodation" on the other.

3. *A net striking force*. The United States may have enough bombs to rain ten tons of TNT on every man, woman, and child in the Communist bloc, but it has no deterring power at all unless it can "deliver" them. What counts in the last analysis is not the size of the stockpile but the number of bombs that can actually be dropped on the target. This number is determined by the number of bombers and missiles the United States has at the outset of the conflict—minus those which would be destroyed in an enemy attack preceding the United States' strike; minus the bombers that will be shot down before they reach target and the missiles that will malfunction; minus, also, any vessels lost through unforeseeable effects of the postnuclear attack environment on United States "means of delivery." (For instance, communications jams may render much of the United States retaliatory force useless.)

In short, one can retaliate only with the force that will survive after an attack, and it is only this *net* force that the enemy takes into account when calculating his risks. The following measures must be taken to guarantee that a gross (preattack) deterrence force will have a net deterrence value.

(a) *A wide variety of weapons systems*. The power of any single weapon, whether Polaris submarines, Minuteman missiles, or giant B-70 nuclear jet bombers, could be neutralized by the enemy on Judgment Day. Thus the United States must have formidable weapons of many types if it is to have even relative assurance of having a retaliatory force when the crucial moment arrives.

(b) *Hardening*. Weapons must be made invulnerable ("hardened") so that they will not be damaged or destroyed under attack. Big bombers loaded with nuclear bombs and missiles of the longest range are of little use as deterrents if the enemy can put them out of commission with his first bombardment. Hence, Kahn says, the United States must—

—develop an adequate warning system, so that its planes can take to the air when an attack is imminent;

—keep part of its bomber fleet constantly airborne, so that it will not be an easy target on the ground;

—disperse the remainder of the bombers among many bases, thus making a coordinated enemy attack more difficult and increasing the bombers' chances of survival;

—shelter the missiles in concrete silos, so that they will not be damaged by blasts from indirect hits (there is no protection from a direct hit);

—station missiles on moving platforms (trucks or railroad cars), so that the enemy cannot predict where they will be;

—hide some of United States bombs and missiles under water in nuclear submarines;

—protect command positions from being hit, so that someone will always be able to trigger the counterblow; to achieve this, headquarters will have to be hidden in the depths of the earth, on the bottom of the ocean, or above the clouds.

RAND experts add still more items to this list, some of which are of a highly technical nature and many of which are classified. But the above selection should be enough to illustrate the general notion of hardening, and to indicate the monumental effort that maintaining a net force necessitates.

4. *Insurance against the unknown*. Even such extensive preparations as those recommended by RAND may turn out to be of no avail. Military history shows that planning and programing often prove quite futile once war actually comes. Hence, in addition to providing for all these needs, the United States must prepare for the unforeseen. This can be done by developing many types of weapons whose exact use is at the moment unknown but which may suddenly become crucial parts of some hurriedly improvised weapon system. Kahn sup-

plies several persuasive examples. The Hound Dog, for instance —a jet-propelled, air-to-ground missile—was an unplanned combination of an old X-10 frame, a guidance system originally developed for a fighter plane, and a J-52 jet engine constructed for some other purpose. Similarly, the two weapon systems on which much of the present American military system relies— the ICBM and the Polaris submarine—are also reported to have resulted from such improvisations.

Since no society, however, is rich enough to produce weapons *ad infinitum,* the proponents of Multideterrence advocate that for some of these weapons only the first two stages of the procurement process be undertaken. Research (determining how a weapon can be produced) is the first of these, followed by development (building one model to see what production problems are involved, making tests and working out snags, exploring potential uses, and preparing blueprints for mass production). The third and most costly stage, production, can be postponed until such time as need for the weapon becomes evident. Obviously only one in ten, or perhaps even one in a hundred, such samples would eventually be mass produced. But the cost of research and development is low compared to that of mass production; and thus, with a relatively small investment (only $1 billion, say, for the first B-70) one can purchase some "insurance" against the unexpected.

5. *Ability to strike first.* Under most conditions, America would not attack first. Yet if we knew that we were about to be attacked, or if a major commitment of the United States were challenged (for example, in case of an attack on Western Europe), the United States might decide to strike first. At any rate, it is noted, the American *ability* to strike first makes the Russians more cautious, forces them to undertake counter-preparations, and therefore is valuable even if never used. Strike-first readiness can be overdone; the United States may appear so threatening that the enemy may decide to launch a preventive attack. But some such preparation, Kahn suggests, is not too risky and is definitely worth making.

All these measures, awesome and ingenious as they are, are insufficient, RAND spokesmen emphasize. In themselves they will not deter an H-bomb attack, guarantee the United States' resistance to blackmail, or ensure the United States' survival as

37

a nation if it is bombed. Besides the various weapons systems, insurance for postattack reliability, hardening, insurance for the unknown, and strike-first capability, America must develop an extensive system of civil defense.

6. *Civil Defense.* Such measures as RAND experts deem necessary are to be developed in two stages, the first to be undertaken immediately, the second to be activated in two or three years, as expected increase in Russian military superiority brings about a worsening in the Western position. The first set of measures is priced at about $500 million, or about ten times the present civil defense budget. The second stage would be even more expensive. The first stage must include the following.

(a) *Radiation meters.* Fall-out has neither color nor smell; one may encounter it unwittingly and fail to survive. Thus the survivors of a nuclear attack must have radiation meters in order to distinguish between lethal and less contaminated areas. Moreover, the meters not only save lives but also serve an important psychological function, according to Kahn.

> The radiation from fallout has curious and frightening effects. Most people already know, or will know in a post-attack world, that if you get a fatal dose of radiation the sequence of events is about like this: first you become nauseated, then sick; you seem to recover; then in two or three weeks you really get sick and die.
>
> Now just imagine yourself in the postwar situation. Everybody will have been subjected to extremes of anxiety, unfamiliar environment, strange foods, minimum toilet facilities, inadequate shelters, and the like. Under these conditions some high percentage of the population is going to become nauseated, and nausea is very catching. If one man vomits, everybody vomits. It would not be surprising if almost everybody vomits. Almost everyone is likely to think he has received too much radiation. Morale may be so affected that many survivors may refuse to participate in constructive activities, but would content themselves with sitting down and waiting to die—some may even become violent and destructive.
>
> However, the situation would be quite different if radiation meters were distributed. Assume now that a man gets

> sick from a cause other than radiation. Not believing this, his morale begins to drop. You look at his meter and say, "You have received only ten roentgens, why are you vomiting? Pull yourself together and get to work."[1]

Thus the radiation meters provide a reality test for a strange new world.

(b) Utilization of *existing structures* for *fall-out protection*. A survey is recommended to examine and label existing structures all or parts of which can serve as fall-out shelters.

(c) Preliminary research and development of a variety of *shelter construction plans*, to be put into production during the second stage of the civil defense program.

(d) *Evacuation cadres*. As many as 200,000 people must be hired on a part-time basis for training in evacuation and survival techniques and in the organization of restoration work. These cadres, aided by a larger army of volunteers, would serve as the mainstay of the postwar society.

(e) *Research for the second phase* of the civil defense program, to determine what further preparations are required as a result of the presumably deteriorating world situation.

(f) Construction of *model shelters* in every town in the United States, for purposes of demonstration.

(g) *Educational and technical assistance* to guide and encourage local authorities, associations, and private citizens in spending money of their own civil defense efforts.

An increasing part of the first stage of this civil defense plan has been introduced by now in the United States. We are coming close to the time when, according to Kahn, we will have to introduce the second part of the program, which calls, among other things, for: massive, nationwide construction of shelters; "stockpiling" of food, fuel, and other essential reserves; dispersion of industries; moving underground important civilian installations, such as power plants; possibly even relocating parts of the urban population in the countryside. In addition, certain "active" civil defense measures are needed, including antimissile missiles and conventional air defense, such as fighter planes and antiaircraft guns—the latter because the enemy

---

[1] Herman Kahn, *On Thermonuclear War* (Princeton, Princeton University Press, 1960), pp. 85–86.

might use bombers against our cities, saving his missiles for military targets. Required also are a variety of warning systems.

Civil defense is necessary for two reasons, Kahn points out. First, because all the means of deterrence put together might fail to deter. Despite all of them (and, as we shall see, in part because of them) nuclear war may break out and a well-developed civil defense will reduce our losses. The recommendation of large expenditures for civil defense thus follows from the basic diagnosis of the Multideterrence strategy: nuclear war need not spell the end of a society, especially if the society is well prepared. While an unprepared United States might suffer eighty million casualties, a prepared one might suffer "only" forty millions.

Civil defense also serves a second purpose, it is suggested, as a central element of deterrence itself. The more poorly a population is protected, the more likely a nation is to succumb to blackmail and the less credible is its alleged retaliatory power. Thus, in Kahn's view, an inadequate civil defense may in itself invite an enemy provocation or attack.

While for the RAND strategists civil defense is one of the many essential components of deterrence, for their critics the civil defense item is perhaps the most controversial one on the list. They argue that developing a thorough system of civil defense will actually help trigger a nuclear war. This is, at first glance, a curious claim. How can a plan that merely promises civilian protection contribute to the beginning of a war? The nuclear deterrence or "balance of terror" position claims that each side holds the civilian population of the other as a hostage. It is as if each were threatening, "You had better not bomb my people, because if you do, I'll bomb yours!" Hence, developing civil defense implies that you are trying to sneak your hostages out of the enemy's custody. The enemy can make only one interpretation of this, especially if he himself has had no intention of attacking you: he assumes that you are preparing to attack him! Why, otherwise, would you be spending many millions of dollars on civil defense? Because in nuclear war the odds are almost overwhelmingly in favor of the attacker, the enemy under this circumstance might decide to attack you first and thus nuclear war might begin because one side suddenly increased its civil defense tenfold.

RAND experts, however, counter these arguments by suggesting that the Russians are, in point of fact, "cheating" on the tacit "agreement" to use the civilians as hostages—that actually their civil defense preparations are proceeding apace. Kahn reports that the Russian population has gone through two civil defense training programs and that the government has distributed printed civil defense instructions. He frankly admits that for the United States to develop a civil defense system under present conditions might increase the probability of nuclear war, but he is willing to take this risk in order to protect the United States' population and deterrence power.

The true extent of Russian civil defense preparation is a question of fact, not of conflicting strategies, but it should be noted that many reports assert that the Russians have done very little.[2] Even Kahn's assertion of Russian civil defense activity sounds extremely unimpressive. Printing instructions and conducting some courses (in which the number of participants is quite unclear) is not much different from the program the West followed before the 1961 build-up of shelters and "survival kits." It is hard to believe that the Russians could prepare shelters for millions of people, move industries to the countryside, exercise mass evacuations, and the like, without the West's having some knowledge of it.

[2] The *New York Times* reports from Moscow as late as July 8, 1961, under the heading "Soviet Lag Seen In Civil Defense; No Practice Alerts Held—Attack Risk Played Down": "With every report of practice alerts by Civil Defense authorities in the United States, Moscow's propaganda journalists write caustic, jeering charges that people in the United States are suffering from nuclear jitters, that 'the death merchants in the Pentagon are stirring up war hysteria.'

"Nothing of the sort happens here or anywhere else in the Soviet Union. It does not seem likely to happen in the foreseeable future. . . .

"There are no outward signs of even the most elementary preparations for civil defense against nuclear blasts or fall-out. Nowhere in Moscow or any other city visited by foreigners can one find signs pointing to shelters. In Moscow, Leningrad and Kiev, the deep subway systems are considered excellent shelters for large segments of the population in case of an ordinary air attack. But these could hardly be considered safe from the radiation effects of a nuclear attack.

"No practice alerts are held in Moscow. Posters giving instructions on the rudiments of civil defense work—how to fight fires and give aid to wounded—are extremely rare. They are found only here and there on the bulletin boards of factories or in workers' union headquarters. And most of them are several years old.

"There is no propaganda about civil defense. There is no such thing as an effort on a city-wide basis to organize block crews or house wardens for civil defense. . . .

"Foreign military experts assigned to embassies in Moscow say that in extensive travels around the Soviet Union they have seen little or no evidence of any construction work on shelters that would protect the civilian population from nuclear attack."

On the other hand, Leon Gouré, RAND analyst, sees Russia as engaging in an extensive civil defense program. See his *Civil Defense in the Soviet Union* (Berkeley and Los Angeles, University of California Press, 1962).

Even if the United States really spends less than Russia on civil defense, for the United States suddenly to increase the expenditure tenfold, as is suggested, could only be perceived by Russia as a threat. It is not unlikely that the Soviet Union will assume the United States is planning to attack them—which, of course, will lead them to consider making a preventive attack. At the very least, such a United States action would lead to an accelerated civil defense effort on Russia's part. This, in turn, would require prompt activation of the much more extensive and costly second phase of the American civil defense program—engulfing much of society and even more of the economy in the widening arms race.

## Multideterrence Critically Assessed

The advocates of Multideterrence have been assailed for amorality (advocating a nuclear war), for "free" use of figures, and even for poor prose style. But Kahn and his colleagues are military strategists, whose business is amoral by definition; even if somewhat different figures are used, the over-all picture they present does not change much; and it is certainly not a matter of an essay contest. The central question is this: if we accept the Multideterrence advocates' main assumptions—the feasibility of nuclear war and the danger of nuclear blackmail—can we also accept the strategy they propose?

The following critical examination leads me to suggest that paying a huge price for a monstrous military machine will yield no increase in security but a vast increase in risk; for a possible small improvement in the United States "posture," we may *all* be shoved over the brink. It turns out that to be able to continue such an accelerated arms race—even according to RAND —we must reach agreements with the Communists not unlike the disarmament agreements that Kahn and his colleagues consider completely utopian.[3]

### MAD RATIONALITY

The construction of the vast, complex, intricate military apparatus that Multideterrence requires demands high-speed computers to calculate its moves, teams of experts and electronic brains to think through its tactics, and hundreds of millions of

[3] For a discussion of these agreements see pp. 32–38 and Ch. 5.

dollars per year to keep it going. Kahn, in his extensive discussion of this apparatus, brings the whole deterrence strategy to its logical conclusion. The machinery of deterrence is rational—that is, the parts are all interdependent, and each one is "justified" by the others. If one has bombers, for example, they are useless unless runways are supplied; if there are runways, they must be protected from bombs, hence antimissile missiles are essential; both the bombers and missiles need someone to command them, hence the need to protect the headquarters and maintain "jam-free" communications networks at all times. Thus, each item "makes sense" because of its contribution to the others.

The proponents of Multideterrence point out that the whole deterrence machine breaks down unless every one of its parts is present and functioning. There is simply no getting away with partial measures. In fact, half-deterrence is more dangerous than full deterrence, because it gives illusory strength and security. One becomes aggressive or complacent, while actually being highly vulnerable. Once the enemy discovers his opponents weak spot, he can paralyze him.

The crucial question, then, is not whether one or another item on the Multideterrence list is necessary; for, given the Multideterrence strategy, they are all equally necessary, and there is no point in asking: Could we do without a nuclear bomber? Do we really need more Polaris subs? Assuming that we spend the many hundreds of millions of dollars each year that this machinery requires; assuming we build all the weapons, weapons systems, flying commands, underwater bombs, antimissile missiles, radiation counters and what not—what will it give us? Will it pay off? If this enormous ultra-complex system, this gigantic investment of resources, of human energy and ingenuity, would yield a relatively assured peace—or at least a substitute for nuclear warfare—many of us might seriously consider buying it. In the bargain we might have to give up a large part of our income, reduce our investment in schools, medical research, and economic development, not to mention private consumption. We might even have to turn our society into something resembling an immense fortress, live in concrete-walled bunkers, put our sons into trenches, subordinate many of our basic freedoms to security regulations, and sleep with our shoes on. Again, if this garrison state would keep us from mass murder, and from being mass murdered, it might be worth the price.

But it will not. First, like any supercomplex mechanism, in this apparatus of automats and explosives, human commanders and computers, electronic beams and buck privates, something —something basic—is quite likely to go wrong. The very fact that the parts are interdependent means that when one goes, the whole system might be undermined. The larger, the cleverer, and the more complicated the military machine, the more likely it is to break down. It is simply impossible to have any assurance that such a system will function reliably. Let us suppose that the Russians invent a device to neutralize the American radar system ("fooling" the radar with decoys has been suggested) or develop a drug that neutralizes fall-out the way a base neutralizes an acid; for that matter, let us imagine any other Russian technological breakthrough of the magnitude of their invention of high-thrust missiles or a major security leak which reveals to the Russians our main defense gap. What is there in the strategy of Multideterrence to stop them from exploiting their advantage to the hilt?

One can cite numerous cases—from France's Maginot Line against Germany to the greatly feared poison gas deployed in World War I, from the American defense installations at Pearl Harbor to Hitler's "ultimate" weapon, the V-2 rocket—when all human calculations and preparations failed. Too many times the "safe" defense provides no safety, the "ultimate" weapons are lost along with those who relied on them. In earlier wars, in which the means of destruction were primitive by comparison, such failures were rarely decisive. But now, a gap may cost some twenty million deaths beyond the forty millions or so provided for in RAND's neat calculations.

Americans, placing their confidence in Multideterrence, seem unaware that in a nuclear war one flaw may prove fatal. They are mentally handicapped in realizing such facts by traditional American overconfidence, many past victories, no major defeats, long security, and 150 years of hegemony in the Western hemisphere. There is the implication that the United States, if it desires, can build a force that will stop the Russians and maintain American security while continuing to realize national objectives. But if this vast apparatus cannot yield such security, especially if, as we shall see immediately, its very construction enhances the likelihood of nuclear war, then this machine is not only not a rational system, it is a systematic madness. There is no more safety in a stockpile of bombs, missiles, and guns than there is in one powder keg. And the larger and more complex the stockpile, the more likely this Pandora's Box will be to spring open of its own accord—and the more awesome will be its contents.

## WAR BY MISTAKE

Many observers agree that a nuclear war might take place in the next ten to fifteen years—by accident. It might be accidentally touched off in at least four major ways.

*War by Mechanical Failure or Human Miscalculation.* Among the less likely but still quite possible mistakes are those due to mechanical or human failure. A malfunctioning test missile may fail to be destroyed in mid-air, as intended; a nuclear stockpile may blow up accidentally and the explosion may be misinterpreted as an attack; a trigger mechanism may short-circuit and shoot off when no one intends it to; and so on *ad infinitum.* Everyone who has ever had anything to do with machines or weapons, especially complex ones, knows how frequently they go awry. The fact that mechanical accidents in the past have been relatively harmless is probably due to the fact that the bombs were not fully armed (which they may well have to be in the near future because of the decline in warning time) and that their total number until recently was relatively small.

Ever since there were wars to fight and decisions to make, great leaders have sometimes miscalculated. *If* Napoleon had not decided to engage his forces at Waterloo, *if* Hitler had not attacked England and Russia at the same time, if. . . . But in the nuclear era, such miscalculations can spell not only defeat but cataclysm—and there is nothing in Multideterrence to avoid it. In the nuclear era, as in any period, one never has satisfactory information about the enemy, especially about an enemy as security-conscious as the Communist bloc. In addition to imperfect or invalid information, or psychological quirks, internal political pressures, such as an approaching presidential election, may tamper with a decision maker's discretion and judgment. Singly or in combination, such factors may distort his thinking to the point where he feels safe in ordering a nuclear surprise attack or—equally disastrous—mistakenly believes his country is about to be bombed and hence orders a preventative strike.

*Unauthorized Action.* With the number of triggers, switches, and dials constantly mounting, with the tense period ahead of us almost guaranteeing that one side or the other will accumulate a number of setbacks and frustrations, it would not be surprising if some individuals should decide to try and pull a trigger "on their own." Thus, a group of Communist pilots incensed at increasing "softness" in the Kremlin or a group of SAC pilots who are also members of an aggressive dissident group, may deliberately unleash a war. It takes *one* commander of a Polaris submarine to shoot *sixteen* nuclear bombs into Russia; it takes two madmen per Minuteman to send a nuclear bomb from a home base to Moscow. The more triggers there are—and according to Multideterrence the number is increasing rapidly—the less selective we can be about the personnel who man the triggers. (Already, there was a John Birch Society *general* in the United States forces stationed in Germany.) The more dispersed the bombs are geographically, as maintaining a net force requires, the less carefully supervised is the staff which has access to the triggers. If there is no need to worry about unauthorized behavior on the American side, what about that of the other side? Their triggers, after all, are multiplying as fast as ours are.

*War by False Alarm.* We have already suffered several narrow escapes from nuclear war caused by false alarm. In the recent past, the alert was sounded because American radar screens recorded the rising of the moon, because meteors fell, because a flock of geese veered in their winter flight, and because some B-47s were flying off course. The B-47 incident is worth describing in some detail because it carries a significant lesson for the future.

Heessen looked up when the yellow lights flashed on and the bell rang. Four vapor trails had been sighted over Nunivak Island, heading SES. They had been seen a full hour and 27 minutes earlier and the report had come

through the Air Defense Control Center at Elmendorf.
. . . The young captain immediately called Captain Joseph
Wood, intelligence duty officer. . . . [Wood called Colonel
W. M. Burgess, ACD's Deputy Chief of Staff, Intelligence.]

Burgess hurried to headquarters. He went over the situation carefully with the two captains and then woke up
Berquist and told him about the Nunivak contrails. The
general did not waste time in getting to the command post.
Again, everything was checked. . . .

By now the tempo of activity had been shoved into high
gear. Telephone lines were loaded with calls back and forth
with the three defense forces. Conferences were held over
classified circuits.

The general officer on duty at the U.S. Air Force Command Post in the Pentagon, Washington, D.C., was informed of the situation.

At 2:20 A.M. Bergquist called Major General Frederic
H. Smith, Jr., Vice-Commander of ADC. "We have something hot—I think you'd better come over," Bergquist said,
his voice calm but firm. . . .

Smith checked on what the others had done. An estimated time of arrival for the unknown plane had been
computed. They would, if they were going at 400 knots,
hit the Seattle radar net at 4:30 A.M. Colorado time. It was
then 3:00 A.M., an hour and a half to go. . . .

It was 3:10 A.M. when Wood walked over to the two
senior officers. "Eastern has just called in and reported five
unknowns coming in over Presque Isle." Presque Isle is in
Maine.

Smith looked up quickly. "This triggers it. The Air Defense Command goes on full Air Defense Readiness immediately," he said.

The time was 3:11 A.M. April 17, 1952. Air Force headquarters in Washington was notified, the Joint Chiefs of
Staff alerted. President Truman was awakened.[4]

It turned out, however, that some American B-47s were flying
off course. With no damage done, the incident could be written
off as a false alarm; but this was in 1952. Armaments technology

[4] Arnold Brophy, *The Air Force*, quoted in Kahn, *op. cit.*, pp. 422–423n.

since then has developed with large speed. In 1952 Captain Wood and his superiors had time to call up their senior officers, who could call up still more senior officers, who in turn issued orders to check with various observation posts, compare reports, and even to wake up the Joint Chiefs of Staff and the President. They had about four hours' leeway. In 1961, a Russian satellite circled the whole earth in eighty-six minutes! The "checking time" in the missile era has already telescoped to a rapid fifteen minutes, and it will be even shorter in the near future. As a consequence of the reduction of checking time, it is now almost impossible to consult senior officers and staff experts, much less render advice to the President. Why even bother to wake him up anymore? What could he accomplish in a maximum of ten minutes? Call a meeting of the National Security Council or the Cabinet? Confer with his staff? Carefully ponder the implications of his fatal decision?

The checking time is already so short that now, or in the very near future, the President will have to make *contingent* decisions; that is, he will have to decide *before* an emergency arises the specific conditions that will *automatically* lead to an order to strike. Whether he will retain the formal right to order the retaliation is of minor importance, because he will have to make up his mind ahead of time. All that will matter is that the radar sets show the anticipated series of blips coming from the anticipated direction. Unless, then and there, contradictory reports come in from other sources, the country's military striking force gets set to retaliate what might well be a nonexisting attack.

The reduced checking time has several dangerous consequences. It increases the opportunity for a group of radar watchers or listening device monitors or intelligence officers to deliberately engage their country in war by feeding exaggerated, slanted, or false information to headquarters. It leaves no time to gather and compare information from a variety of sources. It increases the likelihood of error caused by extreme haste. It means that, before long, lower-ranking officers will, for all practical purposes, be making the final decision.

The major danger of false alarms is, not that the armed forces are mistakenly put on alert, but that an alert may touch off a catastrophic chain reaction. The President or his deputies will alert SAC; much of SAC will become airborne; missiles

48

will be taken out of their shells and readied for fire; bombs will be cocked. With the development of electronic eavesdropping and satellite surveillance, the Russians cannot fail to notice such preparations; but there will be no way for them to know that they result from a false alarm and not from preparation for a surprise attack. The Russians, sensibly, will make counter-preparations. These in turn become visible to the United States and confirm its initial suspicions. In this way, it is quite possible for both countries to be sucked into a nuclear war which neither began. Such a war will cause even more casualties on both sides than a war which was initiated deliberately, because neither side will be adequately prepared (for example, by evacuating some of its population from the vulnerable cities).

Can we not be saved in the future from war-by-accident, as we have been saved in the past? One answer is that it is highly objectionable to allow millions of lives to depend on the chance happenings and the kind of "lucky breaks" that have saved us so far. Not every radar monitor will cry, just in time, "But it's the moon!" More important, in the past the technique of "peeping" into other countries was limited. It was quite possible to alert SAC and man the missiles without Russia's knowing about it instantly. With the development of surveillance satellites like the Midas, which "reads" foreign territory like an open book, and with the development of various electronic monitoring devices (the United States is already using both means of surveillance), any arms alert can immediately become known to the enemy. The enemy reacts by sounding a counter-alert, which in turn generates a counter-counteralert; this moves the opponent into a still more advanced alert. Then, one mistaken move, one nervous pilot or trigger-happy missile commander. . . .

The consequences of such "misunderstandings" were devastating long before the atomic age. King Arthur's last battle is a case in point.

It seems that King Arthur's son, Mordred, revolted against his father. After some fighting the two contenders met, with all their troops, on the field of Camlan to negotiate. Both sides were fully armed and desperately suspicious that the other side was going to try some ruse or stratagem. The

49

negotiations were going along smoothly until one of the knights was stung by an asp and drew his sword to kill the reptile. The others saw the sword being drawn and immediately fell upon each other. A tremendous slaughter ensued. . . . When the battle was over everybody except King Arthur, Mordred, and a couple of knights lay dead.[5]

And this took place when the "ultimate weapon" was the sword!

*War by Brinksmanship.* Multideterrence strategy involves brinksmanship, an activity which, as engaged in by both the United States and Russia, is in my opinion most likely to be the immediate cause of World-War-III-by-miscalculation. Brinksmanship is a foolhardy game wherein one party declares that unless the other party grants a particular concession, the first party will carry out some threat that promises to do damage to both parties. The wife who threatens to walk out unless she receives a dishwasher and the key executive who promises to quit his job unless he receives a raise are both engaging in brinksmanship. Playing this game successfully requires that the threat be one that could seriously injure the threatened party and that the party engaging in brinksmanship be quite willing to carry out its threat. Brinksmanship can fail in two ways. The husband, for instance, may be indifferent to his wife's exit or confident (he can never be certain) that she will not walk out; or he may balk, whereupon, if the wife does not walk out, she has gained nothing and lost much of the future "credibility" of her threats; or she may actually leave, in which case she neither gets what she wanted nor preserves a marriage that she had no intention of ending. If tension is high between the man and wife and both have staked their prestige on sticking stubbornly to their respective stands, they may then go through with a divorce that both will regret.

International brinksmanship is played with nuclear bombs and bombers. The odds for not being "called" are low; the damage, if "called," is immense; concessions, if gained, are small. The United States and the Soviet Union engage in such brinksmanship dangerously often. In some cases, this game has been successful. When the Communists were dragging out the armistice negotiations in Korea while limited hostilities continued,

[5] Kahn, *op. cit.,* p. 525.

the United States let it be known to Peiping through Prime Minister Nehru that if the armistice were not signed "soon," the United States would "lift its self-imposed restrictions,"—a statement that implied nuclear bombing under the then-in-force Massive Retaliation doctrine. This was in May, 1953. Two months later the armistice was signed—although other factors may have helped to bring this about. Russia's announcement that it would rain rockets on Israel, Britain, and France if the Suez invasion in 1956 were not halted was certainly one of the factors that quickly stopped it. On the other hand, United States brinksmanship was highly unsuccessful in Indochina, as was Russian brinksmanship in the Congo.

It should be noted that the Communists have several advantages in this game—advantages which should make the West sensibly refrain from playing.

First, the Communists are far less vulnerable to domestic public opinion than are leading Western governments; unsuccessful brinksmanship creates fewer problems at home for a Communist government. Hence the Russians can engage in brinksmanship more often and, more important, they can lean further over the brink than the West can—that is, they can afford to make bigger threats.

Second, the West is more convinced of the Communist (especially Communist Chinese) resolve to engage in a nuclear war than the Communists are of Western determination to do so. Communist threats are thus more credible, and consequently more effective, than Western threats.

If these are not reasons enough for the West to avoid brinksmanship, there are some compelling reasons why both sides should abandon it. When brinksmanship works, someone wins something; but when it fails—and it fails readily—the loss to both sides is large. If the threat is not carried out, the ensuing loss of prestige becomes in itself a strong motive for carrying out one's next threat. The motive is utterly irrational; it is based on considerations of saving face rather than on the international situation *per se*. Moreover, if the threat is made good, the cost is terrible. A third or more of the American people are offered as stakes when their government threatens nuclear bombing to defend a Berlin or Quemoy and Matsu. All the achievements of the Bolshevik Revolution hang in the balance when the Kremlin threatens to bomb in support of some African rebel. For, if the threat is carried out, retaliation is bound to follow. In short, the victims of brinksmanship are eventually *all* who engage in it.

## ACCIDENT INSURANCE?

To reduce the damage from a war initiated by mistake, Kahn suggests various procedures based on communication with the enemy, on tight self-control, and on "arms control."

A direct communications line between the two camps would allow each side to telephone the other, if necessary, and say, "I'm sorry, old boy, one of ours just got away and is coming your way. I'd appreciate it if you could forget the whole thing, but if you insist on wiping out one of my cities (or even an extra one for revenge), I'll understand and explain it to the folks." The promise to permit retaliation must be made in order to avoid the impression that if the accident victim avenges himself, his strike—even if limited—will be met with a massive counterblow. Otherwise, the accident victim may retaliate in the first place by an all-out blow, to reduce the ability to retaliate the retaliation.

Such strategy makes perfect sense if the two sides are playing at chess; white takes one black pawn, even if in the process he has to let black take one or even two of his pawns, but white will not agree to let black take his rook, much less his queen. Such accident insurance may be an effective safeguard if we view life through the cool, rational glasses of a games theorist. It is something else, however, when we view it through a flickering radar screen propped up against a wall of suspicion.

Accident insurance presupposes that the United States and Russia can reach an agreement about the rules of the game and that each side trusts the other to play fair. It is implied that when the telephone rings in the White House and the head of the Kremlin explains, "Sorry, old man . . ." the President can be certain that only one missile is coming and that it is not carrying a bomb large enough to cripple the entire United States. It is likewise assumed that when the Russian leader answers the telephone, hears that Leningrad is accidentally doomed, and kindly agrees to accept Los Angeles in return for it, he will not give vent to his "irritation" by bombing San Francisco and Denver as well. One might well ask: If the United States and the Soviet Union can so thoroughly trust each other in such deadly matters, why cannot they trust each other on other matters and in much calmer situations? Why did we not trust them, for instance, when they claimed that they had stopped testing bombs?

Second, accident insurance assumes that the American president is a free agent; that he does not have to face Congress, the voters, or the press; that he can let Los Angeles be annihilated and excuse the Russians with, "Sorry, a mistake"—and still be an American president; that he can let the Russians deliberately "take" Los Angeles, just because one crazed American pilot dropped a bomb on Leningrad. (Shooting down the retaliation missiles would violate the rules of the game and trigger a large nuclear war. It would probably also be "cheating" to warn the doomed population.) Clearly, this sort of assumptions border on the ridiculous.

Moreover, such plans ignore the fact that cities are not pawns in a game. They are filled with men, women, and children. They are the centers of our cultural, economic, and political life. Undoubtedly it is "better" to wipe out a city than an entire country; but what a terrible price to pay for accident insurance —and such a mistake might not be an isolated one. If we continue relying on ever-increasing means of multideterrence, further accidents are bound to happen, with mounting frequency as there are more and more bombs and triggers. Even if accident insurance were really effective, even if it were politically feasible, is not the price of accidents too high? After all, this "insurance" policy merely gives the victims the "right" to cause damage in return; it does not restore lives or rebuild cities, nor does it purify the air from fall-out. One can, thus, state categorically that accident insurance absolutely lacks psychological, sociological, political, and moral validity.

## THE NTH COUNTRY

It is widely agreed that, unless the big powers do more than pile one deterrence onto another, unless some global control over nuclear production is devised, more and more governments will acquire H-bombs in the near future. In the so-called $n$th country problem, $n$ stands for the unknown number of countries which soon will be armed with nuclear weapons. In 1960, a German scientist devised a cheap method for producing fissionable materials, thus smoothing the way for smaller and poorer nations to build stockpiles of nuclear weapons. Communist China will probably possess bombs not later than 1963. The National Planning Council has reported that eleven nations will be able to enter the once exclusive "nuclear club" in the next five years. The potential members include East and West Germany, Japan, Communist China, and Czechoslovakia.

It is true that only mass production of bombs and missiles turns a country into a nuclear power capable of threatening the existence of the United States or Russia. But enough bombs and missiles can be imported from other countries (from France to Israel, from the United States to Denmark, from China to Albania) to turn many a small nation into a nuclear power quite capable of destroying other small nations and involving the big ones.

What will happen when the ownership of nuclear arms becomes widespread? Theoretically, it is possible that the dispersion of these all-powerful weapons will make everyone so apprehensive and cautious that there will be fewer armed conflicts than before and more insistent demands for worldwide disarmament. But history suggests that an outcome of this sort is quite unlikely. Other weapons—tanks, machine guns, poison gas—were once viewed as all-destructive, but none of them abolished war, nor did their possessors manage to prevent their use.

Many arms experts, from advocates of Massive Retaliation to Unilateralists, agree that the emergence of many nuclear powers is likely to have disastrous consequences, none of which the Multideterrence strategy is equipped to forestall. The major ones are as follows.

While large countries are likely to survive and recuperate from nuclear war, smaller countries (such as Israel and Syria) may be totally destroyed, or may at least cease to be viable societies.

The more nuclear countries there are, the more decision makers there will be who can touch off nuclear war and the more likely it is that war will be precipitated by mistake, accident, miscalculation, or brinksmanship.

The widespread dispersion of H-bombs means that some of

them will fall into the hands of leaders who are far more irrational and aggressive—and have less to lose by starting a war—than the leaders of the current nuclear powers. Thus, while Russia might try to avoid war, a Hoxha of Albania might precipitate one; similarly, the United States would not want to initiate nuclear war, but someone like Chiang Kai-shek might.

Nuclear weapons ownership will give many countries a fingerhold on the nuclear triggers of the two superpowers. If a nuclear war breaks out between two lesser nations, the conflict might easily involve the United States and Russia, whether or not they want to become involved. If Communist China continued to feel that Soviet Russia is too "soft" on the West, it could bomb the United States itself, and thus pull Russia into a global nuclear war, Russia being unlikely to risk the defeat of its major ally.

It is even possible that a third power, expecting to benefit from the devastation of the two superpowers, may drop a bomb on one of them. Missiles can be very anonymous, especially when launched from an unidentifiable submarine.

Finally, unless definite steps are taken to control the production and distribution of nuclear weapons, rebel groups or governments will be able, some time before 1975, to afford their own nuclear arsenals. H-bombs can already be hidden in a trunk and shot out of a bazooka by one man.

Not all the consequences of H-bomb dispersion are likely to mean the destruction of civilization; most of them would "merely" turn some area of the world into a radioactive desert. (The fall-out resulting from a succession of small wars, however, might be enough to do away with all of us.) Other consequences, such as the provocation of war between the two superpowers, might lead more directly to global disaster. The spread of nuclear arms is the surest road—via many small disasters, several middling ones, or one big one—to Doomsday.

Multideterrence is not only utterly incapable of averting these dangers; it actually serves to increase them. The need to produce more and varied bombs at an ever accelerating pace, the need to disperse them to prevent them from being hit by the first strike of an enemy—both needs accentuated by Multideterrence—makes the nuclear arming of $n$ countries more and more "necessary." And once the small countries of one bloc have obtained nuclear arms, those of the other will inescapably find that it is "in the interests of national security" for them to do likewise. Soon the whole earth will be populated with big bombs and triggers. Multideterrence sees some hope in "arms control" to tackle this problem. But as we shall see, arms control has as much validity as accident insurance.

## ESCALATION AND DOOMSDAY

Multideterrence strategy is based on the assumptions that mutual annihilation is not the only alternative to accommodation; that the bombs we now have cannot destroy civilization; and that even if there were Doomsday bombs, no power would use them.

The latter two assumptions, however, are invalid. First, it makes little difference whether we now have Doomsday bombs or not (although recent developments seem to indicate the existence of bombs that can wipe out civilization on one continent, if not on the entire globe). Even if present-day bombs can annihilate only Russia, China, the United States, and Western Europe, they will still blot out half the people on earth and much of what the remaining survivors hold dear. *In either case —let experts quibble over the exact facts and timetables—we still face, sooner or later (and even "later" is very soon), the possibility of complete annihilation.*

Secondly, if nuclear war does occur, the Multideterrence advocates argue, no one will use the big bombs even if he has them; the danger of self-annihilation is too great. Nuclear blackmail is a less risky, more promising course for a nuclear power.

There are good reasons for rejecting this position, however. One is the fact that premiers and presidents need not always be as rational as Multideterrence requires them to be. Today both superpowers are governed by fairly level-headed leaders, but someday a Hitler or a Stalin may lead again. Even the United States knows an increasing number of advocates of a "preventive war" who advise the President to order a massive nuclear attack on Russia.

But even if level-headed leaders prevail, "escalation" might bring nations that possess the big bombs to use them. Escalation refers to the process by which, step after step, as if being carried up a moving escalator, a country's leaders may be brought to "raise" the level of war by resorting to more and more powerful weapons, until they ascend to the last position and unleash the most devastating bombs in their possession.

Escalation might play itself out as follows. One morning the radios outside New York might announce that the world's greatest metropolis is a pile of radioactive dust. The Russians claim that the destruction is an American accident—(the result of one of the SAC planes' having crashed, or the Birch Society's having tried to provoke the United States into attacking Russia); the CIA claims it to be a Russian trick to weaken America psychologically without risking the all-out retaliation which would follow a larger attack; the English explain it as a Russian accident—the outcome of a Russian submarine, on training maneuvers near the United States seaboard, believing it had been ordered to fire. Could an American president resist the pressure to destroy in return at least one Russian city? And how would the Russians respond to such *deliberate* bombing, following what they claim, perhaps rightly, was an American accident? How, in turn, will the United States react when the Russians retaliate? And so on—to the last escalation.

Or let us imagine a limited war—in Korea or Southeast Asia or Berlin. Both sides are using only conventional arms, but the Americans are rapidly losing. The American top field commander obtains permission to drop atomic bombs on Communist military targets. The Russians retaliate in kind. But since some of the most important United States military bases are located in or near cities, some cities are devastated. To this the Americans respond by bombing some Russian cities. The Russians had not expected the United States to attack its civilians. Millions of Russians die; there is demoralization, chaos, general paralysis. As a last resort, rather than face total loss, the Kremlin pushes the button that triggers the big bombs. The United States is in ruins, but it has some big bombs stationed in Turkey, Japan, and Alaska. When the men in charge of these bomb sites learn that their country has been completely devastated, they pull the triggers, as they have been instructed, and Russia is also doomed.

Thus, escalation can take us not only from cold war to hot,

57

from limited war to world war, and from conventional conflict to nuclear attack—it may also lead us that one step further to nuclear cataclysm.

Moreover, under certain circumstances last escalation might be very tempting, for it *does* after all grant the loser a last chance for survival, if not for victory. His country is in ruins, his forces are demoralized, the enemy is breaking through his last lines. Pulling the biggest trigger gives him one slim, final opportunity to save the day, pull his scattered army together, and perhaps even be the sole survivor of a nuclear war. The loser might well calculate in addition that the enemy, already sure of his victory, might be caught off guard. Devastating the enemy's country might yet undermine the morale of his troops and cut off supplies he counts on for the final offensive. However slight the possibility, even a not irrational leader might give it a try. He has nothing to lose; but if he succeeds, he has a great deal to gain.

Or, with no chance whatever to win or to survive, a defeat-crazed leader—like Hitler in his burning bunker when the enemy closed in: a dictator about to lose the last remnant of his semi-global empire—might still unleash his doomsday bombs. Men in such straits may vow, "I shall drag them all into the grave with me." Samson's suicide-homicide is probably the first recorded case of pulling the last trigger. Captured and blinded by the Philistines, Samson was bound to the pillars of a house on whose roof the Philistines were feasting. Taking hold of the pillars and calling, "Let me die with the Philistines," Samson "bowed himself with all his might; and the house fell upon the lords, and upon all the people that were therein. So the dead which he slew at his death were more than they which he slew in his life."

Deterrence strategies assume that people make rational responses; but men with their backs to the wall are not in a "normal" psychological state. If there are buttons to be pushed, such men may very well push them.

There is nothing whatever in Multideterrence to deter last escalation, whether the motives behind it be rational or irrational. True, the proponents of this strategy have attempted to devise some insurance against it. First of all, they point out, one way to prevent last escalation is to deter intermediate escalations. (If the enemy is kept off the middle of the staircase, we need not fear that he will arrive at the top.) We do this by convincing him that whenever he raises the level of warfare (by using more or deadlier weapons), we are more than ready to meet his challenge. If for each successive level we possess an adequate counterforce, we can deter the enemy from escalating, for he realizes that the more he escalates, the larger his losses will be when he is finally blocked.

Moreover, say the Multideterrence strategists, last escalation can also be forestalled if the objectives in any given conflict are deliberately limited, with the proviso that the enemy realizes that this has been done. That is, there must be a public announcement that only conventional armaments will be used or that troops will push no further than, say, the 38th Parallel (The Korean War is often cited as the classic example of deterred escalation.) By publicly limiting military objectives, one refrains from pushing the enemy to the wall, for he realizes that as long as he does not escalate, he will suffer at worst only a limited setback, not total defeat.

The hazards of such measures are many, however. First, it requires that the enemy have high faith in our promise to honor the self-imposed limitation, even if we are winning; *and* it requires that we rely on the enemy's pledge not to escalate in situations where we are facing "limited defeat."

Second, these measures require that our side be stronger than the other at each possible level of conflict, so that at no time will it pay the enemy to escalate to a higher level. Such a military "posture" is rarely, if ever, attained, and to bank our hopes on it is visionary.

Third, this antiescalation strategy assumes that the seventh and eighth "limited setbacks" have the same psychological effect on the loser as the first and second. Realistically, however, it is clear that if one country—say, the United States—loses an increasing succession of rounds (such as Indochina, Laos, the space race, and several more), it will feel more and more threatened. No matter how limited each individual setback is, a long series will make the loser begin to react like the man with his back to the wall. Accumulated frustrations, fears, and desperation, intensified by internal political pressures from voters and groups disgusted with the loss of prestige and the erosion of strength, may make a country resort to escalation, even if the enemy has kept to the rules of the game.

## MULTIDETERRENCE *and* ARMS CONTROL?

It may be a good sign for critics of reliance on armed deterrence that even Kahn, the most influential of the Multideterrence advocates, freely admits that the whole vast machine, even if constructed just as designed and right on schedule, gives at best only short-run protection against disaster. We must also work for arms control. In *On Thermonuclear War,* Kahn writes: "If we are to reach the year 2000, or even 1975, without a cataclysm of some sort (in particular, if we are to obtain the time to work out the rivalry peacefully), we will almost undoubtedly require extensive arms control measures in addition to unilateral security measures."[6] That is, we must reach some agreement with the Russians which, without significantly weakening either side, effectively controls the arms race, particularly the manufacture and distribution of nuclear weapons.

This raises a central question that the theories of armed deterrence—whether Containment, Massive Retaliation, or Multideterrence—do not answer: does not the arms race itself create conditions which prevent us from arriving at the agreement that even proponents of Multideterrence—which intensifies the arms race by adding arms to arms— see as absolutely essential for human survival? The unilateralists, who stand at the opposite pole, rejecting reliance on armed deterrence, make the incongruence between a continued arms race and interbloc negotiations, their starting point.

## Chapter 3

## Unilateralism—A Hopeless Hope

UNILATERALISTS advocate disarmament by the West even if the Communists do not, believing that this is the only way to change the present disastrous course of the arms race. At first glance this position seems completely absurd. After a second

6 *Ibid.,* p. 224.

look, one can understand why some highly thoughtful people hold it. Nevertheless, a critical examination reveals why they hope against hope.

## The Unilateral Diagnosis

One of the achievements of the unilateralists, widely acknowledged even by their opponents, is that they have pointed out, emphasized, and clarified the dangers of armed deterrence, which is the ultimate foundation of all strategies devised to date by American foreign policy experts. The unilateralists point out that the increasing probabilities of accidents, miscalculations, and unauthorized attacks; the increase in the number of countries possessing nuclear arms; the possibility of escalation; and the increase in international tension make nuclear war in the near future virtually a certainty. The history of mankind tells of numerous attempts to build up an armed force to deter an aggressor. Deterrence has often worked for a while; rarely has it prevented the imminent outbreak of war. If a war follows the present "deterrence" build-up, it will be fought with weapons of such great destructive power that they endanger the survival of the human race itself. A single plane can now deliver a bomb with an explosive power as large as the total amount of high-power explosives dropped on Germany and Japan in *all* of World War II; the United States alone has 2000 nuclear-armed bombers, not counting missiles. Both sides now have enough nuclear bombs to kill every person alive many times over—enough to strike with a blast of ten tons of TNT every man, woman, and child. While nuclear bombs have been "cleaned," by reducing their radioactive fall-out, the fall-out is still great enough to subject many survivors of a "clean" blast to the agonizing death of radiation poisoning. Such "survivors" will envy those who died under the bomb.

Most unilateralists feel that the present arms race leads to the annihilation of all life. Some add, countering the Multi-deterrence argument, that even if there is only a "small" nuclear war, one in which the United States suffers from ten to sixty million casualties, Western civilization will never recuperate. Societies are organic units. You cannot cut off a third and say to the rest, "Grow back." Once a society is severely damaged and demoralized, it cannot recuperate. Culture, civilization,

61

and modern economy, all city-based, will be particularly hard hit. There will be gangs of delinquents and desperados fighting each other for food in oases of radioactive deserts. Nobody will be motivated to work and reconstruct; effort will become meaningless after such great, deliberate man-made destruction. People exposed to such nuclear horrors, many of whose relatives first vomit, then get better, then "really get sick and die," will become asocial, cynical, and psychotic. Says the eminent psychologist and unilateralist, Erich Fromm: "[Nuclear destruction] will create such a panic, fury, and despair as could only be compared with the mass psychosis resulting from the Black Death in the Middle Ages. The traumatic effects of such a catastrophe would lead to a new form of primitive barbarism. . . ."[1] That is, one need not assume complete annihilation in order to realize that a nuclear war will lead to total disaster.

Even under the most optimistic conditions, if armed deterrence "works" well enough to prevent even a "small" nuclear war, we still will have to pay a terrible price. We will have to invest ever larger amounts of resources, talent, and energy in the monstrous war machinery. In order to avoid security leaks, which will become more and more dangerous, we will have to introduce more and more security measures and restrict even further the freedom of individuals to expose, question, criticize, and reject government policy. Soon we will be living in a garrison state.

Finally, sitting forever on powder kegs that may explode at any minute is bound to take its toll.[2] Says Fromm:

> To live for any length of time under the constant threat of destruction creates certain psychological effects in most human beings—fright, hostility, callousness, a hardening

[1] Erich Fromm, "The Case for Unilateral Disarmament," *Daedalus*, Vol. 89, No. 4 (Fall, 1960), p. 1018.

[2] A recent medical report illustrates one threat to our health—that is, to our sanity.

"An American Medical Association publication came up yesterday with another phobia: nucleomitophobia, or fear of atomic energy and all its works.

"The publication *Today's Health*, put out at AMA headquarters, reported that public officials were receiving what it called a rash of calls for help from frantic persons who think they are radioactive.

"It also quoted Dr. Milton A. Dushkin, medical director of the North Shore Hospital in Winnetka, Ill., a Chicago suburb.

"He said that, for example, people were 'seeing' submarines in Lake Michigan that shot mysterious rays to the shore, and ghostly flying objects that somehow charged women's hair curlers with radioactivity.

" 'It's a product of the age,' explained Dr. Dushkin." *New York Times*, September 23, 1961.

of the heart, and a resulting indifference to all the values we cherish. Such conditions will transform us into barbarians—though barbarians equipped with the most complicated machines. If we are serious in claiming that our aim is to preserve freedom (that is, to prevent the subordination of the individual under an all-powerful state), we must admit that this freedom will be lost, whether the deterrent works or does not work.[3]

Thus, according to the unilateralists, the arms race is totally illogical. Our participation in it is "justified" by the need to protect the Western way of life; but, in fact, this very participation destroys our way of life. The new means of destruction are so devastating that they make the institution of war obsolete. It is no longer a question of sacrificing some lives to defend the lives and values of the large majority and of future generations. Life itself, the life of all, is imperiled. Hence, to follow the course of armed deterrence is sheer madness.

Russians and Americans, East and West, are caught in the same dilemma. Russian lives as well as ours are suspended; Soviet ability to improve the lot of its citizens and to pursue values dear to them is also at stake. The arms race itself, in good part, explains why we find no way out of the corner into which we have backed ourselves. The ever greater amassing of arms by each side generates countermoves that further increase the arms build-up in a deadly spiral, making the most vicious circle in which the human race has ever been caught. The arms race generates mutual suspicion and hatred, and thus, by its very existence, it not only produces the dangers we must remove but also stops us from removing them. It not only propels us into a deadly competition but also prevents us from leaving it.

## What Can Be Done?

Before the unilateralist proposals can be presented, it is crucial to realize that there are many variants of the unilateralist position (though their total number of advocates is not large). There are religious unilateralists (many of them Quakers), Socialist unilateralists, and unilateralists without other persuasions; there is a comparatively large unilateralist movement in England, and there are small, campus-based groups in

[3] Fromm, *loc. cit.*, p. 1019.

63

the United States; there are philosophers, such as Bertrand Russell; psychologists such as Jerome Frank and Erich Fromm; and a military commander, Stephen King-Hall. Organizations favor this modern form of pacifism, including the American Friends Service Committee, the Campaign for Nuclear Disarmament (CND), the Committee for Non-Violent Action, the War Resistors League, the Fellowship of Reconciliation, and others.

One view is shared by all of these groups. They firmly believe that the present arms race will lead to disaster and that disarmament is the one and only way out. Since negotiations are deadlocked—since we will not give up because they will not, and they will not because we will not—the only way to stop the disastrous drift is for the West to disarm *unilaterally*. To allay the Communists' suspicions of such a move, the West should permit them uninhibited inspection. A crucial point of the unilateral argument is that simultaneous disarmament by both sides—under conditions and in stages decided upon through bilateral negotiations—is unfeasible because of mutual distrust. The unilateralists insist on one-sided disarmament now; they are hopeful that the other side will reciprocate, but they do not make reciprocation a condition for action. This position is held by all unilateralists; they differ, however, respecting the extent of unilateral disarmament, the rationale supplied for the limit chosen, and the procedures of disarming.

## ENGLISH AND AMERICAN UNILATERALISTS

The unilateral disarmament movement is much stronger in England than in the United States. Whereas the Marchers for Peace and demonstrators in the United States numbered a few thousand in 1960, their English counterparts that year numbered close to a hundred thousand. Whereas in the United States the various peace groups (by no means all true unilateralists) are chiefly made up of students and professors, intellectuals and beatniks, in Britain they are supported by a few members of Parliament, some labor unions, and much of the left wing of the Labour Party; during brief periods, unilateralism was even adopted as part of the Labour Party's platform—that is, as a policy the Party would carry out if elected. The Party still favors the establishment of a Non-Nuclear Club for antibomb nations. In the United States, no significant political group or leader endorses unilateralism.

These differences in the popularity enjoyed by unilateralism in the two closest Western allies are based partly on differences in tradition, more on differences in location, and chiefly on the kind of unilateralism advocated.[4] England traditionally has been more tolerant of various pacifist movements and of conscientious objectors than the United States. More important is the fact that England is much closer to the Soviet Union and that its population is concentrated in comparatively small areas (790 persons per square mile, compared to 49 in the United States). Short-range Russian missiles and bombers, which are believed to exist in abundance, could easily turn the British isles into a pile of rubble. Khrushchev remarked recently that six of his bombs would suffice to level all of Britain.

Britain developed its own bombs and tried to build its own striking force, primarily to assure its defense independent from that of the United States (the latter might choose not to bring on itself a nuclear disaster if the Russians attacked only England) and to enable England, the former big power, to pursue an independent foreign policy. But with an economy that is basically weak and much smaller than the United States', England found that it cannot afford its own nuclear striking force and thus cannot retaliate or deter independently of the United States. Finally, its weak economy would make recuperation unlikely, following even a comparatively "small" nuclear war. Thus, in an English-Russian nuclear war, England's ability to retaliate would be minimal, its devastation maximal, and its chances of recuperation small.

Moreover, the British are not convinced that the American State Department, the CIA, and the President always act with the greatest possible political wisdom; they fear that England might suffer a nuclear holocaust because of an ill-advised American move. A nuclear-disarmed England, especially if it were to withdraw from NATO and other alliances with the

[4] David Riesman and Michael Maccoby point to additional sources of difference: the British politicians are less cut off from British intellectuals, scientists, and writers, than the Americans; the country is smaller, and hence people feel more insecure; they know that a war which hits home is like; and, finally, "perhaps a deeper difference between us and the British lies in the fact that American men seem constantly pursued by the fear of unmanliness, and therefore feel the need to present themselves as hard and realistic." *Commentary,* June, 1960, p. 463.

United States (a course many unilateralists have lately advocated), would attract no more Russian nuclear bombs than any neutral country.

The chief difference, however, between unilateralism in England and in the United States—a difference often hidden behind similar slogans—is that American unilateralists favor disarmament by the United States—which practically means disarmament of the West—whereas the English unilateralists largely favor disarmament of England alone. This British position to a large degree is not unilateralism at all. It does not remove the basis of the interbloc arms race; it cannot break the circle of mutual distrust; and it does not reject armed deterrence (either on the part of the West or the United States.). Hence, it does not raise many of the extremely difficult problems inherent in the American advocacy of unilateral disarmament. All that the English unilateralists offer, from the Russian viewpoint, is a relatively minor repositioning of nuclear forces, insignificant because the development of long-range missiles has made nearby bases obsolete. It is true that England might save itself by such a repositioning, for if she has no nuclear bombs (and the Russians take her word for it), she will not be a target (at least not a prime one) in a United States-Soviet nuclear exchange. English unilateralism thus appears to be a movement of people concerned chiefly with the safety of their country, although a few English unilateralists advocate unilateral disarmament of the West.

Advocating unilateral disarmament of the West is a far more drastic position. But only such disarmament, if the various unilateralist assumptions are valid, would stop the arms race, supply a substitute for armed deterrence (nuclear or total), and give the Communists the free choice of whether to disarm as well or to respond with a "unilateral" attack. Hence only those who advocate Western unilateralism have to face the difficult questions unilateralism raises. Therefore it is not surprising that so few people in the much larger United States support what looks like the same policy. Actually, the largest American peace group, SANE (Committee for a Sane Nuclear Policy), does not advocate unilateral disarmament, total or nuclear. Instead, it favors some unilateral measures, such as withdrawal from friction points and a permanent ban on the testing of bombs, to help reduce tensions and to open the way to fruitful negotiations and multilateral disarmament. Only a few groups in the United States, such as the Committee of Non-Violent Action and the Peace Makers, come close to supporting a true unilateralist position.

## TRADITIONAL VERSUS NUCLEAR UNILATERALISTS

The traditional unilateralists (formerly called pacifists) include some religious groups, especially many Quakers, and various humanists who, on secular moral grounds, arrive at the same conclusion: that the use of violence to advance one's interests or to enforce one's beliefs is evil under any conditions. Any violence corrupts the person using it, and its very exercise completely devalues whatever might be achieved. Therefore, every human being should completely renounce the use of weapons, large or small, nuclear or conventional, for retaliation, deterrence, or any other purpose. Some Quakers go even further: they preach the abolition not only of pistols and cannons, nuclear bombs and knives, but also of hate. "Our truth is an ancient one: that love endures and overcomes; that hatred destroys; that what is obtained by love is retained, but what is obtained by hatred proves a burden."

The pacifists stress that in order to forego violence it is not necessary to give up defense of one's values and way of life. There are other, nonviolent, defenses. Answering aggression with love is one; passive resistance is another. One can resist a totalitarian ruler by lying on the ground and refusing to move. If many hundreds of thousands adopt this strategy, what can a tyrant do? Kill them all? Carry them away one by one? Even the worst human being finds it difficult to stab someone who does not resist. The pacifists claim that nonviolent resistance ultimately led to the British retreat from India; no Indian guerrillas or anticolonial fighters could have achieved more. If necessary, it is better to sacrifice everything, even to die, than to kill.

Unlike the traditional unilateralists, the nuclear unilateralists do not object to violence in principle. They agree that in prenuclear war the use of violence was sometimes justified. (Lord Russell, for instance, supported the Allies' war against Nazi Germany.) "Conventional" violence is conceived as one

67

method, in addition to economic power and psychological (or ideological) warfare, by which nations pursued their objectives *vis-à-vis* other nations. If one nation blocked the advance of another, believing its power superior, war enabled them both to assess their relative power and to adjust accordingly. The stronger one got its way, the weaker one retreated, punished though, as a rule, not destroyed. But nuclear weapons are so destructive that using violence can no longer be justified regardless of the goals pursued. Since there are no sides left after a nuclear war, such a war cannot possibly lead to accommodation.

Thus, whereas the traditional pacifists (or total unilateralists) base their position on moral grounds, the nuclear pacifists rest their case on logic. The difference, however, is not as deep as it seems. First, each group is quite willing to use the arguments of the other to support its position. Second, many (though not all) nuclear pacifists agree that escalation from conventional to nuclear war is quite likely and that total disarmament is necessary, therefore, to avoid nuclear wars. In short, both groups agree that war should be abolished; no circumstance can justify it.

In addition to moral and logical arguments, the unilateralists frequently use other arguments—psychological analogies and economic analyses—to point to some sources of the arms race, identify factors that prevent its cessation or even curtailment, and indicate ways and means to remove such obstacles to peace.

PSYCHOLOGY OF THE ARMS RACE AND DISARMAMENT

The starting point for the psychological analysis of disarmament is a question. If the arms race so obviously leads to individual and collective disaster for friend, foe, and neutral alike, why do we not try to stop it? Several theories are advanced, which for the most part complement rather than contradict each other.[5]

One way to prevent ourselves from seeing a danger is to deny reality. Denial is a well-known psychological phenomenon; it typically emerges under conditions of high stress. When stress is minimal, we are realistic and happy and continue in the path

[5] Among the leading authorities in this field are Jerome D. Frank, Erich Fromm, and David Riesman. Much of the following discussion has benefited from their various writings.

we have chosen. When stress is medial, we are still realistic and try to abandon our path and look for a more satisfactory one. Under conditions of high stress, we are stricken with panic and tend irrationally to withdraw from reality; we deny that there is a danger and rigidly hold to our fatal path.

High stress, of the kind psychologists feel is generated by a world populated with nuclear bombs, makes people deny the dangers of nuclear war, optimistically assume it can be deterred, and rigidly adhere to the arms race line. An objective examination of reality may confront us with an unbearable fate—the fear of which not only inhibits us from seeing things as they are but also prevents us from finding a way out of the fear-ridden state.

Our repressed fears and latent anxiety, it is suggested, account for four psychological phenomena: stereotyping, paranoia, prestige obsession, and schizophrenia; all of these, according to various psychoanalysts and psychologists, distort our international behavior.

We stereotype by seeing events as either black or white; by choosing from our experience those elements that fit into our mental image and ignoring those that might force us to change our mind. Stereotyping is common to relationships among races, ethnic groups, and nations; in particular it affects those hostile to each other. Blocked or distorted communication between hostile groups prevents each from correcting its false image of the other.

Stereotyping often goes hand in hand with another psychological phenomenon, that of paranoia, or feelings of persecution. Whatever our adversary does or suggests (for example, if he offers complete disarmament coupled with complete inspection) we either ignore or interpret as a device to further his own interest (for example, we interpret Russia's disarmament proposals as a propaganda gambit). We could, of course, stymie the Russians rather easily by agreeing to their proposals (thereby, to continue the example, either gaining disarmament or exposing them as liars), thus destroying their propaganda advantage. But a paranoiac is likely to find a hidden trap in this suggestion, too.

The paranoiac believes that the entire world is seeking to destroy him. He lets his behavior be guided by apprehension of events that are logically possible but extremely improbable, rather than taking the course of a normal person, who guides his behavior primarily by events that are fairly likely to occur. If we feel that whenever we cross a street we are sure to be hit by a car—which is, of course, a possibility—then we can never cross a street. And if we feel that any stranger we meet may try to kill us—which is again a possibility, but very unlikely—then we have to stay home. Psychologists point out that efforts to tie up every possible loophole in negotiations with the Russians over cessation of nuclear tests and disarmament are paranoid. The character of modern weapons is such that a completely effective inspection plan is impossible; hence, by constantly pointing out possible but unlikely violations inherent in a particular plan, we are acting like paranoiacs.

When confronted with a threat, real or imagined, we respond aggressively with a counterthreat (for example, increasing our arms orders), to which the other side responds with a counterthreat (expanding *his* armaments). Thus, regardless of whether the original response was made to a real or to an imagined threat, the vicious circle continues and leads to the same result: an ever accelerated arms race and eventually Doomsday.

The same repressed fear also makes us see any concession to the other side as submission, cowardice, resignation, or, to use the political term, appeasement. It labels such behavior as disloyal or treacherous, and it impedes negotiations, which require open-mindedness, flexibility, and willingness to make concessions while defending major values and positions.

Such a frame of mind leads to prestige obsession. Every normal person has some concern with the respect of others for his integrity and position. But only a power- and prestige-obsessed person will regard every matter as one affecting his principles and status. True, small matters can acquire such generalized meaning *if seen* as standing for important principles or issues. A teen-ager will not say "uncle" even if the gang threatens to break his arm, because he has staked his self-esteem and status on a refusal; but a mature person selects the issues to which he will attach such meanings. Only a highly infantile person will let others pressure him into a position where every issue, significant or not, becomes a matter of principle, where rational behavior, such as negotiation, becomes impossible. This, it is suggested, is our present mental state.

Finally, psychologists detect signs of schizophrenia in our ability to discuss coolly, and even to plan, mass destruction of others and ourselves in magnitudes that dwarf the most shocking devastations of World War II. One big nuclear bomb can create more human misery than all the concentration camps put together, not only in immediate victims but also in the misery of people who will slowly burn up or vomit themselves to death. Only people whose thoughts have become dissociated from their emotions can make such plans. It is such dissociation that characterizes the schizophrenic patient.

What, the psychologists ask, can be done? How can one break the vicious circle—the stereotyping, the paranoid orientation, the schizophrenic state? Increased communication with the other side is highly recommended. Exchange visits of Russians and Americans and participation in such joint ventures as the International Geophysical Year are favored remedies. Also recommended is the creation of new shared endeavors, such as joint space exploration and Russian-American teams for underdeveloped countries. Ultimately, world law and world government are deemed essential.

Psychologists have indicated that bilateral disarmament, agreed upon by both sides, is unlikely, for all the processes discussed above create such a high level of hostility, mutual fear, and suspicion that negotiations inevitably break down and the mutual recriminations that follow reduce rather than increase the chances of disarmament. Hence what is needed—as Jerome Frank, for instance, recommends—are unilateral moves that will break down this psychological state. These moves must be very clear and very simple, so that the other side will be unable to reject them as insincere, as traps, or as propaganda devices.

In sum, the psychological analysis of our current self-destructive behavior indicates that repressed anxiety about the dire consequences of an approaching nuclear war stops us from preventing the war. We deny the danger, rigidly adhering to a disastrous course. We block communication with the Russians by stereotyping and by giving paranoiac interpretations to their

71

moves, and they do the same to ours. Our schizophrenic tendencies permit us to proceed with the horrible preparations. Both sides are in the same predicament: mutual fear, reinforced and heightened by a vicious circle of suspicion, blocks the settlement of the interbloc conflict through negotiations and multilateral disarmament.

Hence the prognosis: only a one-sided, dramatic move—unilateral disarmament—can break the deadly barriers. The move has to be of such a magnitude that it will be extremely difficult for the other side to reconcile it with its distorted frame of reference. Giving up a base here or a position there will not do; a major act, such as giving up nuclear weapons, or all arms, is required.

## ECONOMICS OF THE ARMS RACE AND DISARMAMENT

The arms race is explained by Marxists, pseudo-Marxists, and other radicals as deriving neither from the nature of the international situation nor the psychology of those exposed to it, but from the nature of the capitalist societies. The unilateralists point to an opening that will allow overcoming this barrier to disarmament.

The essence of the radical analysis is that the arms race promotes the interests of the business circles who reap profits directly or indirectly from weapon production. These circles include not only the arms manufacturers and those who supply them with parts and raw materials but also every one of America's millions of stockholders; for whenever preparations for war decline, the entire American economy—and with it, at least in the past, those of many industrial Western countries—suffers a recession. The Great Depression was not really overcome, these analysts point out, until the arms build-up for World War II started; the postwar recession ended only when the arms race for the Korean war spurred the American economy; subsequent smaller ups and downs of the economy have been closely related to ups and downs in the tension of the cold war. For instance, the Wall Street stock market experienced merry rallies after the breakdown of the 1960 summit conference in Paris and the 1961 Berlin crisis. The rallies were led by "defense" stocks, but other stocks benefited as well.

Workers also benefit from the arms race. The close association between employment and international tension, unemployment and relaxation of this tension, is well reflected in the following figures. In 1939, 17.2 per cent of the American labor force was unemployed. The war reduced unemployment to 1.2 per cent in 1944. Unemployment rose after the war to 3.9 per cent (1946), was reduced by the Korean war to 2.5 per cent; rose after this war was terminated to 5.0 per cent by 1954, and continued to rise to 7.0 per cent in 1961. In the same year, between 6,500,000 and 7,500,000 American jobs depended on defense spending. Were these jobs abolished, the United States would have the same percentage of unemployed as in 1939— about 17 per cent.

No less important in explaining many international actions by the United States and its over-all strategy, it is suggested, are business investments abroad. United States foreign investments amounted to $44.8 billion in 1959. Earnings from these investments are 60 per cent higher than from investment in the United States (13.8 per cent versus 8.5 per cent); and much of this investment is held by the powerful 100 top American corporations. It is common among radicals to explain specific United States foreign acts by reference to big business interests abroad: intervention in the Middle East (for example, in Lebanon) is explained by the interests of various oil companies; intervention in Latin America (for example, in Guatemala), by the interests of the United Fruit Company, whose property was nationalized by the Arbenz Government; intervention in Cuba in 1961, by the interests of the sugar industry, whose property was confiscated by Castro, and so on.

Authorities as diverse as Dwight D. Eisenhower and C. Wright Mills mention two other groups with vested interests in the arms race, though not as owners of means of production. One is composed of generals in the Pentagon and lesser senior officers, wherever stationed. It is said that such men would obviously object to disarmament, which would leave them unemployed, with only a useless vocation to their name. Said Eisenhower in his Farewell Address (January 16, 1961): "We must guard against the acquisition of unwarranted influence, whether sought or unsought, by the military-industrial complex. The potential rise of misplaced power exists and will persist."

The second interest group includes the thousands of scientists and technicians who are employed by the military services or who, while on campus, are awarded large military research grants. With the diminution of defense expenditure, many of them would lose income, travel grants, and prestige.

The radicals accuse these professionals of supplying the anti-disarmament business and military groups with ideologies to cover up their naked self-interest. The RAND Corporation, subsidized by the Air Force, which produced Herman Kahn and his book, is a typical one of many examples. As Harrison Brown and James Real have stated:

> Ten thousand scientists and technicians have devoted all of their lives to the invention and construction of weapons. A majority of those who went to work *after* World War II are convinced that weaponry is a way of life for themselves and expect the U.S.-Soviet contest to continue forever. Many of them are articulate and highly valued consultants in every walk of American life, from the Congressional committee to the P.T.A.[6]

C. Wright Mills, whose *The Causes of World War Three* stresses the role of the "military metaphysics" in the drift toward nuclear disaster, states:

> Technologists and scientists readily develop new weapons; preachers and rabbis and priests bless the great endeavor; newsmen disseminate the official definitions of world reality, labeling for their publics the shifting line-up of friends and enemies; publicists elaborate the "reasons" for the coming war, and the "necessity" for the causes of it. They do not set forth alternative policies; they do not politically oppose and politically debate the thrust toward war. They have generally become the Swiss Guard of the power elite. . . .[7]

What do the various social analysts feel can be done to counter these pressures toward war? Most radicals are highly dubious about the possibility of doing anything constructive within the framework of capitalist society, in particular that of

[6] Harrison Brown and James Real, *Community of Fear* (Santa Barbara, Calif., Center for the Study of Democratic Institutions, 1960).
[7] C. Wright Mills, *The Causes of World War Three*, (New York, Simon and Schuster, 1958).

the United States; they believe that changing international relations must begin with a revolutionary change at home. Only when public ownership of the means of production abolishes the profit motive will the true incentive for the armaments production and race disappear; only when employment is controlled by the government (there is no unemployment in a Communist society) and not by the business cycle, will the socioeconomic conditions of disarmament be met. To work for peace, radicals say, therefore requires working for a socialist revolution.

"Unilateral" economists have worked out several schemes for alleviating pressures toward armament within the framework of a capitalistic society. For instance, various peaceful functions are suggested for ex-armament industries, programs are recommended to keep the economy running at full speed by spending the funds saved by cuts in the military budget. Increased investment in schools, medicine, and underdeveloped countries are the favorite recommendations. In addition, economist Kenneth E. Boulding has pointed out that disarmament may require as much investment as the arms race, if not more, because of the cost of inspection, monitors, international armies, and international organizations.

Similarly, programs have been suggested to retrain army officers for peaceful vocations while maintaining their salary, status, and security. For instance, military pilots could be used by civilian air lines; various military staff members might make good college teachers; and medical researchers developing nerve-gas and bacteriological weapons could do as well fighting cancer and mental illness.[8] It is also estimated that about 40,000 militarily trained personnel will be required to staff disarmament inspection programs. In short, the basic radical analysis is accepted, but not its solution. Disarmament, the unilateralists suggest, can be brought in line with the economic self-interests of members of the capitalist society.

Objective assessment of the economic forces that serve to perpetuate the arms race is extremely difficult. It would require a book at least the size of this one to disentangle truth from half-truth and to analyze the various complications involved.

[8] For various plans, see Seymour Melman, *The Peace Race* (New York, Ballantine Books, 1961), especially Chapter 9.

It may be true, for instance, that officers have a vested interest in a military career; on the other hand, many officers are truly devoted to their country and might be willing to sacrifice their careers—they might certainly be willing to expose themselves to the pains of retraining for civil careers—in order to serve its best interests. Moreover, the American government did reduce its military budget after World Wars I and II and the Korean war, though economists knew that such reductions were likely to bring about recession or depression. As for American investments abroad, the situation is even more complex; we shall discuss this point at some length in Chapter 10.

The various programs advocated to alleviate the anticipated resistance to disarmament by businessmen, officers, and scientists are, on the one hand, somewhat naive; but, on the other hand, they indicate that the situation is not beyond remedy. It is somewhat unlikely that SAC pilots would be welcome in the civilian air lines, already overstaffed as a consequence of the introduction of jets. It is also questionable if army colonels would relish teaching college freshmen, even if the salary were equivalent. Yet, it is true that locating alternative employment and subsidizing retraining where necessary will ease the transition. If it is true that disarmament, at least initially, requires considerable personnel with military skill and considerable equipment for which ex-military assembly lines can be used (for example, observers' towers, satellites, and monitors), then the economic crisis caused by disarmament would be less severe than has been suggested. It seems safe to conclude that if we investigate the problems involved and plan ahead for them, the transition to a peacetime economy can be eased; the anxiety of vested-interest groups can be alleviated; and with it, resistance to disarmament can be reduced, though not eliminated.

## Unilateralism—A Critical Assessment

The essential aim of bona-fide unilateralism, defined as a one-sided disarming of the West (not just of one Western country), is to break the suspicion barrier by a major—that is, militarily significant—sacrifice, not merely a gesture, and to reject force as an instrument of national policy. "War is an obsolete social institution" is the true unilateralists' motto.

Two questions have to be asked in evaluating this position. First, is a genuine unilateral program acceptable to the American people and their government? Second, what would be the consequence of unilateral disarmament if it is implemented, and how acceptable are the various possible results?

## POLITICAL FEASIBILITY

Does unilateralism, as a political program, stand a chance of being adopted by the American government as its foreign policy and strategy? After giving this question the most careful examination I am capable of giving, I conclude that it does not. Not only is unilateralism completely alien to the American people and their leaders, but the forces supporting it are also politically impotent.

The limited appeal unilateralism has is not accidental; *the very factors so effectively pointed out by unilateralists as barring interbloc negotiations also bar the acceptance of their plan by the American people.* Many Americans are indeed infested with suspicions of the Communists, fears over bombs secretly hidden by the other side, paranoid feelings over China, and so forth. Hence, suggesting that they should put their trust into the Russians' conscience (or "inherent nonexpansionism") to the degree that they will allow their government to disarm unilaterally is utterly unrealistic.

The American man on the street, the typical American voter, hates Communism intensely. According to a poll taken by the American Institute of Public Opinion (AIPO) in 1955, 55 per cent of the American people were willing to engage in atomic war in order not to lose Quemoy and Matsu. As many as 81 per cent would have the United States stay in Berlin even if it means war with Russia, according to a 1959 poll. The more frustrations Americans suffer on the international front or in space competition, the more aggressive their mood becomes. After the ill-fated American-supported invasion of Cuba, itself an expression of this mood, President Kennedy made his first "tough" speech about Communism, declaring that the United States would fight it regardless of cost and perils. According to

77

an analysis of mail received in the White House, this proved to be the most popular speech he had made to date.

The American people do not know what war means. Their country has not suffered physical devastation for a century. In all the wars in its history, the United States was never defeated. As a result, its people have built up an enormous conviction of invincibility. They are much more likely to authorize their government to push the nuclear button than to allow it to disarm. To suggest that American politicians and leaders can convince their people to substitute nonviolent action for armed defense, passive resistance for the Marines, is Utopian. Unilateralism is an expression of emotion, wishful thinking, and good intention, but it is no more politically potent than these are and has no chance of being implemented.

When the political impotence of the unilateralist program is criticized, its advocates frequently give two answers. One is that unilateralism is morally right, and that political inexpedience is therefore no excuse for abandoning it. Such a position might be quite legitimate when it comes to most other issues. Nobody, for example, would insist that prohibitionists, who believe that drinking liquor is a sin, should stop their fight just because they are unlikely to succeed. But when the issue is nuclear war, the unilateralists' lack of political insight and skill dwarfs the peace movement. The limited funds, leaders, and supporters that could help push through a more realistic program, are riding the windmills. Unilateralists refuse to save life unless it is saved their way. *Trying to save their souls by uncompromising morality, they may well lose humanity.*

The second answer to the argument of impotence is that the unilateralists are out to educate a small minority; that, as the international situation deteriorates, more people may be ready to see the light. Without such a vanguard there is no hope at all. This argument is typical of unsuccessful radical movements waiting for the revolutionary opportunity, which often serves only as a rationale for continuing an unfruitful program. In fact, as the international situation continues to deteriorate, as it has for the last several years, the public becomes more and more aggressive and the pacifist program becomes less and less adequate.

Even if unilateralism were viable as a political program, the

78

American peace movement is quite incapable of putting it across. Small to begin with, split into numerous groups and constantly splintering, full of personal feuds, undermined by the "support" of local Communists (real and imagined) and religious pacifists whose aim is the "abolishment of hatred and the rule of love," the peace movement is hardly able to advance any program, not to mention as "unsalable" a one as unilateralism.

Trying desperately to be heard, the peace movement has turned to various attention-getting devices, from entering nuclear test areas to refusing to take shelter during civil defense drills. These devices do indeed gain attention, but rather for the advocates of peace than for their ideas, in the process depriving their platform of the respectability essential for political success in a predominantly middle-class society.

Aside from the publicity stunts, which affect the image of the whole movement though they are supported by only part of the membership, the tactics of unilateralism can be likened to those of movements trying to obtain fluoridation of town water or approval for school bond issues. Lectures are given, pamphlets are printed, discussion groups are organized, local secretaries are elected. It seems that such methods are ineffective in changing opinion on even local political issues (most fluoridation and school bond drives fail); but these methods are surely inappropriate when it comes to so major an issue as national strategy. Fluoridation and school bonds are local issues, decided by local authorities, over whom the voters have some direct effect; national strategy is worked out by teams of experts and decided upon in confidential meetings of bodies such as the National Security Council and the President's formal or informal Cabinet. Rarely do the American people know specifically what these strategies are, and rarely do they have a chance to vote on them before they have been implemented. Thus Truman made what was probably the most fateful decision of the twentieth century, to drop atomic bombs on Hiroshima and Nagasaki, before the American public even knew that such bombs existed. Extremely few people today know whether, and under what conditions, the American government would initiate nuclear war. Most Americans will not even believe that their government is preparing the means required for chemical and bacteriological warfare; hence they are hardly in a position to influence the decisions concerning their use.

Let us assume, however, that the unilateralists united their movement; concentrated their efforts on winning over already organized groups instead of unorganized, politically weightless individuals; established an effective lobby in Washington; reduced their aims from abolishing hatred to "just" unilateral disarmament; and then one day succeeded in doing the impossible—making the American government follow their ideas—what would happen then?

## UNILATERALISM AND THE COMMUNISTS

Let us assume for a moment that the United States has decided to shoot all its nuclear and atomic bombs to the other side of Venus and to dismantle all its military machinery. The Russians are invited to send as many inspectors as they wish, to check wherever and as often as they like. The Communists (this includes the Chinese, who are unlikely to trust the Russians in such a matter) become convinced, after thorough examination, that the United States has really disarmed. What then?

The Communists might bomb the United States, but I quite agree with the unilateralists that they are unlikely to do so. Why should they risk world condemnation, and the pangs of their own conscience, when they can get all they want without bombs?

They might send over an occupation army. This, thinks unilateralist Jerome Frank, is unlikely because an occupation would require considerable personnel and resources, "especially if they knew they would be met by a population fully determined to resist them by nonviolent means and well-trained to do so."[9] But to judge from the experiences of the Roman Empire, Nazi Germany, and the Soviet Union itself, it is not so difficult to control large countries, once their military might has been cracked. The Communists would find such occupation less demanding than other victors have found it because they are likely to have at least some local support. Their great skill at using instruments of persuasion would help to enlist the sup-

[9] *Sanity and Survival* (Berkeley, Calif., Acts for Peace, n.d.), p. 15.

port of others.[10] The likelihood (or, rather, unlikelihood) that the American people would resist by Gandhilike methods has been pointed out. Americans are much more likely to band together in small guerrilla groups, trying to no avail to stop the expansion of Communism by means that their government has just relinquished.

The third possible course for the Communists is the one they are most likely to take: to annex the rest of Asia, Africa, and Latin America, leaving Western Europe and United States-Canada to themselves for a while. Even now many of these countries, with masses of poor peasants and workers, are ripe for Communism. They neither could nor would resist Communist occupation once the United States had removed the military rim containing the Communist bloc.

Finally, the unilateralists expect the Russians to reciprocate by disarming also. Perhaps, one cool afternoon, for the sake of mental exercise (there is certainly no hurry), Khrushchev asks his advisers to give him one reason why he should disarm. They are hard put to find one. As the only armed power in the world, the Communists can take over whatever part of the world they desire, whenever they desire. They can cut their military budget, but why give up armaments? They do not have to use weapons; they do not even have to threaten. The fact that they are the only force left is well known and is by itself quite sufficient. They can rely on propaganda and ideological campaigns, *in which they were frequently more successful than the West,* to bring their way of life to Asia, Africa, and Latin America, where the most advantageous conditions for receptivity to Communism exist. They can decide what to do with the rest of the world later.

In short, unilateralism will save life and avoid war—an achievement not to be taken lightly; but the Communist way of life will pervade the earth. Inherently less irrational and hence more stable than Nazism, it is likely to reign for many generations.

Erich Fromm has stated that the chief potential cause of

---

[10] The problems involved in and the consequences of combining force with persuasion are extensively analyzed in the author's *A Comparative Analysis of Complex Organizations* (New York, The Free Press of Glencoe, 1961).

war is mutual fear (of weapons), not expansionism and efforts to block it. He feels that the idea that "the Soviet Union is out to conquer the world for Communism and that, if the United States disarmed, Russia would be all the more eager to achieve her wish for world domination . . . is based on an erroneous appreciation of the nature of the present-day Soviet Union."[11] Western disarmament, together with internal developments in the East (such as increased concern with a higher standard of living and increasing Sino-Soviet tensions), would suffice to eliminate the motives for Communist expansion.

The Communists themselves, however, do not claim that fear of the West is their prime reason for their expansion efforts. They have a way of life which they see as better and more just than that by which the non-Communist world lives. Since the Russian Revolution of 1917, they have promised to bring this way of life to the rest of the world and have consistently worked toward that goal. They have exposed themselves to many deprivations in order to advance this goal. Now that the way is finally open and all risks are removed, why should they fail to carry out what they see as their historic mission? Moreover, the Soviets believe that they cannot become a true Communist society as long as there are capitalist societies in the world. Conversion of the world to Communism is thus not only part of their historical assignment (which Marxists take very seriously), but also a condition of success in their own country. Khrushchev is apparently willing to delay achievement of the Communist goal considerably in order to avoid a nuclear war and in order not to risk what he has won so far. He also believes, and he has increasing support for his view, that he can achieve this goal gradually without risking a nuclear war. But with the removal of the risk implied in the West's armed deterrence, which not only stops his bombers but also reduces his nonviolent expansion, he could hardly fail to go ahead with what is as dear to him as the Bill of Rights is to an American.

Well, say the unilateralists; well, says Lord Russell; well, says H. Stuart Hughes, retreating to the last line of defense: If the worst outcome of unilateral disarmament is Communist world domination, whereas the worst outcome of the arms race is

[11] Fromm, *loc. cit.,* p. 1021.

annihilation, Better Red Than Dead. Nuclear annihilation is a certainty (if the arms race continues); Communist domination is only a risk. Every person in his right mind would prefer a bad risk to a worse certainty.

The position of the Multideterrence strategists is that this is a false dilemma, that an alternative exists to both Communist world domination and annihilation of all life. That alternative is the risk of destruction of some life to defend freedom. But we have seen that the danger of losing all of life and all of civilization is, or soon will be, entirely real; and the unilateralists have pointed out that defending freedom by bombs leads to a garrison state, to a victory of totalitarianism without war.

The crucial questions then are: Is there no other alternative? Is there no route less fraught with risk? Is there no more acceptable choice than that between the arms race (whether or not life is in jeopardy) and Communist domination? The answer, as presented in the next chapter, is a qualified yes. A politically feasible policy for a peaceful "settling" of interbloc conflict exists. It is a policy that may not succeed, but it involves so few risks that it ought to be tried prior to either deadly multideterrence or submissive unilateralism.

## Chapter 4

### What Is to Be Done— The Gradualist Position

WHAT IS to be done? We have seen past strategies which have not worked and Utopian remedies that will never work. To put it in a nutshell: advocates of Massive Retaliation, supporters of Multideterrence, and to a great extent old and new Containment men, would risk life itself to advance national interests and to defend the Western way of life. Unilateralists of various shades and brands would sacrifice national interests and jeopardize the Western way of life in order to preserve life itself. Both schools are willing to pay high prices and to take grave risks. But there is a course which risks neither life nor

83

liberty—the course offered by Gradualism. There is no guarantee that it will succeed and there cannot be one. But the unique advantage of Gradualism is that it does not require guarantees. The United States has little or nothing to lose if this strategy should fail; the world has a great deal to gain if it succeeds. Moreover, if the policy should fail, the United States is still free to turn to some more dangerous and more costly strategy.

Gradualism is oriented toward elimination of international violence while preserving both the national security and the values to which we are committed, through (1) reduction of international tension, (2) reversal of the arms race, and (3) an interbloc political settlement. Gradualism is implicit in the platform of the Committee of Correspondence, which declared in its widely circulated and subscribed Bear Mountain statement that it favors "unilateral steps toward disarmament," but did not so much as mention unilateral disarmament. The Committee is composed of American intellectuals and has followings on about thirty campuses across the United States. Its members include some traditional unilateralists, who support the Bear Mountain statement as a minimum program, but also such level-headed and responsible persons as William Davidon, Albert Hozelitz, Robert Pickus, Mark Raskin, and David Riesman. The most important contribution to the psychological analysis which the Gradualist approach draws on was made by Charles E. Osgood, president of the American Psychological Association. Gradualism is also implied by a statement circulated by Toward Peace, an effort conducted by a large number of civic groups, religious organizations, labor unions, and pacifist organizations. SANE, a widely known peace action organization, seems also to be approaching what I call a Gradualist line.

Gradualism derives its name from the fact that it is built on several interdependent steps or grades; the activation of each successive step depending on the success of the preceding ones. This exposition of Gradualism begins with an analysis of the present international situation in which it has to be applied. I then present the strategy itself and specify the conditions for its effective application. Finally we face the question of what is to be done if, after all, it fails.

# The Gradualist Opportunity

The successful application of any strategy requires that it be based on an adequate analysis of the objective situation and that it be geared to take advantage of the opportunities that arise from its changing features. I have therefore to show that Gradualism is both politically acceptable in terms of the internal politics of the West, and highly responsive to the changing international reality.

## THE PRESENT STATE

*The power balance has changed in favor of Russia,* which has moved from a secondary world power position to a primary one, from nuclear inferiority to nuclear parity; indeed, many believe that with the development of their rocketry the Russians have achieved nuclear superiority.

In 1960 and the beginning of 1961 it was widely agreed that the Russians were ahead of the United States in the development of the main type of "means of delivery," that is, long-range missiles. The "missile gap" was widely believed to exist. After the Soviet air show in 1961, many experts felt that the Russians are also ahead in air power, not just space power. Russian tests of nuclear arms in the latter part of 1961 indicated, according to the Bethe report to the National Security Council, that they are not behind in this area either. (The claim that the Russians' tests were conducted only to spread terror among the neutral countries was quietly dropped since they obviously tested new nuclear weapons). But at the end of 1961 a sudden reversal of all these estimates was suggested. Intelligence reports not only made public but were even publicized to indicate that the Russians have only forty-five long-range missiles and a comparatively small air force.

The layman, who has no access to classified information, must still find it difficult to believe such reports. First of all, the earlier figures of 500 to 2000 Russian missiles by 1962 were given by the same intelligence agencies that now find only forty-five missiles. Why is the estimate of forty-five more trustworthy than 500 or 2000? Second, present intelligence counts seem to be largely based on counting the number of launching

85

pads; but if the Russians have moved on to mass production of what is widely believed to be the next step of rocketry—that of missiles that can be launched from railroad platforms or trucks —it is not surprising how few launching pads were found. Finally, the Russians would be more than stupid to use a third of their missile force to put Sputniks into the sky, if they really had only a small number of missiles. The Russian space shots clearly indicate the existence of powerful and abundant production of long-range, high-thrust missiles. In the following analysis I assume that (a) the Russians have largely increased their power position vis-à-vis the United States in the last decade, and that (b) by now their nuclear might is at least at par if not superior to that of the West. Their superiority in conventional arms is rarely if ever questioned.

*The Communist Chinese are more aggressive than the Russians, but they are not yet ready for a major war.*

*While the power of the West has relatively declined, the West still has enormous power,* especially for an "all-out" war.

Both sides are aware of (1) *the consequences of limited wars, nuclear or conventional;* (2) *those of all-out nuclear war;* (3) the high probability that a limited war will occur; and (4) the likelihood that a limited war will escalate into an all-out nuclear war.

The fact that Russians also realize these facts is revealed in the strategy they exercise. *They take minimal risks in their continued efforts to expand.* Despite their strong feelings about West Berlin and the many years of tensions there, they have not applied their military might in any one of the many ways open to them, from keeping the land routes blocked to supporting a "revolution" started by "local" Communists. When the situation looked risky in Laos, they agreed to an armistice, although it was generally believed that if they had not, the West would not have interfered militarily and the Pathet Lao guerrillas probably would have taken the entire country. The Russians preferred an armistice to the small chance of another open armed clash with the United States. Similarly, they did not send direct military support, even in the form of "volunteers" (not to mention rockets) into any one of the many fronts to which the West sent troops, despite the Communist promise to do so. They did not march to the aid of Nasser in Egypt or Lumumba in the Congo, or the FLN in Algeria. While they constantly nibble at the West, they are extremely cautious; they rarely take large bites, and almost never at two places at the same time. The Berlin crisis was warmed up in mid-1961 only after the Laos one was carefully chilled.

These instances of hypercaution indicate that the Russians still are less sure of their present might than we are and than we think they are; that they know they are not quite ready yet; and that they have considerable respect for the West's actual as well as potential military might.

The Russians realize that the very success of their nibbling may endanger the state of nonwar. The West might regard each loss in itself as "minor," hence not "deserving" a major military effort. But the accumulation, especially the acceleration, of "minor" losses may have the same effect as a major loss. It might alarm Western public opinion to the point that it would encourage Western governments to utilize the superior GNP[1] of the West, particularly that of the United States, to accelerate the arms race. Worse, unwilling to pay the price of a really big arms race, frustrated by an accelerated accumulation of losses, the West might in a moment of desperation push the button that unleashes the nuclear striking forces. After all, as the Russians see it, only one nation has ever employed an atomic bomb.

## THE COMING YEARS

Many of these factors will change in the near future, though no one can predict exactly when. But because overoptimism can have such tragic consequences, one should act conservatively. It is better to abolish the arms race a few years too early than one day too late.

In the next few years the United States position is likely to become weaker, especially if the Communists continue to keep their nibbling level low. The Russians will probably retain, if not increase, their technical-military lead, for the United States appears unlikely to spend the enormous amounts of resources that any attempt to catch up would cost. China will develop its gigantic force, now just potential, and add it to that of Russia. As the West's position will continue to weaken, more countries in Asia, Africa, and Latin America will shift from a pro-Western

[1] Gross National Product, the base of a country's economic power.

to a neutral position (Brazil and Thailand were leading this movement in 1961), and more of the neutral countries will ally themselves with the East as the power balance continues to change in its favor (though not all of them will formally join the Communist bloc or establish a military alliance with it). The United States' declining power in the United Nations is one expression of this process.

China will become more and more independent of Russia's aid, more able to support its Communist allies, and will be militarily more potent, and thus will constantly increase its influence in the Communist camp. While at the same time it will lose some of its "toughness," especially if it is more readily accepted in the world community, it is nevertheless very likely that increases in its power will be more rapid than decreases in its aggressive outlook. The total effect of the coming power of China will hence be a decline in Russian leadership, matched by a continuous and important gain in Chinese leadership, and an increase in the Communist bloc's "toughness" and readiness to take risks.

In sum, if my assessment of the present power distribution and its future shifts is valid, the next three to seven years supply our one great opportunity to "settle" without a major war. It is tempting to say that this is our last chance, but such a statement assumes that the worst will happen. One does not have to assume a Doomsday in order to suggest that we should not miss this opportunity. Even if we can settle later, even without first having an exchange of nuclear disaster, it is likely that the later we settle, the more concessions we will have to make.

I keep referring to a "settlement," and the reader must by now want to know what such settlement implies. The following two sections of this chapter are devoted to answering precisely this question.

## Views of Settlement: American, Russian, and Chinese

It is very difficult for a proud young nation, never yet defeated, to realize that the scale of power is tipping against it. But there is no question that if the present trends continue, the power of the West as compared to that of the East will keep on declining. The earlier the West settles, therefore, the better will be the terms, from its standpoint. It is also vital to note that from the viewpoint of world safety, the later a settlement comes, the more chance there is of at least a "small" nuclear war, and this possibility alone makes an early settlement highly advisable. Furthermore, if a settlement has to be reached in any event, the earlier we settle, the less will be wasted on the arms race.

The only condition under which the West could prefer to stall would be if it had good reason to believe it could improve its position in the near future. But the odds are against the West's pulling ahead in the arms race, even if it did decide to increase its efforts. That the Russians have a lead is enough to favor them. The West could spurt forward by turning to its superior GNP; in the past, however, unless the crisis was very evident, continuous, and close to home, a democratic government has been unable to gain public support for the heavy taxation and national debt required for an armament marathon. The Russians are likely to keep their pressure low enough so as not to alarm the American public, as they have done so effectively in the past. Moreover, today as in the Eisenhower days, advisors and senators still may whisper in the ears of the President that a preventive war against Russia, using big nuclear bombs, is not only much more likely to succeed than a multifaced arms race but is also much cheaper. We need a settlement to protect us from such homicidal-suicidal urges.

Finally—and this is probably the most crucial point—we have a limited number of years in which to work out a settlement. If those years are devoted to an accelerated arms race, we might very well miss the big chance while still building ever-increasing piles of arms and counterarms. Sooner or later, probably some time between 1968 and 1972, the entire situation will have changed. When the Communist bloc is more influenced by China, the United States may well have an adversary who will not be willing to settle without first testing its claim to superiority in a nuclear duel.

## WHAT ABOUT THE RUSSIANS?

Most people assume that if the odds are against the West, they are in the East's favor, and hence that the Russians will try to settle as late as posible (short of a major nuclear war) or not at all. If the West sits at the negotiation table under the present conditions, it is suggested, the Russians will methodically pick the West to pieces.

But let us take the Russians' viewpoint for a moment. First, the Russians share with the West many of the hazards of the arms race. A war will cost them millions of lives, too. There is no way to guarantee that the devastation of their country will be less than that of the United States; they do love their country and know what a war means. Second, after many years of tightening their belts, they have other uses for their resources than buying arms. The longer and the larger the arms race, the more they have to pour into it. While they do not spend more than the West does in absolute terms, they already spend a much larger proportion of their national income on the military. And while they are more accustomed to such deprivations than is the West, they are also more tired of them. Hence an accelerated arms race would be much more painful to Russia than to the West.

The Russians share a third predicament with the West, though it affects them differently—the coming power of China. The later Russia settles with the West, the more likely it is to lose its leadership to China, and the more likely China is to determine the time, conditions, and nature of the settlement. The Russians may not like this at all, especially since the Chinese are willing to risk more—and the stakes include the Russian state and achievement!

Finally, the Russians must realize that the very change of the power balance in their favor is dangerous for them. They are surely aware of the West's accumulated frustrations, and they must surely know that if they make the American people feel cornered, the Americans might lash back in a way which will result in the Russians' winning all the battles but losing the campaign. What good will be their careful, gradual expansion, their patient nibbling at the West, if suddenly their heartland is devastated and their whole bloc disintegrated? Under these conditions, it makes a lot of sense for them to settle under what the West might view as relatively reasonable terms.

Above all, the Russians do believe (and as we shall see below, not without reason) that they will do much better in a disarmed world than in an armed world. They feel they are much more successful in ideological strife than the West and that the sociological condtions for the spread of Communism are ripe in Asia, Africa, and Latin America, as well as in southern Europe. Their chain of frequent successes only strengthens this belief. They should therefore be willing to settle. We shall see that this assumption can be tested without undue risk.

## WHAT ABOUT THE CHINESE?

The Chinese are not willing to settle, and show it. If they had free command of the Communist bloc, they would follow a much tougher line with regard to the West. This was the major struggle in the 1960 Communist Congress in Moscow, where the Russians favored a more cautious policy, while the Chinese complained bitterly about Russia's "softness" toward the West. The Chinese are "tougher" because they have less to lose than the Russians: they have built comparatively little as yet. They may also be much less concerned over potential population losses than the Russians, since there are 669 million Chinese, compared to 209 million Russians. Chou En-lai, premier of overpopulated China, is reported to have told a Yugoslav diplomat that an all-out nuclear war would leave 10 million Americans, 20 million Russians, and 350 million Chinese. Like many nations in the early stages of industrial revolution, the Chinese are less educated and more barbarous than either the primitive or the highly industrialized countries. Knowing less about the West, they might believe there is no nuclear fight left in it, especially after the American bluff was called in Indochina.

The crucial fact is, however, that *at this stage* they cannot fight alone. They are highly dependent on technological and economic aid from Russia; they have no nuclear bombs, no missiles, and only a World War II-type military machinery. Nor can they gain the support of most other Communist countries. The Russian superiority position was well reflected in the 1960 Communist Congress debates. Whatever the face-saving resolutions made public, the fact is that all Communist countries with the exception of tiny Albania (as backward as China in industry and education) supported the Russian line, including even China's neighbors, North Korea and North Vietnam. In short, China may not be willing to settle, but for the next few years it will not have much choice. The longer the West and Russia wait, the more power and voice China will have. Once it will

combined. The West and Russia are confronted with a big op-
it will have more force than all other Communist countries
complete its basic industrialization and build its nuclear power,
portunity to settle, and China is at present unable to hinder it.

## The Gradualist Policy: What Needs to Be Done?

It is possible to test the assumptions which underlie the claim that we face an opportunity to "settle." It seems pointless to speculate about Communists' intentions or deduce the impossibility of negotiations from theories about "suspicion barriers" and paranoia when one can go and find out, *without* undue risks. This is the essence of Gradualism. It suggests a strategy that will create a situation in which the Russians' willingness to settle can be tested; in which the West will be psychologically able to settle; in which the West's willingness to settle will be demonstrated; and in which the settlement itself will be worked out as a Gradualist strategy.

In full contrast to the basic unilateralist assumptions, Gradualism assumes that it is not necessary to disarm unilaterally in order to break the stalemate; there is no need to strip oneself naked to indicate that one is willing to talk. The West can negotiate without first significantly weakening its military might, and without laying the world open to Communist domination, by following a strategy that will reduce the international tensions, the nonrational barriers that now block successful interbloc communication and negotiations. It is the present international situation that makes such a psychological strategy appropriate.

Unilateralists, especially of the psychological branch, often seem to consider the entire problem one of a twisted state of mind, mutual fear barriers, and vicious circles of suspicion. It seems to me that one should not underplay the import of objective elements, such as weapons capacities, their distribution among the contenders, economic capabilities, and geopolitical factors. Each of these, as well as the psychological factors, plays a central role. However, as the situation is developing at present the objective factors, as I have tried to show in the preceding pages, enable settlement and require it. Hence the removal of psychological blocks becomes crucial now. It is *now* that our fears, suspicions, and stereotypes are inappropriate, however realistic they might have been in other periods and stages.

There is a strong tendency to apply past strategies to the present and future. Most Americans did not believe that the Russians would put a sputnik in the skies, because they thought the Soviets to be as technologically backward as they were ten or twenty years earlier. Because in the past we saw no possibility of settlement, we are apt to see none now; we are apt to see the chance to settle only when it is gone. Several American foreign policy experts stated that there was a big chance to settle in 1953, after Stalin's death, when there was great turmoil in Russia and its leaders were unsure of their course. However, we continued to project the Stalin image on Russia until it was too late.

It is for these reasons that I think the unilateralist psychological analysis of our attitude applies to the present state and to the near future. We really think that the Russians are out to destroy us; we find quotations in Lenin about "just wars against capitalism" and remember Khrushchev's saying that Communism will bury us. We do not realize that the Russians find quotations in Dulles and Eisenhower speeches and writings that refer to a "crusade" against the evil of Communism and to our intentions to "liberate" China, Eastern Europe, and the Russian people—which, translated into Russian terms, means that we are out to dissolve their bloc and imperil their security. We feel that we defend freedom and they enslave people; they feel that we are capitalist exploiters and warmongers while they are carriers of social justice, the basis of true freedom as they see it. We are alarmed by the Russians' development of rocketry and by Communist "subversions," but we do not realize that the Russians feel quite as threatened by the ring of military bases the United States has set around their mainland. It is safe to generalize that whatever we feel about them they feel about us. What is needed, and what might work under the present conditions, is a policy that will break this vicious circle of suspicion and remove the mental blocs and psychological barriers of both sides, so that each will see the situation as it really is and be capable of acting on this insight. *Reduction of international*

93

*tensions* is hence a primary need to be fulfilled by Gradualist policy.[2]

But we cannot stop there. Removing mental blocks will in itself not solve our problems, but will merely permit a solution to be worked out. The second need is to *slow down, stop, reverse and finally abolish the arms race*. Gradualism can serve this need, too.

It is essential to realize that the two needs are closely related. We are interested not only in the reduction of tensions but also in the reduction of the capacity for violence. As long as there are triggers, somebody might pull them; and as long as there are tensions, somebody might provide triggers. Gradualism seeks to reduce, first, suspicions and tensions and, second, the capacity for violence. Moreover, Gradualism weighs carefully the sacrifices each goal demands, lest we give all we have to gain the first and find ourselves without means to insure the second.

Reduction of tensions and reduction of arms will have to be accompanied by an overhaul of the international system. Reduction of tensions is likely to be followed by new tensions, and arms reductions by rearmament, unless lasting international institutions are founded in which differences of interest and opinion among nations can be settled without resort to violence, as they are settled in any community.

Reducing tensions and arms and building up international institutions is an enormous task. Obviously it cannot be carried out in one act; it will have to be phased out in a number of stages and steps. Moreover, as we shall see, it involves no small risk, and hence the need to provide safeguards for the sides implementing the Gradualist policy. Even if there were no objective needed for these safeguards, they would have to be supplied to overcome some of the irrational fears of the participants.

Gradualism is based on a sequence of stages; we cannot emphasize this too strongly. The later phases are activated only after earlier ones have been successfully completed. The reader might be quite shocked to learn that at phase *n* the United States will consider giving up this or that strategic position, unless he remembers that phase *n* comes only after several uni-

[2] For the first exposition of psychological gradualism see Charles E. Osgood, "A Case for Graduated Unilateral Disengagement," *Bulletin of the Atomic Scientists*, April, 1960, pp. 127–131.

lateral steps by the United States have been reciprocated and after a number of earlier concessions have been made by both sides. In such a context concessions now considered "impossible" will seem, and will be, quite reasonable.

The main stages of Gradualism are as follows.

1. First, the United States *unilaterally* takes some *symbolic* steps to reduce international tensions.

2. After a number of these, it makes some *concessions,* expecting the Russians to *reciprocate.* These concessions are of some, though rather limited, political and military value. A second round of concessions is not initiated until the first round has been reciprocated. But no negotiations are held to assure reciprocation or to determine its scope.

3. Finally, when unilateral symbolic moves and reciprocated concessions have markedly reduced international tension, the United States suggests *multilateral negotiations.* Only at this stage, when the other side's willingness to engage in *simultaneous* and *balanced* concessions is established, can one expect significant arms reduction to take place and important political questions to be settled. The third phase is likely to be long and to require the development of nonviolent means of international competition and, even more, of viable international institutions.

The sequence is constructed in this way on the assumption that the objective situation calls for settlement but psychological factors on both sides block it; hence these factors must be overcome before the situation can be viewed as it is. Once these irrational barriers are successfully removed, negotiations can be opened. This third phase is essential because the unilateral-reciprocation process is too slow, cumbersome, imprecise, and precarious for the settlement of major issues. It is a first-aid device; it is helpful when fruitful negotiations are unattainable; but the major surgery will have to be carried out on the multilateral negotiation table.

## Psychological Gradualism: A Treatment of the Cold War

### The First Phase: Unilateral Symbolic Steps

The first phase involves the introduction of several—though limited in number—symbolic moves to indicate the West's desire to reduce international tension. None of these steps weaken the power of the West.

*Declaration of New Policy.* The West starts by making it evident that there is a major shift in strategy. This would probably happen as follows. The White House and the State Department for a time reply to all questions on policy that American foreign policy is being reviewed and that the United States is in the process of formulating a new strategy. Since Gradualism requires considerable anticipatory planning, the requisite large number of staff conferences, meetings of the National Security Council, and the like, call public attention to the imminent change. Then, on some special occasion chosen to lend emphasis to the import of the announcement, the President of the United States declares the new policy. He is likely to emphasize that other strategies have been advocated, but that he has decided to try Gradualism first, to see if international tensions can be greatly reduced and to test whether their removal opens the door to settlement. He outlines the strategy, making clear how far the United States will go in its unilateral contributions, and he points out that at a later stage the United States will have to wait for reciprocation, and ultimately for multilateralism, before settlement can be achieved.

Before specific examples of Gradualist concessions can be supplied, I must point out that the actual steps to be taken need to be planned by a large staff of public opinion experts, psychologists, military personnel, and political advisors. In addition to their large variety of skills, specializations, and rich experience, this staff will have access to classified material about the United States and the other side. Only such teams will be able to work out the details of this policy, and then only after careful research and deliberation. The following are examples which merely illustrate the general character of Gradualism. One might reject each example and still approve of the policy as a whole.

*Shift in Propaganda.* The very announcement of the adoption of Gradualism will reduce tension by indicating a willingness to settle under reasonable conditions. Of course, this in itself does not suffice. As a next step, the United States might *reduce* and *change* the nature of its propaganda during the "experiment" period. It might reduce its attacks on beliefs central to Communism and halt broadcasts calling on citizens of these countries to reject their governments. It might stop referring to the Communists in offensive terms; in particular, it might stop likening them to the Nazis.

All propaganda means available should stress the United States' efforts to settle and its hope that peaceful coexistence will be established in the near future. The United States might stress its hope that the other side realized the sincerity of the shift in its policy and will be willing to review its own.

*Side Effects of Accident Control.* Several steps which are urgently required in any case might be given more public attention at this stage and thus reduce tensions. Many of these concern nuclear-accident control. It is in the interest of the United States to reduce the probability of accidents, both because of their tragic results and because they may precipitate a war when the country is not ready and when its forces are not alerted. For instance, it has recently been made public that the firing mechanism of Minuteman missiles is now equipped with a lock that cannot be released by one man. This reduces the possibility of an unauthorized attack by one individual (so long as he is not the commander of a Minuteman unit). Similarly, the United States should declare that if an imminent accident comes to its attention (a pilot runs away with a bomber armed with a bomb, or a missile is misfired), it will broadcast the fact immediately on a specified wave length and give full details, such as the direction of the flight, so that the other side will be in a better position to prevent or reduce the potential damage.

Other unilateral steps will have to be devised. In the heat of the propaganda war, we have built up many claims that have symbolic but little real value. Each of these should be given a fresh examination to determine whether the United States could give it up unilaterally without incurring any real damage.

*Preparation for Phase Two.* These early moves will be followed by a rapid succession of steps aimed at initiating the transition to the next phase. First, the West will make a number of concessions; after each it will be announced that the Russians are expected to reciprocate, but reciprocation will *not* be made a condition for continuation. It will be wise to choose some

97

steps for this stage that the United States knows the Russians are likely to reciprocate, either because such reciprocations have occurred in the past or because they have been more or less agreed upon.

Based on past experience, the following steps are likely to reduce international tension and to be reciprocated.

1. The United States might extend the right of Soviet diplomats to travel in the United States (reciprocation in the past has worked mainly the other way around—a reduction of the traveling limits by Russia has led to a reduction by the United States).

2. The United States might release Russians detained in the United States. After President John F. Kennedy entered office in January, 1961, the Russians released two American fliers who were shot down flying an RB-47 reconnaissance plane. A few days later, the United States released a major Russian spy. It was reported that the exchange was not prenegotiated. This exchange supplies a fine illustration of the way reciprocation follows unilateral moves. It is also worth noting that this step, which had no military import whatsoever, was widely credited with reducing international tensions at the time.

3. The United States might remove its objection to the seating of Outer Mongolia in the United Nations. It is known that the Soviets would then remove their objection to the seating of Mauritania, which the United States supports.[3]

Several additional steps will have to be devised. While the United States will announce, following each one of these steps, that it expects Russian reciprocation, it will neither make this a condition for its next step nor state the nature of the reciprocation it expects.

We shall see below how the United States might respond if the Soviet Union were to ignore the American concessions or to reciprocate only to some American moves. But first let us assume that the Russians reciprocate more or less as expected, and that some reduction in international tension has been attained. We are now ready for the second phase.

[3] These lines were written in July, 1961. At the end of October, 1961, the General Assembly elected Outer Mongolia and Mauritania as the 102nd and 103rd members of the United Nations. This step helped to reduce the tensions generated by the 1961 Berlin crisis. It would suggest that other such steps could be implemented just as well and to similar effect.

In the new phase, the United States offers (and is willing to reciprocate) comparatively important political and military concessions, still without demanding specific or simultaneous reciprocation and without necessarily engaging in any kind of negotiation. The central difference between the two phases is that the *magnitude* of each step in the second phase is such that the United States will have to wait for reciprocation after each one (or at most two) in order not to weaken its relative position.

Again, each single example supplied below can be questioned. Some will feel, for instance, that the recognition of Communist China and its admission to the United Nations belongs in the earlier phase of unilateral concessions (some argue that the United States not only would gain by such recognition but is also obligated to offer it in any event). Others will feel that it belongs to the next phase, of negotiated simultaneous concessions. I therefore emphasize again that these examples merely illustrate the general nature of this phase. The actual concessions to be made will have to be worked out by experts.

*Cutting Travel and Commerce Limitations.* The West might remove bans on travel and commerce with the Communist bloc, and expect them to reciprocate in kind. It seems that the West has to offer travel and commerce as a package deal, because the Russians are much less interested in opening their society to travelers and the West is less interested in removing the ban on commerce. But over the years the Russians have increased permissions to enter their country. (There were more than 10,000 American tourists in Russia in 1961, compared to 2500 in 1957, the first year of any large-scale tourism there.) There is a constant increase in the standard of living in Russia; educational and propaganda efforts have largely succeeded in building up the commitment of many of the citizens to their government. They may, therefore—especially in order not to lose what Gradualism has already achieved at this stage or still has to offer—open at least large parts of Russia to traveling.

The United States might feel that the Russians and the Chinese will gain from the removal of the ban on commerce. But it is widely known that the ban is not effective; the Russians buy virtually all the United States goods they want through intermediaries in various neutral countries. The bans probably increase the prices they have to pay, and probably occasion some difficulty in obtaining certain products. But all in all, with some limitations on fissionable material, the United States could safely remove the ban.

A side effect of the removal of these bans would be increased contact between West and East, which is in itself considered desirable for the reduction of international tension and which is expected to work in favor of the West, already so much more open.

*Disengagement.* Disengagement is often suggested as a means of reducing the volatility of the international conflict, but actually it is more important as a device to reduce tension (though it does serve both functions). It is suggested that both sides withdraw from the boundary between the American and the Sino-Russian spheres of influence, so that a neutral buffer zone will emerge to prevent direct contact. Austria is such a zone; so is Finland; some believe Laos is becoming one; it has been suggested that a unified disarmed Germany would be a buffer. The United Nations has in effect produced such a buffer on the border of the Gaza strip between Israel and Egypt.

One function of disengagement is to reduce border incidents that might escalate into wars. Actually the number, scope, and severity of incidents, and especially the way they are defined by the opponents—"regrettable incidents"; "major insults"; "reason for war"—depend not on the actual incidents but on the orientation of the parties to each other. Hence while some bona-fide incidents can be prevented by disengagement, its more important function is to reduce tension. Disengagement symbolizes willingness to reduce tension by giving up one tool of cold war, the creation and exploitation of border incidents, and it indicates willingness to give up control over territory and populations to attain that end.

Disengagement has become a more acceptable technique since the increase in the number, accuracy, and payload of long-range bombers and missiles has decreased the need for military bases close to the enemy. The United States bases in Europe are rapidly becoming obsolete; the short-range Russian missiles would make them inoperative in the first minutes of a war, and there is no way to protect them. Since the Russians have built up a considerable propaganda claim against the American foreign bases—demanding, for instance, that they be closed as a precondition or first stage of disarmament—it would be relatively easy to close some of these bases, as a tension-reduction device.

The United States might thus reduce its forces in country X, completely remove them from country Y, and close its bases in country Z, expecting the Russians to reciprocate accordingly. Selecting countries for the disengagement will require the most careful consideration. Many factors will affect such a decision, including the strategic significance of the country for the Western bloc; the stability of its economy, its political structure, and the strength of its military force; the size of its Communist party; and the orientation of its government toward such disengagement.

No less important is the existence of a reasonable reciprocation for the Russians to grant. Thus, for instance, disengagement from West Germany would be warranted on all these counts but the last. Russia cannot be expected to disengage itself from East Germany, though this might seem a "natural" reciprocation; West Germany would remain in the Western bloc after Operation Disengagement (even if this included Germany's leaving NATO), but East Germany, it seems, would be lost to the Communist bloc within hours after the last Russian tank left its gates. On the other hand, if disarmament of both Germanies were added to the bargain, the Russians might prefer a disarmed, unified Germany, at least formally committed to neutrality, over an armed West Germany in NATO and a smaller, weak East Germany in their camp. While at present the West relies heavily on West Germany for the defense of Western Europe, at this stage of Gradualism a disarmed Germany might be acceptable, especially if disengagement had been successfully exercised elsewhere.

Other places where disengagement might be exercised by both sides, in order to abolish what have become symbols of international friction, include Berlin (before, instead of, or as a stage of, a total German disengagement), Korea, and Southeast Asia. Finally, the United States might reduce its troops in Western Europe, and the Russians theirs in Eastern Europe.

*Reduction of Conventional Arms.* At present, reduction of

conventional arms is quite unacceptable to the West, because it has much less conventional military power than the East, and should be unacceptable to the East, because cuts in the conventional forces of the West increase its reliance on nuclear bombs. But as Gradualism proceeds, especially since by that time United States conventional forces will be larger (President Kennedy ordered their increase in 1961) and more concentrated (because of disengagement), the United States might take some cuts, expecting in reciprocation *larger* Soviet cuts in conventional arms (the Soviet accepted the principle of disproportionate cut in 1956).[4] It is quite likely that large reductions of arms will have to wait for the next phase, but small cuts, for purposes of tension reduction rather than arms reduction, may be possible in this stage.

## THE THIRD PHASE: SIMULTANEOUS MATCHED CONCESSIONS

Assuming that the two earlier phases have been successfully completed, both sides will then be ready for the all-important and much longer third phase. Suspicion and fear would by then be reduced to a level where fruitful negotiations are possible. From now on concessions will be made simultaneously after negotiation, according to an established timetable, and accompanied by inspection; moreover, they will be matched in military import (though probably not identical in substance). The shift to this type of international interaction is essential because *major* settlements are exceedingly difficult to attain on a unilateral-reciprocated basis. Unilateral action puts a premium on small concessions in matters that do not significantly affect the military and political position of each side, concessions small enough to prevent significant losses in the event the other side should not reciprocate. Hence *major settlements tend to depend on bilateral or multilateral negotiations*. Part II of this volume is devoted to the armament "settlement," and Part III to Gradualism in the political area.

[4] The present conventional arms build-up is not necessarily contradictory to my projection. It provides the United States with a conventional force that could then be used for an arms-reduction program. Without such a build-up, a plan like ours would have to start with rather large Soviet cuts, accompanied by small or no American cuts, because of the very considerable differences in the size of the conventional forces of the two blocs, before the 1961 United States build-up. I am indebted for this point to David Riesman.

## Conditions for Effective Gradualism

Many of the essential conditions for effective Gradualism were specified in a study by Professor Osgood. He states:

A unilateral act (1) should, in terms of capacity for military aggression, be clearly disadvantageous to the side making it; (2) should be such as to be clearly perceived by the other side as reducing his external threat; (3) should not increase an enemy's threat to our heartland; (4) should be such that reciprocal action by the other side is clearly available and clearly indicated; (5) should be announced in advance and widely publicized to ally, neutral, and enemy countries—as regards the nature of the act, its purpose as part of a consistent policy, and the expected reciprocation; (6) but should not demand prior commitment to reciprocation by the other side as a condition for its commission.[5]

The following considerations might be added.

### CONTINUITY

It is essential for the success of Gradualism that no half-hearted attempts be made and that the policy be followed as planned, even if at the outset it seems not to work. The United States will have to carry through the first steps aimed at reduction of tensions regardless of the Russian response. Initially, as the unilateralist psychological analysis suggests, the Russians are likely to be highly suspicious. Like the Americans, at this still highly tense stage, they believe that whatever concessions one side makes include some traps for the other. Closing the military bases can be defined as an economy measure or as the junking of obsolete weapons; cutting conventional arms can be interpreted as increased reliance on nuclear bombs or as the sign of increased fire power of each soldier. When such traps cannot be pointed out, one can always claim that the concessions are merely propaganda stunts. But when the initiator of unilateral tension reduction does not respond to or reinforce the suspicions of the other side, but rather continues with his

[5] Osgood, *loc. cit.*, p. 131.

tension-reducing acts, it becomes more and more difficult for the adversary to maintain his distorted interpretation. This is especially true when the moves are clear and given to minimum misinterpretation. For instance, it would be difficult to imagine any hidden trap in the unilateral removal of the ban on travel of Russian diplomats in the United States or in disengagement from Quemoy and Matsu; accordingly, these moves would do much to win the confidence of the Russians and of world public opinion.

This is not to suggest that the United States will go on indefinitely with such unilateral steps. After a while, it will have to stop and wait for reciprocation. But so long as the predetermined series of steps has not been exhausted, it should be carried out as planned, whatever the reaction.

## CONSISTENCY

Another important condition for the success of Gradualism is the avoidance of any step that is "out of character" with the others, for this might undermine the entire campaign. Consistency is not an unmitigated virtue; the excessive stress on the need for a consistent foreign policy is liable to produce a rigid one. But the first two phases of Gradualism are *public opinion* campaigns, in that their success depends in part on the pressure of public opinion on nonreciprocating parties. For, especially in the short run, public opinion is very sensitive to inconsistencies, real or apparent. Thus, the atmosphere of relaxation (the "Camp David spirit"), built up during Khrushchev's visit to the United States, and in preparation for the Eisenhower-Khrushchev summit meeting in Paris in 1960, was sharply undermined by the U-2 incident. Whoever was to blame for it, this one "out of character" incident was enough to cancel all the reduction in tension achieved in the preceding months. Another illustration to the same effect is the invasion of Cuba of 1961. Through the election campaign and the first months of his administration, Kennedy had built up an image of competent leadership and liberal foreign policy. He supported the rebels of Angola against the colonial government of Portugal; he encouraged the ambition of the people of West New Guinea for independence from the Netherlands; and he insisted that progress

104

toward social reform and democracy be prerequisites for United States economic aid to Latin American countries. Then United States intervention in Cuba undermined the image Kennedy had so painstakingly constructed.

It is clear, then, that in effecting a Gradualist policy we must carefully evaluate each act of foreign policy to be sure that no deliberate or unwitting act (perhaps through the failure of some intelligence activity) will wreck the results of the policy just when it is about to succeed. Particularly dangerous are groups or allies, averse to relaxation or convinced that it is not in the interest of the United States, who might deliberately or unwittingly spoil the entire effort.

Should an "out of character" act occur, the United States should be prepared to declare immediately that it was only an incident, that the United States will continue with its earlier policy as designed, and that it will add a number of additional unilateral steps to overcome the increased suspicion such an incident would create. If after this another incident should occur, the psychological effects on which the success of Gradualism is based are likely to be lost, at least in the critical near future.

GENEROSITY

While the United States should declare from the beginning that it expects reciprocation, it would undermine the whole strategy and render it meaningless if the United States were constantly to complain that the Russian reciprocations were smaller in value than the initial contributions of the United States. The spirit appropriate to the first stage, and to some degree to the second, is that of generosity. One who gives a gift parts with it freely; he hopes to get one in return someday, but he will neither make this a condition for his giving nor will he constantly remind the other of his obligation; nor will he publicly compare the value of what he receives with what he gave. It is essential to remember at all times that the purpose of these two phases is not to obtain particular concessions or to bring about particular exchanges, but to reduce interbloc tensions. Since the initial concessions are only symbolic or limited, such generosity would not imperil national security. In the third phase of Gradualism, in which the safety and central interests of the nation are affected, generosity will, of course, have to give way to caution.

## EDUCATION

It is exceedingly important to accompany Gradualism with an educational campaign, best directed from the White House, to make this policy acceptable to the American public. The fears and paranoia that impede settlement are as rampant among Americans as among Russians; the hindrance they offer is actually greater in the United States, because the nature of the democratic process requires, at least in the long run, the public support of major policy changes. One purpose of such a campaign would be to reduce the feeling widespread among Americans (but not in other Western countries) that all the justice is on the West's side, while *the other side is completely evil*. This conviction of righteousness generates a crusading spirit, a supermoralist demand for a fight to the finish. It will be necessary to remind the public that the West is not so pure and the Communist not so satanic; that the United States has pulled one or two "fast" ones; and that the Russians have kept their word—sometimes (for instance, with regard to disengagement and neutralization of Austria in 1955). The related view that *every* concession to Russia is appeasement is probably the most important single bar to settlement.

Finally, such an educational campaign will in itself be viewed by allies, neutrals, and opponents as a contribution to the reduction of international tension. And it will advance the belief in the sincerity of the new American policy.

## No "RIDERS"

The surest way to ruin Gradualism's chances for success is to try to use it to achieve more than the specified goals. Thus, for instance, if disengagement were oriented toward helping countries in the Communist bloc to break away from it, and such considerations were to guide its application, this purpose would soon become evident to the Russians and would nullify both Gradualism and the chances of "liberation." If, as a consequence of disengagement, a Communist-bloc country should break away, the West has gained an "unanticipated bonus"; but such a consequence should not be an intended goal of Gradualism. The same disastrous effect would result if removal of the commerce ban were used to lower the price of some crop crucial to the Communists' export by dumping surplus commodities on foreign markets. Several disarmament talks in the past were stalemated when the West tried to gain, in addition to arms reduction, such political goals as the unification of Germany or the cessation of Communist ideological expansion. Gradualism will have to be geared strictly to the reduction of tension at first, and then to working out a settlement.

## A "LAST" CHANCE

It should be abundantly clear to the Russians, from the United States' exposition of Gradualism to the world, that the United States considers this large, extensive, sincere attempt at settlement a *major test*, and that, should it fail, the United States will be very unlikely to try again. While the United States should never give the appearance of an ultimatum, which would be counter to the very concept of tension reduction, it should be evident from the nature and scope of the effort that this might well be a last opportunity.[6]

## Russian Responses and American Reactions

If the Russians reciprocate, sooner or later, by granting concessions of more or less equal magnitude, the policy will proceed as designed. However, the American policy makers should be prepared to find that once they decide to play ball, the Russians, old hands at peace campaigns, may not leave the initiative completely in the hands of the Americans. They may initiate unilateral moves of their own, as they did when they suspended the testing of bombs in 1958 and when they released the RB-47 pilots in 1961. The United States should be ready to offer generous reciprocations. This would be the best way to

[6] As this book goes to press, Professor Osgood has sent the author two unpublished documents in which he extends his study of psychological gradualism. He further analyzes the means of inducing reciprocation and provides criteria for selection of unilateral steps as well as criteria for evaluation of reciprocation. These documents illustrate effectively how research might contribute to the development of an alternative strategy to armed deterrence, and further strengthens my conviction that Gradualism is a feasible policy.

make Gradualism effective. Attempts to keep a monopoly of initiative will build tensions rather than reduce them; hence, in this period Russian initiative should be welcomed.

On the other hand, the Russians might go on with "business as usual," refusing to reciprocate and labeling the policy as an American public-relations stunt. The United States will in this case carry out its first sequence of steps and then wait for some period of time to allow world public opinion to exert whatever influence it has and to give the Russians a chance to consider the effect of their refusal to reciprocate. If after a period of time returns are still withheld, the United States, perhaps after one last gesture, will declare that the policy has failed. There will be little need to explain why or to place the blame.

*It is crucial to realize that Gradualism is a "minimum regret" strategy; even if it should fail, the United States will have risked little and lost nothing.* Even if the Russians were to refuse to reciprocate, the United States will have demonstrated the sincerity of its desire for peace (which has often been doubted by neutral countries and even by some allies) and will have satisfied its own mind that it had sincerely and deeply explored the Russians' intentions. The United States would then, of course, be free to turn to other strategies.

Even if Gradualism should fail, the other two major alternatives, the more extreme and more dangerous policies of unilateralism and an accelerated arms race (or multideterrence) will still be available. If you support unilateralism, why not try Gradualism first? If it does not work, you will have tried a less "expensive" step first (expensive in terms of the danger of Communist world domination) and will have lost nothing. On the contrary, the international atmosphere will be much more conducive to unilateral disarmament and the likelihood of reciprocation greater. The Gradualist test does not have to be long; it can easily be carried out in a year, or two at most, within which period it would be possible to judge whether the policy is taking effect.

If you believe that multideterrence or preventive war is the solution, you would certainly want to make sure you had exhausted every other possibility before embarking on so hazardous a course. Again, the short Gradualist phase would neither significantly retard your plans nor impair your ability to effect these policies.

It is sometimes suggested that it would be impossible after reduction of tension to rebuild the resolve of the West or to regain public support for the expense of the armament program. But the opposite is true. If the United States were to build up public expectation of the last big trial, if it really made generous and consistent symbolic concessions, and yet made no headway —then the public abroad and in the United States would be that much more willing to support a strong, highly accelerated arms race and a superlatively "tough" line toward the Communists.

The *implicit* threat that a failure of Gradualism will lead to a crash arms race of the multideterrence type is much more conducive to reciprocation and settlement than the alternative expectation that the West will resort to unilateralism. However, as we have seen, the question is strictly academic, because unilateralism has no chance whatsoever of becoming a United States policy. Hence, for all practical purposes, whatever one's moral preferences, the failure of a genuine, extensive, consistent Gradualist attempt will lead to an accelerated arms race, if not to a "preventive" war. The fear of such a development would doubtless be an important factor in the other side's decision to reciprocate and thus make Gradualism a success. (On the other hand, if one were fairly sure Gradualism would fail, fear of the consequences of the ensuing frustration could be a reason for not adopting the policy.)

There is a third possibility, in addition to complete failure or complete success. The Russians might go along for a while but then break the sequence, using some real or manufactured incident or "injustice" as an excuse. I do not expect this to happen for, as I have tried to point out above, it is to their interest as well as to that of the West to follow through on each stage of the Gradualist sequence. If a partial failure should ensue, nevertheless, the points made above with regard to a complete failure apply.

One point, however, must be emphasized. If after a few successful steps the Russians raise some complaints about an unfair expectation (the United States expects too much in return for

109

a concession), or about our failure to reciprocate a gesture of theirs, or about an aggressive act of a third party which the United States claims is independent but which actually is in the West's camp (for example, France), most serious consideration should be given to the Russian claim before it is rejected. We must always remember that the Russian viewpoint is truly different from ours, and that in all likelihood neither side sees things as they really are. One should follow Linus Pauling's reformulation of the Golden Rule: "Do unto others 20 per cent better than you expect them to do unto you, to correct for subjective error."

## Conclusion

The kernel of my argument so far is this: Unilateralism finds it necessary to risk liberty to insure life; armed-deterrence strategies are willing to risk life to assure liberty. Gradualism wishes to test whether we are compelled to take either of these grave risks. The objective international situation appears to be moving toward conditions for a possible settlement between the Russians, as the present leader of the Communist bloc, and the United States, as the Western leader. China, whatever course it might want to pursue, is not yet able to impose its will on the Communist bloc. Gradualism removes the psychological barriers that hinder negotiations without taking undue risks. Should it be effective, it might lead to a negotiated settlement, without risking either life or liberty. Should it fail, the more hazardous extreme strategies are still available. *It is a "maximum gain," "minimum regret" strategy.*

I now turn to some major questions. Assuming that Gradualism works, what kind of arms reduction should the West work for? How should the various steps be "ordered"? And, if we finally reach a state of arms reduction approaching disarmament, would this not bring world domination of Communism by ideological and economic means? What is the optimal policy for the West in a disarming world? Arms reduction is the subject of Part II of this volume, political strategy the subject of Part III.

# PART TWO

# THREE ARMAMENT STRATEGIES

## The Peril of the Unmatched Race

IF WE ARE to sit down with the Russians to try to negotiate a "settlement," we must first know what we want. Our most urgent goal is a safer world; our long-run goal, a better one. A safer world can be reached only through disarmament—remote as that may be—since even conflicts fought with conventional arms can "escalate" into nuclear wars, resulting in mass murder of an unprecedented order and the possible elimination of all human life.

Achieving peace, however, will not be easy; even complete disarmament will not assure it. History teaches us that *after disarmament frequently comes, not peace, but rearmament.* The world, for example, was practically disarmed after World War I. When rearmament is bilateral (or multilateral) it leads to new wars; when it is unilateral, it opens the world to domination by the power that first violates the disarmament pact. The age of nuclear bombs greatly intensifies this danger. In the past, the victim in a violation of a disarmament pact could hope to arm itself after it had been attacked—to catch up and win—especially if it had an economy and manpower superior to that of the violating party. Now a country that has a nuclear monopoly, and is brutal enough to use it, will in all likelihood inherit the earth. Thus, the temptation to violate a disarmament agreement is almost irresistible, if only as a hidden safeguard against the possibility that the other side may do the same.

There is wide agreement among specialists of many disciplines, philosophers, politicians, and among practically all those who have given serious consideration to the matter, that stable peace requires even more than abolishing the capacity to wage war—it requires the curbing of the underlying conflicts which cause nations to take up arms. While the specific plans advanced differ, the gist of the solutions advocated are similar: what is needed is a world organized like a state, with a world legislature to enact a set of laws forbidding the use of violence and an international police force to enforce the world law, and so on—in short, a world government.

But just as there is no stable disarmament without world government, there is no world government without some development of a global society. Governments do not function in a vacuum; they require the support of the people. One can force some people to comply some of the time, but one cannot force most people to comply most of the time. A viable world government, not a League of Nations or a United Nations, can emerge only when there is worldwide sharing of at least a minimum of basic values and sentiments, which that government can express, implement, and be supported by.

The crux of the problem is that the development of a world government and a global community is a long-run process, *a matter of generations*. It is often argued by speakers and writers favoring unilateral disarmament that we cannot afford to wait, that we *need* a world government most urgently. One must hence point to the well-known fact that the urgency of one's needs is often quite unrelated to the speed with which they can be fulfilled. It is difficult to point to historical, political, and sociological processes which lead to the fulfillment of this need; and to the degree that we can chart these, we must realize the tragic but valid fact that they are slow processes.

Meanwhile, the world carriage is harnessed to a pair of unmatched horses. The arms race is like a runaway mare, madly galloping at an ever increasing speed and taking further fright at every sound and shadow; unless tamed, it might well draw us over the cliff in the next one or two decades, if not earlier. On the other hand, sociopolitical processes proceed like a slow, stolid plow horse, as if we had all the time in the world. The unmatched pace of the arms race and the sociopolitical processes prevents use from reaching basic solutions to the problems of the nuclear age. Unless we slow down the arms race and accelerate the sociopolitical processes, unless we synchronize the pace of the two, we will not have a safe course for generations to come.

In the following chapters we will first review alternative programs to reduce the arms race; then, in Part III, we will discuss the nature of the sociopolitical processes and the ways in which they can be accelerated.

It should be stated at the outset that the author is far from optimistic. Too often in human history, neither leaders nor people have realized the danger awaiting them around the next bend; moreover, even when many have called the devil by his name, nobody has succeeded in stopping the carriage from heading straight into his arms. It is quite possible that at least one nuclear war will occur before the nations that populate the earth will draw the necessary conclusions from their fateful brotherhood on a small planet in an age of big bombs.

Arms control, multilateral disarmament, and arms reductions are three methods by which to tame the wild race. In examining each one we ask: if carried out as planned, what *scope of the problem* will it solve? There is little use in schemes that, even when functioning perfectly, only modify the arms race.

Since all three plans require guarantees that they will be carried out as agreed, the *nature and extent of inspection* that each plan necessitates are compared. Since the sides can hardly be expected to be saintlike, the *effect of violations* will have to be assessed; does the plan leave the side that acts in good faith at the mercy of the side that "cheats," or does it provide satisfactory protection or *safeguards*? What *sanctions* are available to punish violations?

In addition, we would like to know to what degree the various plans are *acceptable* to the Soviet Union and to the United States as well as to other countries. It is easy to imagine fine solutions to our problem—for example, all countries will disarm completely and unconditionally tomorrow—but so long as the steps to such solutions are completely unacceptable to both or even to just one of the superpowers, they are less than useful.

Finally, since armed conflict is only part of the problem, we will have to ask how the solution of this conflict relates to the evolution of a global community. Does it encourage or hinder such development? Is the pace of the arms plan synchronized with the pace of sociopolitical progress?

Arms control and multilateral disarmament are rejected in the following two chapters as unsatisfactory on several of these

113

grounds. Awareness of their shortcomings supplies highly critical standards for testing the plan advocated here, graded arms reduction and inspection. While it seems quite adequate on all these counts, it proves to have its own Achilles' heel; this, however, can be overcome by sociopolitical gradualism, advocated in Part Three of this volume.

The reader may wish to note that, whichever his favorite, up to now not one of these plans is being carried out. The arms race is continuing, accumulating an ever-increasing and deadlier momentum.

## Chapter 5

## Arms Control—Making Arms Safe?

GAINING control over the arms race, rather than being controlled by it, must be our objective. Arms control offers to curb the race without abolishing the arms, and promises to build security and peace by reliance on arms, rather than by their annihilation. An assessment of the objectives, methods, and effects of arms control points to shortcomings which suggest that the cure it offers is both ineffective and hazardous. But we have further interest in these shortcomings—they highlight dilemmas a true remedy will have to solve.

### Limited Cure

There is a large variety of arms control plans, though all share the same general objective and method: they claim to reduce the dangers of the present arms race by imposing limitations on the armament held by both sides. These limitations are to be negotiated and agreed upon by the East and the West; abiding by such agreements is to be checked through inspection. They differ in the specific objectives they pursue and in the means they intend to apply. The two major schools of arms control are the stabilization and the limited-prevention school. The former school advocates either total stabilization or merely nuclear stabilization; the latter, the prevention of annihilation-wars or just wars-by-accident. The four arms control methods differ in the extent of the cure they offer and the difficulties they encounter, but only total stabilization aims at complete elimination of international violence; the other three do not even intend to do so. Total stabilization, however, is not only the most difficult plan to safeguard, but would probably also have the most hazardous side effects.

## TOTAL VERSUS NUCLEAR STABILIZATION

The stabilization school in general suggests that wars could be avoided if both sides had equal military power. This could be achieved by equalizing present arms stockpiles, by eliminating production of arms, and by providing adequate safeguards for compliance with arms agreements. Then neither side would fear attack from the other; like two automobiles of equal horsepower, trying to push each other as they face bumper to bumper, neither would be able to move the other an inch.

This general approach becomes more complex when we consider the alternatives of total stabilization and nuclear stabilization. Proponents of *total stabilization* would neutralize all arms through equalization and thus eliminate wars completely. After all, they remind us, we are concerned not with the abolition of weapons as an end in itself but with peace; if peace can be best assumed by equalizing armament, instead of by disarming, we should retain weapons rather than seek to destroy them. By remaining armed, this approach holds, we avoid the chief danger of disarmament, the total helplessness in the face of violations; by equalizing arms, we avoid the danger in the arms race—situations in which an attack might seem to pay off.

Proponents of *nuclear stabilization* point to the huge difficulties involved in implementing the inspection of all weapons and to the deep conflict of interests and beliefs which exists between the blocs. They feel that these differences will from time to time seek expression through force, when other outlets fail. Therefore, unless we leave room for such expression, the whole system of arms control would be undermined. Hence this approach favors stabilizing only nuclear arms, thus neutralizing the primary danger in the arms race, while "allowing" for limited wars.

In order for nuclear stabilization to be effective, objectives

115

of warfare, as well as weapons, must be limited. The sides might fight over the control of a third country, parts of a border land, or rights of sea or air passages; they must not, however, seek total victory, since this might lead to the use of nuclear arms by a desperate losing side. This limitation of war would be backed up by the equalization of nuclear arms, which would make it highly unlikely that nuclear war could be of advantage to either side.

## Two Types of Limited Prevention

The second school of arms control is less optimistic. It does not believe that wars, even nuclear wars, can be eliminated. At best, some state of more limited prevention can be reached. One might be able to assure that future wars would not be wars of total annihilation, even when fought with H-bombs,[1] and not occur unless deliberately triggered. Thus, this school attempts to trim the arms race, to eliminate those results that neither side could possibly desire—mutual suicide and war by accident.

To avoid mutual annihilation, limited-prevention plans suggest that both sides forego the production of Doomsday bombs and other means of warfare (such as chemical and biological) that have similar devastation potentialities. Other limited-prevention plans try to reduce the probability that wars would be caused by accidents, such as by misinterpreting enemy defensive moves as preparations for an attack (with the danger lying in the temptation to strike the first, pre-emptive blow) or seeing a declaration of war in an isolated bomb dropped by mistake or by unauthorized command.

Both the stabilization and the limited-prevention schools draw on historical precedents to illustrate and support their position. Stabilization proponents are fond of pointing to the "balance of power" system, established at the Congress of Vienna, which kept peace in Europe for a hundred years (1815–

---

[1] For a while nuclear war and suicidal war were viewed as synonymous; a nuclear war was believed to lead to the annihilation of mankind. Under the influence of various RAND studies and the wide attention gained by Herman Kahn's book, *On Thermonuclear War*, it became known that nuclear wars might have varying degrees of devastation, from "small" wars (ten million casualties) to medium wars (destruction of a third of the United States and the Soviet Union) to suicidal wars in which both sides, and possibly all of mankind, would be wiped out.

1914). While the system is too complex to be done justice to here, we can say that basically it avoided wars by assuring that at each phase no European power had a significant military advantage over the others, and hence could not effectively attack or even threaten other countries.

While the stabilization school goes back to the nineteenth century to find historical precedents, the limited-prevention school points to World War II and the Korean war for cases in point. Poison gas was not used in either war and atomic weapons were kept out of the "limited" war in Korea.

In summary, it might be said of the stabilization and limited-prevention viewpoints that the first attempts to eliminate wars, the second to limit them; the first to make war irrational, the second to avoid irrational wars. Both schools impose some arms limitations and wish to curb the arms race; the first school limits both sides to equal piles of arms; the second trims deadly weapons or accident-prone postures from the arms race.

## The Need for Inspection

Unlike their historical antecedents, current schemes for arms control require inspection to enforce the observation of arms limitation agreements. In the prenuclear age, violations were not fatal; the party attacked by a violator of an arms reduction pact could often increase arms production sufficiently to retaliate and even win. In the age of nuclear mass bombing, the first strike might be crippling, if not fatal. Hence the need for inspection is great.

Present plans differ, however, in the amount and kind of inspection they prescribe and, thus, in the difficulties they encounter. *Prevention of accidents* requires least inspection. To some degree, such prevention can be attained by each side without the cooperation of the other. For instance, even now when the Soviet Union or the United States tests a missile or places a satellite in orbit, a course is chosen which does not require shooting the missile in the "enemy's" direction, in order to prevent his mistaking it for an attack. But many other elements of accident control require multilateral agreements and inspection. One major source of a possible accidental war is the spread of nuclear arms to other countries. The larger the number of bombs and triggers, the higher the probability that

117

an accident will occur. Also, the dispersion of bombs would allow a third country to drag the superpowers into a global war by nuclear provocation. To avoid these sources of accidental war, it is widely agreed, both superpowers should maintain a nuclear monopoly. But since secret distribution of nuclear weapons to one's allies, or secret production by them, would give enormous advantages to the violator of such an arms-control agreement, global inspection is required.

*Stabilization* plans demand that each side allow an initial inventory inspection to demonstrate that he does not hold a larger amount of arms than the other side and a continued inspection to assure that no additional weapons are produced or imported after the initial equalization. *Nuclear* stabilization could be made relatively effective by inspecting only the stock of means of delivery, primarily missiles and bombers, without which a massive nuclear attack is hardly feasible. *Total* stabilization, on the other hand, requires not only all the kinds of inspection listed above, but, in addition, inspection of all other military research, development, and production, from Doomsday bombs to hand grenades, as well as inspection of all military installations and national borders (the latter to prevent weapon import, which is at present chiefly a problem with conventional arms).

To illustrate the extent of inspection required by both stabilization plans, an inspection system suggested by Henry A. Kissinger is reported in some detail. It should be noted that this system aims to inspect inventories of missiles only. To carry out this plan, each side would have to divide his territory into large units. Some areas would be free of missiles and open to complete inspection; other areas would contain bases for mobile missile launchers.[2] Twice a year, all the launchers would be at a fixed location, to allow the other side to count them, to assure that their number is not larger than the agreement permits. In order not to deprive the enemy of his missile protection during the count (because when it is known where his missiles are, they and the whole country can be erased), there would be a *number* of armed territories, and inventory

---

[2] The plan takes into account the trend to make all missile-launching sites mobile, to make it difficult for an enemy to pinpoint them. See Kissinger, *The Necessity for Choice* (New York, Harper & Brothers, 1960), pp. 222 ff.

would be taken in one territory at a time. The armed territories would be separated from each other by "open" areas, in which constant inspection would assure that the mobile launchers are not moved out of an area before an inventory is taken. To prevent missiles' being carried out by air, all flights from the area inspected would be grounded for the inventory period. To control seaborne missiles, all vessels would be required to report to ports. Ports would have to be under constant surveillance to prevent evasion. Kissinger obviously thinks it is difficult to "forget" to bring in a few hundred trucks, which hold rocket launchers, to the semi-annual inventory, in a country which has millions of vehicles; further, he seems to think that Polaris submarines have to report in person to port to be refilled.

When the proponents of arms control tackle the problem of total stabilization, their plans for inspection become even more elaborate than those proposed by Kissinger, though their claims that those plans might ever be installed and effective are much more moderate. The total control of arms would require the inspection of all relevant research, development, production, and distribution processes. Since every laboratory might conduct research work on new weapons, every laboratory—or every room that might include one—would have to be inspected. It is suggested that research inspection might be omitted because there is a lengthy interval between a research breakthrough and the development and production of weapons. Development, for instance, requires testing, and tests can be relatively easily monitored. But it should be pointed out that weapons *need not* be tested for development; or they might be tested by very small-scale models, to avoid detection. Many experiments, such as those required to test and develop chemical or biological arms, can be conducted in a small laboratory; they do not emit tell-tale radioactive beams, and they are practically impossible to distinguish from ordinary medical research. With regard to manufacturing, even under extensive inspection it is rather easy to turn production for peaceful purposes into production of nuclear arms. If a violator, for instance, were to "steal" only 3 per cent of the fissionable material produced yearly for peaceful purposes, he could produce *each year* "on the side" ninety-eight nuclear bombs, each equivalent to the Hiroshima bomb. Only the tightest network of inspection could hope to detect such small diversions of fissionable material. The same holds even more strongly for diversion of the material needed for the production of conventional arms. Inspection for total stabilization would require random checking of factories, store rooms and laboratories, not only those of the super-powers, but of all their allies and allies' allies, to counteract "subcontracting" of armament production.

Thus, in summary, checking adherence to arms-control agreements requires extensive inspection. The "preventive" arms-control plans have highly limited objectives, but require rather extensive inspection; the more ambitious stabilization schemes, especially that for total stabilization, require inspection as extensive and intensive as that demanded by total disarmament. Unlike total disarmament, however, total stabilization leaves the world filled with arms and military establishments, with money being wasted on military budgets, and with the world leading a life in the shadow of the bombs, with no way out.

One might claim that if these plans supply us with a relative security, they are the best we can expect under the circumstances. Hence, the assessment of the value of these plans rests not only on the evaluation of the effectiveness of inspection which, it is granted, cannot be made foolproof, but also on the effects of violations. The arms-control advocates have, or think they have, an answer to the danger of violation.

## Safety in Numbers?

### THE SAFETY OF HIGH PILES

The stabilization school has developed a powerful argument in favor of safety in numbers, which to a considerable extent applies to other arms-control plans. The claim is made that sitting on high, equal piles of arms is safe, while sitting on small or declining ones is not, even if cuts are balanced. Having no piles at all, according to this logic, is the most dangerous state of all.

In a world without arms, if one side had hidden a few nuclear bombs, it would have absolute power over its opponent by merely threatening to use them. A few hidden bombs would be almost impossible to discover, even under the most detailed inspection system. The same danger would exist in partial, nuclear-only disarmament or in major arms reductions. If both sides were to "stabilize" on a low level—for example, each side keeping ten bombs and ten missiles—the one that hides five bombs and five missiles would have a crippling advantage over the other.

On the other hand, stability at a high level—for example, each side possessing 500 missiles—is a different matter altogether. To gain a decisive advantage under these conditions, a violator would have to hide hundreds of bombs and missiles. The inspectors would be likely to find at least a few. Moreover, to mount an attack that would neutralize most of the opponent's 500 missiles, to prevent his retaliation from being devastating, would require extensive preparations, certain to be detected. Hence, the aggressor would have little confidence in his plan, and attacks would be unlikely.

The "limited prevention" school of arms control has no room for any major arms reductions. It merely advocates putting some restrictions on the arms race. It basically sees safeguards where Multideterrence strategy finds them: in a large and varied amount of effectively developed, deployed, and—if necessary—employed weapons systems.

## CRIPPLING BREAKTHROUGHS

But how safe is safe? It seems quite inevitable that several technological breakthroughs in the next years will completely undermine any security system based on safety in numbers. The United States is working day and night on an antimissile defense; no doubt the Russians are doing likewise. The United States is reported to be developing a combination of radar, computers, and antimissile missiles that might be effective—at least until a counterdevice is found—in stopping most missile and bomber attacks.[3] It is also reported that experiments are

[3] Such development was predicted by the alert *New York Times* military editor, Hanson Baldwin, as early as June 3, 1956. The first full-fledged test of antimissile defense, the Nike-Zeus, was conducted by the United States Army in December, 1961. At the moment the Nike-Zeus radar is still unable to distinguish between missiles and decoys, which are likely to be shot together with a barrage of attacking missiles, to fool the defense. But the United States is working on this problem and the Russians are probably doing the same. Another weapon, which the public still considers an "infallible" attack weapon, is the Polaris-carrying submarines. Actually, the United States is developing a new submarine finder (Project Artemis), which

121

being conducted to find a space spray, possibly sand, to stop missiles. When the missiles, which fly at enormous speed, hit these small particles, they are diverted from course or punctured. Whatever the technological details, it is quite likely that in the next few years one side or the other will find a relatively safe antimissile defense. In the arms control world, the side that first perfects such a device will be able to destroy or cripple the other side, and then stop the retaliatory strike in mid-air.

Other technological endeavors are likely to yield, not later than 1970, a "continental" bomb that can turn a continent into a radioctive desert in one strike.[4] The side which, despite an arms control treaty, secretly builds a few such bombs—extremely unlikely to be detected by even the most effective inspection system—while other countries are diligently counting and recounting his inventory of missile launchers and obsolete nuclear bombs, will surely be the side to win the next war.

Arms controllers realize the grave danger posed by technological breakthroughs. Hence, ideally they would like to halt all military research and to install an inspection system to ensure observance of any agreement to this effect. Since this simply cannot be done, they emphasize the need to include in the arms control agreements provisions for revisions as new weapons emerge. This position reflects the special talent of the advocates of arms control for handling secondary issues with great care, while leaving the principal issue unsolved. In this case, however, the gap is too conspicuous to be overlooked. The issue solved by provision for agreement adjustment is less than minor in view of the crucial circumstance that is unaccounted for. It is true that once a side has revealed that it has made a technological breakthrough and is willing to let it be covered by the arms control agreement, a way can be found to extend the initial scheme to cover it. But the question remains: what about undisclosed technological breakthroughs? Do they not make a complete farce of arms control? Proponents

---

will be able to pinpoint the location of submarines many hundred times more effectively than the existing sonar systems (*The New York Times*, June 1, 1961). Russia is surely working on a similar device. These instruments might enable the enemy to dig out nuclear submarines with nuclear warheads from the depths of the sea, thus making this source of armed safety as "ultimate" or "infallible" as its predecessors, the machine gun, tank, and bomber.

[4] See Appendix for some data to this effect.

of arms control feel that what will not be caught by inspection will be neutralized by the safeguards built into stabilization on a high plateau—that is, "safety in numbers." In other words, to produce *many* extra missiles and bombs "on the side" without being detected is extremely difficult, and producing *some* will not provide a decisive advantage. Hence, violations would be avoided. But the very nature of these technological innovations is that they do not require "numbers"; three continental bombs —to be on the safe side, five—would suffice to give absolute superiority to the side that would construct them.

Many of the designers of arms control schemes are experts in games theory, an expertise that is less than helpful here. Theoretically, in games, either the rules are observed or there is no game; in reality, there is a third choice, one an enemy is most likely to choose, in particular since neither conflicts nor arms are eliminated, but just curbed or stabilized.

The neglect of the third alternative can be seen in the choice Kissinger and his colleagues present—that between an open and a controlled arms race. It can be demonstrated that if these are the alternatives, it makes sense to prefer the controlled race. But there is a third choice: to agree to arms control and not to obey the rules. If the other side violates them too, your violation will save your neck, because when one day the enemy says, "Brother, I've got you—I have twice as many missiles as you. Capitulate—have mercy on your children," you will counter with, "You think you are the only smart one—I have twice as many as we agreed upon myself!" If, on the other hand, the enemy conforms to the rules, your violation will give you both added security (you never know *for sure* the other side did not violate) and a chance to come out ahead in the interbloc competition if and when you so desire. The arms-control advocates correctly observe that there is a "built-in incentive" to agreeing to arms-control schemes, for both sides are endangered by the untamed arms race; their "only" mistake is that they consider this also to be an incentive to abiding by the agreement once it is established.

In sum, the proponents of arms control think that a little cheating will not matter, and a great deal will be difficult because of inspection. I suggest that a little cheating will go a long way, if it leads to a technological breakthrough. Furthermore, while it is difficult to hide a large number of missiles, in countries the size of Russia or the United States it is not insuperably difficult.

## AN UNANTICIPATED CONSEQUENCE: PREMIUM ON SUPERBOMBS

The central feature of arms control plans is that they intend to curb wars but otherwise leave things as they are, including both the interbloc political, ideological conflict and the piles of arms. This fact has the unanticipated consequence that the more effective an arms control plan is, the more hazardous it is and that total stabilization is therefore the most dangerous of all.

Once peaceful means have failed in an open arms race, objectives can be pursued through a large variety of military methods, from guerrilla warfare to city exchange as expounded by Kahn. In the world of arms control other than total stabilization, limited war could be carried out to "correct," through the use of violence, whatever injustice a side felt it had suffered. But under total stabilization, if effectively implemented, both sides would be paralyzed. All the forces would be effectively countered so that no "correction" through violence would be possible. This would seem ideal, until we realize that the underlying conflicts have not been removed, nor have the arms and the fears they produce been overcome. It is much like trying to cure malaria and the related high temperature by stopping the patient from sweating. Both sides will be sitting nervously on their piles of arms, counting those of the enemy, waiting, full of the old animosities and fears. Even if one could stand such a strain, could one trust the opponent's nerves? Would the enemy not strike when he has a chance? The only way out of this tense, frustrating, no-action, no-outlet, no-end situation is by a successful surprise attack with the biggest bombs at hand. Only superbombs, secretly developed, could possibly give a side a decisive advantage. Total stabilization supplies no other out.

## Arms Control and Disarmament

In a disarmed world, both sides have many vested interests in maintaining disarmament: the consumer products that the ex-arms industries turn out, the careers that a new draft would interrupt, the psychological frustration resulting from the loss of peace, and many others. In addition, there can never be absolute certainty that the other side did not also hide some bombs to be safe, so that a nuclear threat might only resurrect the arms race. When A pulls his bombs from a clandestine cache to threaten B, B counters by demonstrating his heretofore concealed cache to the international press. Thus, in no time we would be back in the arms race, where we started. It is quite possible that the fear of this eventuality and the increasingly vested interests in peace would maintain a manifestly disarmed world in which both sides have hidden stocks of nuclear bombs, never to be used.

In an arms control world, on the other hand, wherein the vested interests in peace are not built up or global institutions are not developed, arms are manufactured and military establishments are operative, both sides are likely to work day and night to gain a major technological breakthrough, and, once they have gained it, there is nothing—either in the arms control pact and machinery or in the psychological and sociological state of the opponents and that of the world it sustains—to prevent their exploiting it. Actually, it is the only way out of the state of armed truce arms control tries to perpetuate. Thus, arms control, and total stabilization in particular, not only does not create the kind of psychological climate and vested interests under which international agreements are likely to be observed, global institutions to be developed, and a stake in the peace to be built up, but also establishes a frustrating stalemate, from which the only way out is by use of the biggest bomb.

Arms control may take four different basic forms, but there is one thing it definitely is not; it is not a form of, or a way to, disarmament. At least one authority, Professor Seymour Melman of Columbia University, has suggested that the confusion of arms control with disarmament is not completely unintentional.[5] Arms control, he points out, is advanced, among other reasons, to alleviate some of the pressure of public opinion in the United States and abroad on the Pentagon to do "something" about the arms race. It should therefore be pointed out that while arms control and disarmament share a certain con-

[5] *The Nation,* February 11, 1961, pp. 114–119.

cern with the course of the uncontrolled arms race, and carrying out either requires the cooperation of both sides, they have little else in common. Disarmament seeks safety from arms, while arms control seeks safety through arms. According to all schools of arms control, both sides would maintain a high plateau of armament. No arms control plan can allow even major arms reduction, not to mention disarmament, since this would lead to a low plateau in which the magic safety in numbers, the supposedly ultimate safeguard, would vanish. Thus, arms control is not and cannot be, according to its own premise, a way to a farewell to arms.

## Who Wants Arms Control?

While total disarmament is advocated by the Communist bloc and, more recently, by many in the West, arms control is a plan devised by the Pentagon and its civilian researchers; it will be accepted by the Russians the day the Volga flows up the Rocky Mountains. The United States sees itself as protecting the underdeveloped countries from expanding Communism, a task that often requires the use of arms even when Communism —as we shall see in some detail below—relies chiefly on its ideological power. Hence the United States is more interested, at least at present, in inspection (which would open Russia to the West) than in disarmament (which would expose the underdeveloped countries to Communist expansion). Russia, for the very same reasons, is interested in disarmament, but not in inspection. The inevitable result is the present impasse of disarmament negotiation.[6] Arms control, a strategy devised by American experts, typically calls for extensive inspection but for little or no disarmament. It is true that arms limitations would benefit both sides, but arms control would benefit the Americans so much more than it would the expanding Russians that one must wonder if the designers of arms control plans even considered their acceptability to the Soviet Union. If the Russians could be convinced to agree to extensive inspection

[6] President Kennedy broke a long Western tradition in his speech before the United Nations in September, 1961. He offered for the first time a Western total disarmament plan, not tied to the earlier Western principle of negotiating later disarmament steps only as earlier ones are completed, which was viewed, at least by the Russians, as no commitment to complete disarmament. But Kennedy still maintained the principle of inspecting not what is disarmed, but what is not yet disarmed, which proved to be unacceptable to the Russians.

without real disarmament—if they could, for example, be made to agree to Kissinger's "generous" suggestion that "a build-up of Western local power should be coupled with a reduction of Communist conventional strength and the whole arrangement should be monitored by an inspection system"—the American advocates of arms control might, if not enhance peace, at least carry out a patriotic feat. The Russians, however, have already indicated that they see the whole plan as a cold war maneuver, another step in the campaign to use disarmament as a propaganda weapon. Thus, whether arms control planning is a deliberate or an unintentional folly, it has little, if any, chance of being implemented.

## Conclusion

The large variety of arms control schemes share many characteristics. They do not take care of the roots of our problem, and they demand much in exchange. They would not, even if effectively implemented, establish a stable world peace, bereft of arms and bombs. "Preventive" arms control schemes just trim the arms race of some of its most irrational and dangerous side effects—the dangers of accidental and suicidal war—leaving the arms race itself to continue in its fatal course. The more ambitious plans of stabilization are an attempt at alchemy—to turn the very means of violence, death, and destruction into the foundation of safety and lasting peace. But tin will turn to gold and vodka to whiskey before there will be safety in piles of guns and nuclear explosives.

The extensive inspection called for by the implementation of arms control is a major drawback. Arms control is unlikely to be effective because of the size of the countries inspected, the nature of forthcoming technological breakthroughs, the absence of a psychological climate that would discourage violations, and, above all, the unacceptability to the East of extensive inspection without extensive disarmament. Moreover, there is every reason to believe that if total stabilization—otherwise the only promising arms control plan—were ever implemented, the resulting frustration in containing two dynamic international forces, armed to the teeth, in a strait jacket would put a premium on constructing the most deadly weapons ever conceived and would encourage their use.

In summary, on all counts—scope of inspection, magnitude of violation, and extent of disarmament—arms control simply will not do. There is no plan which can slow the arms race while keeping the arms; there is no more safety in arms.

## Chapter 6

### Multilateral Disarmament— Security Without Arms?

#### The Disarmament War

MULTILATERAL DISARMAMENT differs greatly from arms control, despite several common features, such as interbloc negotiations, extensive inspection systems, and desire to prevent the hazardous drift of the arms race. They differ in the most basic assumption: while arms control wishes to base security on arms, multilateral disarmament plans to establish security by abolishing armament. This principle is also subscribed to by the advocates of unilateral disarmament, but while the latter stands little chance of ever becoming American policy, or, for that matter, any country's policy, multilateral disarmament has been the subject of 300-odd interbloc meetings in Geneva and of general debates in the United Nations and is supported by both blocs.

Global multilateral disarmament has captured the imagination of man ever since the prophet promised that the day would come when swords would be turned into plowshares. Thirty years ago, on the eve of the great Disarmament Conference in Geneva, the then Soviet Foreign Minister, Maxim Litvinov, advanced in the name of his country a plan very similar to the total disarmament proposal recently presented by Premier Khrushchev to the United Nations. The United States itself has advanced several disarmament programs, including the well-known Baruch Plan, and a six-point program presented by President Kennedy to the United Nations. The fate of all these plans has been the same: they never got off the ground. Instead of furthering peace, they served as ammunition in the cold war.

East and West have used and are using disarmament proposals chiefly for propaganda purposes, though the Russians are far ahead in making political capital out of disarmament. Their grand, total, here-and-now disarmament proposal, always on top of their propaganda list, officially submitted to the West in 1932 in Geneva, and in 1959 at the United Nations headquarters in New York, has much appeal.

On the other hand, the West has used its inspection proposals to point up the totalitarian, secretive, closed nature of Communist societies. President Eisenhower's offer to exchange a free aerial inspection—"open skies"—to which no disarmament proposal was attached, was one case in point. The more recent demand of the West to couple a ban on nuclear tests (which provides practically no disarmament) with inspection of Russia is another.

There is much evidence that until recently neither side considered disarmament seriously as a policy to be followed, either because each was aware that disarmament would not be to its advantage or because it did not believe the other side would ever truly consent to disarm. Disarmament is an intricate and complicated operation. It requires careful planning for reemployment of resources and manpower, research and development of inspection instruments, training of inspectors, working out of time tables, and so forth. It is widely known that the United States as well as the Soviet Union has done little on any of these problems. When scientists met in Geneva to discuss disarmament, one side's concessions often proved to be an embarrassment to the other side because it was not prepared for the next move.

On at least two occasions, the West has agreed to steps that some additional examination showed were not "thought through." In October, 1958, the United States responded to a Russian declaration of the unilateral suspension of nuclear tests with a similar declaration. Several American experts believe that this was not to the advantage of the United States. Whether or not this is true, it is clear that the United States did not *plan* to suspend its tests, but was maneuvered into it by the Russians and world public opinion, and the consequences of uninspected suspension were not "researched" when it was declared. Similarly, the United States agreed that 180 inspection stations around the world (twenty-one in Russia) would suffice to discover explosions larger than five kilotons. But shortly after the United States more or less committed itself to this position, its scientists pointed out the possibility of drastically reducing the ability to discover tests by conducting them in some big canyon or man-made crater. The United States had to change its earlier position and demand a larger number of inspection stations. This led not only to some loss of face but also to increased interbloc mistrust and suspicions, so detrimental to international negotiations and agreements.

The Russians' main objection to the American inspection proposals was the larger number of inspection posts the United States wanted to set up in Russia. Many fewer stations, it seems now, are needed for effective inspections. When, finally, a nuclear bomb was exploded underground in December 1961 as part of Project Plowshare (for peaceful use of nuclear explosives), the American scientists were highly surprised to learn that the explosion was detected at a much greater distance than they had expected. If such a test had been set off in the three years of negotiations over banning tests of nuclear arms, it is quite possible that the United States would have reached an agreement with the Russians on effective inspection.

The way negotiations are prepared explains in large measure why the position taken is often so tenuous.

Both the negotiations on the prevention of surprise attack in November, 1958, and the disarmament conference of March, 1960, were prepared by *ad hoc* committees assembled when the conference was imminent. The Coolidge Committee, which was supposed to develop the U.S. position for the 1960 conference, was much maligned and its report finally discarded. The real villain, however, was not the committee but the conception which called it into being. It was against all reason to expect an *ad hoc* committee, most of whose members were spending only part time on their assignment, to resolve in less than six months a subject of such technical complexity and on which opinion has been so divided.

Whatever the cause, when Western diplomats assembled a month before the conference to prepare their program, an American position had not yet been developed, and a

130

week before the talks the Western allies had not yet reached agreement on their proposals. Inevitably the Western program had an air of improvisation. The process by which it emerged was directly responsible for the lack of assurance with which it was maintained.[1]

This does not imply that were the two sides thoroughly prepared and were they to agree to forego propaganda gains from negotiations (for example, by conducting them secretly until agreement is reached), consensus over disarmament could be reached. There are true differences of interest and deep differences of perspective which block the negotiations. The formation of a disarmament and arms control agency by the Kennedy Administration in 1961 is an important step to assure that future negotiations will be more adequately prepared. There is, however, still much room to increase and strengthen this agency and enlarge its assignments, before peace research will be well founded.

Three major issues remain unresolved: the scope of inspection, the scope of disarmament (nuclear only? all arms?), and the nature of sanctions should a violation be detected. These road blocks deserve special attention because the arms reduction scheme advanced below claims to overcome all of them.

## Inspection: An American and a Russian Perspective

### Is There a Foolproof Inspection?

Before the nuclear age, inspection of disarmament was not essential, since building up a conventional force involved violations of a magnitude which was impossible to hide. It was widely known that Germany was rearming after World War I, though probably even informed persons were not aware of the full extent of the arms build-up. The British in Palestine were unable to locate most hidden arms but had a fairly accurate estimate of the scope of the arms caches and their clandestine production. Second, a true blitzkrieg was impossible in the days of conventional arms; a surprise attack did not cripple the victim, and he had a chance to build up his forces for a counterattack.

[1] Henry A. Kissinger, *The Necessity for Choice* (New York, Harper & Brothers, 1960), pp. 282–283.

131

In the nuclear age, an aggressor has so many advantages, and the bombs needed are comparatively so few, that inspection for disarmament becomes absolutely necessary. The Americans were the first to point this out; the Russians only slowly and reluctantly recognized the need.

But is effective inspection feasible? Can one really detect every bomb or missile hidden by the other side? Although experts completely agree that foolproof inspection cannot be carried out, there are many differences of opinion on how effective inspection can be made. Many of the opponents of disarmament stress that a small cache of nuclear bombs will make such a difference in a disarmed world that they deem the entire concept of disarmament a folly, and they support arms control instead. Other experts find a "workable" inspection feasible.[2] By combining a large variety of inspection schemes, from foreign aerial inspection to random site visits, the risks of undetected violations can be reduced markedly; at least, it is pointed out again and again, it can be reduced to the degree that the dangers of violations become much smaller than those of the continued arms race. C. P. Snow gave sharp expression to this view when he stated that the arms race is *certain* to lead to disaster, while the dangers of disarmament are only a *possibility*.

## SOCIAL CHANGE EFFECT

Even if there were agreement over the possibility and advisability of inspection from the viewpoint of the number and magnitude of violations, inspection would still be highly controversial. Inspection, one must realize, is both advanced (by the United States) and objected to (by the Soviet Union) on the grounds that it might serve as an instrument of de-Communization.

Western writers were first to suggest that inspection, even if limited in effectiveness as a method to detect violations, may serve to reduce some of the underlying political-ideological conflict between East and West, the ultimate cause of the arms race. Inspection would require between 30,000 to 40,000 observers living in Communist countries (of which about 10,000

---

[2] See, for instance, a collection of studies, edited by Seymour Melman, *Inspection for Disarmament* (New York, Columbia University Press, 1958).

would be in the Soviet Union alone), unhampered in their movements and contacts with local citizens if they are to do their job effectively. It is suggested that this widespread and frequent contact with Westerners would open the closed Communist world to the West and would break up its monolithic character, thus exposing and making untenable at least the more extreme forms of totalitarianism. It would force Communist governments to be more tolerant and to raise the standard of living of their populations in order to make the West less attractive and to sustain the loyalty of their citizens. Hence, inspection would bring the East closer to the West, reduce the more "objectionable" characteristics of Communism, and thus reduce interbloc conflict.

Sociologists, however, would be quick to point out that most of these expectations are based on wishful thinking or serve as an ideology to make disarmament more appealing to Americans. They have little validity. Ten thousand inspectors (many of whom would be from neutral countries such as India and Mexico) might tour Soviet Russia day and night and have very little effect on its political and social structure. Foreigners have a special status in most societies, especially in Communist countries, which makes them particularly ineffective as agents of social change. Aliens are often kept isolated by a wall of polite, or not so polite, hospitality (as are United Nations inspectors in Jerusalem, Gaza, and Leopoldville), with little entrée into intimate social gatherings, clubs, associations, and elite circles of the host country. Foreigners frequently do not have enough command of the native language and customs to communicate effectively even when they have a chance to do so. There are probably many thousands of non-Communists in Moscow alone (diplomats, journalists, students, tourists), but they do not appear to threaten Communism; they are but a drop in the bucket.

## Inspection and Scope of Disarmament

The import of the social-change effect of inspection, however, does not lie in its sociological validity, for as long as both sides believe in it, it further increases the West's demand for inspection of Communist countries and the latter's objection to this measure. Actually, the source of the very different attitudes toward inspection in the East and in the West lies elsewhere. Since information equals power, the fact the Communist societies are "closed" while the Western societies are "open" has central military import for all wars. Russia undoubtedly gained significantly from its highly successful atomic spies in the critical years when the United States had bombs and Russia did not; the significance of the United States success in breaking the Japanese naval code during the campaign in the Far East is often stressed. But less attention is paid to the large amount of important military information one can gain about the West from public sources, such as directories of factories, newspapers, city maps, train schedules, and the publication of Congressional hearings. The West is again and again surprised when some enterprising journalist, through painstaking clipping of newspapers alone, publishes a highly accurate report of the positioning of United States forces, the number of its missiles, the location of their launching sites and the like. One cannot close the channels of information without "closing" the door on many of the distinctive characteristics of a free society.

In Communist countries, almost all these items of information are not made public but are kept deliberately secret. American intelligence must employ elaborate techniques to gain information about the Soviet Union, while the latter needs only subscriptions to periodicals to learn much about the military power of the United States. A U-2 is needed, for example, to acquire maps of Soviet cities whose American equivalent can be bought in tourist shops. If any Russian can read English, he must *know* where most, if not all, American missile launching bases are; an American needs much more than a knowledge of Russian to *guess* at the locations of their missile sites.

In short, by allowing 10,000 inspectors to roam around freely in their country, the Russians would give up one of their most vital military advantages in exchange for inspection of the already highly open United States. Thus, whatever the Russians think about the social-change effects of inspection, they cannot but realize that by granting uninhibited inspection they might well be giving away a good part of their military might, possibly enough to give the West a distinctive advantage.

This explains, at least in part, the position the Russians take toward inspection. They first rejected it totally as legalized spying; when they came to recognize that the problem of violation is so important that the West will never agree to disarmament without inspection, *they tied inspection to disarmament*. In a disarmed world, they will not need to maintain secrecy, and hence they will be able to afford inspection. But they are quite unwilling, and from their viewpoint possibly unable, to accept *total* (or extensive) *inspection coupled with limited disarmament,* which is approximately what the West has been offering them for the last seven years. For a while the United States offered the Soviet Union simple exchange of aerial inspection ("open skies") without any disarmament, which must have sounded to the Russians like a deal in which an American offered, "I will give you what you have and you give me what I want." More recently, the United States has been willing to join in a declaration of a permanent ban on nuclear tests (that is, limiting to some degree the development of one category of weapons) if the Russians agree to what from their viewpoint is a rather extensive inspection (it includes from twelve to twenty uninhibited "site visits" of suspicious locations, to be determined by non-Communist inspectors). Finally, in September 1961, the United States came around to support full disarmament; but it still demands inspection not of what is disarmed but of what arms remain, which is unacceptable to the Russians.

One can argue that the United States, by virtue of its openness, has already given the East "inspection" opportunities, thus what looks like an uneven deal is just an attempt to even the score. But we are not concerned here with the absolute justice of the position taken by each side, but with the probability that it will lead to disarmament. Clearly, the Russians will agree to extensive inspection coupled with limited disarmament the day "shrimps learn to whistle."

## Violations, Sanctions, and Safeguards

Not less crucial than the difference in interests, perspective toward inspection, and scope of disarmament is the problem of sanctions—or rather, the lack of sanctions. Inspection is of little use if violations are fatal, or, though not fatal, if there is still no way to punish the violator so as to make additional violations "unattractive," thus abolishing the advantages the violator gains. Let us assume that one day a neutral inspector opens the "wrong" door in a hangar next to a Russian airport in the far Ural and stumbles over a hundred hidden nuclear bombs. The very discovery may well paralyze all the truly disarmed countries, and in all likelihood it would put all those with similar hidden caches back into the arms race. The situation would exert much pressure on the country whose cache had been disclosed to use it before other countries could rebuild their defenses or strike a preventive blow.

It is theoretically possible that the countries that observed the disarmament pact would be granted satisfaction through filing a complaint with the United Nations against the violator, by imposing some enormous fine, and by turning over the found bombs to the International Agency for the Peaceful Use of Fissionable Materials. But this seems highly unlikely.

The very thought of the destruction which a country with a nuclear monopoly could inflict, when discovered in a violation, would induce all nonarmed countries either to completely capitulate or to secretly rearm. The very consideration of such a possibility has sufficed to block all disarmament until now. Since multilateral disarmament plans do not offer viable safeguards nor effective sanctions, they are again and again rejected.

In summary, total and immediate disarmament—to be carried out in four, six, or eight years, as various planners suggest —has much appeal for human imagination. It certainly would eliminate not only arms but also waste of human talent, manpower, and resources, as well as many of the fears resulting from the very existence of arms. The major flaw in multilateral disarmament lies in the subjective fear of violations and their objective effect, because hiding even a small number of nuclear bombs would suffice to make the possessor a potential tyrant of the world.

## Social Order, Change, and Disarmament

The danger of violation hangs over all disarming nations; why the special reluctance of the United States to disarm?[3] In part it is due to a deep-seated suspicion of Communist inten-

3 Obviously, no country has disarmed so far, but the Soviets have subscribed to the principle of total disarmament, consistently, since the early 30's; the United States, since September, 1961.

tions. In part the answer lies in the United States reliance on arms not only to stop the military expansionism of the Communist bloc but also to counter the spread of Communism as an ideological-political movement. The world is full of strains and conflicts—native people fight for their independence against colonial powers; races engage in conflicts; peasants cry for land; and workers demand an improved standard of living. Communism as a revolutionary movement appears to have much to offer all these groups. Russia is not recognized as a colonial power, and it therefore commands the sympathy of many nationalist independence movements; it has a major non-white ally, and it therefore appeals to the nonwhite races: it offers land to the peasants, and rapid industrialization to the workers. Communism has much appeal in countries where the level of education is low, where social inequality is high, and where the people have never experienced either Western democracy or the Western standard of living. This description happens to fit most of Asia, Africa, and Central and South America and parts of Southern Europe. Where Communism has strong appeal, it has little need for force in order to make inroads.

Most internal strains and conflicts—especially any such large-scale disorders as the Congo crisis in 1960, Cuba after the 1959 revolution, Lebanon in 1958, and Guatemala in 1956 —work in favor of Communism, even when the Communist bloc cannot send troops or "volunteers" (as it did not, in all the cases cited). The West's intervention in these cases "confirms" the imperialist image of the United States held by many people in the uncommitted nations, an image which the Communists attempt to spread. On the other hand, order often cannot be restored without force. The West—frequently the side supporting order—needed to employ its military might in all these crises. In one instance, it was employed openly through the use of United States marines (Lebanon), once through the use of native rebels (Cuba), once through the United Fruit Co. and the CIA (Guatemala), and once through the forces of the United Nations (the Congo); but in all these cases Western force was used to restore or to try to restore the previously existing order, thus countering Communism. *So the crux of the problem is that the power which supports social change and revolution can benefit from social strains and disorder, and can rely on its ideological power and political agitation, while that power which supports order and the status quo has often to resort to force.*

Note that when the roles are reversed, when strains and disorders occur in a Communist country, and Russia is concerned with maintaining the status quo and order—as it was in Poland, East Germany, and Hungary—it had to resort to force, while the West's influence rested on the power of its ideals.

Yet, when it comes to the large majority of countries—the underdeveloped ones—the West is seen as the user of force, the East less so, because in these countries, most of which are outside the Communist bloc, the Communists support social change, while the West tends to support the existing order. The United States, because of its traditional fear of revolutions, its fight against Communism, its colonial allies, and business interests in the old regimes, again and again resorts to the use of force to maintain the existing order. Hence, it is often claimed that in *a disarmed world Communism would do better than the West.*[4] It is suggested that many countries in Asia, Africa, and Latin America are ripe for Communism because they are full of unresolved social strains. The social needs of these countries could theoretically be answered through social reforms and evolution, but the combination of internal and external forces that support the status quo, largely unresponsive to the changing social needs, blocks most adjustments until it is too late for nonviolent, gradual reforms. If the United States did not support the existing order, these countries might well experience leftist revolutions. Thus the desire to defend the uncommitted nations, which "know no better," from Communism as an ideological force—or from other left-wing revolutions—may well be the ultimate source of United States reluctance to agree to total disarmament, even if coupled with extensive and effective inspection.

But what about the Communist bloc—would it not disintegrate in a disarmed world? It should first of all be pointed out that the belief, widespread in the United States but not in other Western countries, that most people in most Communist coun-

[4] See Richard J. Barnet, *Who Wants Disarmament?* (Boston, The Beacon Press, 1960), p. 70 ff.

tries hate Communism and would denounce it were it not for their armed oppressors is simply not true. The ill-fated Cuban invasion was conceived with this idea in mind; it was expected that when the United States-supported rebel force landed, the "enslaved" Cubans would rise against their "Communist tyrant" to fight for their freedom. No such uprising was forthcoming.

The citizens of most Communist countries have never experienced a democracy. Before Communism took over, they had Nazi totalitarianism, "enlightened" monarchs, feudal landlords, or forced sharecropping. The Communists gave the peasants land, the workers full employment, and education to the children. Often they could not take freedoms away from the people, for they did not have any (or, as it is sometimes put, they had only the freedom to starve under the bridge). Since then, years of Communist rule and education, recent rises in the standard of living, and less exercise of force have made many of the citizens supporters of the regime.

The Communists might realize that in a disarmed world some countries might break away from their bloc; East Germany seems a particularly likely candidate. But the Communists seem quite willing to risk losing two or three countries to gain a chance to spread over three continents! In a disarmed world, moreover, military blocs will disappear anyway; alliances will have much less significance; and breaking away from the Communist bloc would not make these countries necessarily non-Communist. Yugoslavia broke away from the Communist bloc in 1948, but this did not make its internal structure much less Communist than that of bloc-member Poland.

In short, the United States correctly perceives that the nature of the social conflict in many underdeveloped countries is such that, should it presently disarm without devising alternative means to maintain order in these countries, many of them would undergo left-wing or Communist revolutions, though they would not necessarily join the Communist bloc.

This is of course a major reason Russia is so keen on total disarmament. Hence the Soviet Union will accept partial disarmament only if it leads to total disarmament, and inspection only if it is tied to both. The United States demands first of all inspection, which maximizes its gains (opens Russia) and minimizes its sacrifices (because so much of it is open anyway), and

139

is willing from time to time to consider some partial disarmament, but not total disarmament under conditions acceptable to the Russians. Hence substantial or total disarmament will have to be delayed until the United States finds means and strategies, excluding force, which will allow it to support order and other values it is committed to, or until Communist expansionism, geared to social change in the underdeveloped countries, ceases. Both possibilities are related to the progress of various sociopolitical processes to be extensively discussed in Part Three.

In summary, foolproof inspection is out of the question. A major roadblock is created by the Russian demand to tie extensive inspection to extensive disarmament. The American position, which relates disarmament to the pressure of Communist expansion as an ideological power, points correctly to the need to relate, much more closely than disarmament plans do, the solution of the arms race to the settlement of global, political, and social problems. Trying to overcome the symptoms of international violence without curing the underlying sources is probably the final reason for the failure of disarmament programs to command the approval of both sides, and it would lead to their failure even if the sides would sign a disarmament pact.

Arms control does not offer a cure, it might even worsen the situation, and it is totally unacceptable to the Communist bloc; multilateral disarmament attempts too much too quickly, it has no true safeguards, and it is, at least presently, unacceptable to the West. Arms reduction is a plan that begins modestly but has far-reaching ends, that overcomes many of the dilemmas revealed by the preceding analysis of arms control and multilateral disarmament.

# Chapter 7

## Arms Reduction— A Safe Way to Lasting Peace

BOTH SIDES might subscribe to a plan to reverse the arms race and to work toward the eventual destruction of all arms and military establishments. Following a successful completion of tension reduction (through the first two phases of Gradualism), the sides might agree on arms reduction (as part of "the settlement" of Gradualism's third phase). Arms reduction will divide disarmament into two main phases—conventional and nuclear disarmament—each including many steps, such as the closing of military bases, the reduction of armies, the destruction of destroyers, and the like, spread over a considerable period of time. According to the principles of Gradualism, later steps will be carried out only to the degree that earlier ones have been carried out successfully; no undue risk will be taken at any one step. Risks will be avoided by a combination of inspection and safeguards. At all times, inspection and arms reduction will be coextensive, both expanding gradually. Safeguards are built into the plan, in that the more potent weapons are disarmed last; thus, arms to be given up at later stages protect the complying parties from violations at earlier stages. The very last stage is delayed until the formation of the global community—to be accelerated by means discussed below—makes safeguards unnecessary.

Arms reduction is a slow and lengthy process. It is this slow pace which allows the sociopolitical processes to catch up and supply the necessary foundation when the day of total disarmament finally arrives. But if we are oriented toward disarmament, we will be able to enjoy some of its blessings before arms reduction is completed.

Arms reduction is unlikely to be the plan the United States or the Soviet Union will advance as they sit at the negotiation table, since it requires some concessions from both. But the plan might emerge as a compromise in the interbloc negotiations and might well be promoted by the genuine neutral countries. It may never satisfy the idealist, especially the supporters of unilateral or multilateral disarmament, since it requires that some arms and bombs be kept for a considerable length of time; but unlike more appealing programs, it has a chance to be agreed upon and to be carried out. Unlike multideterrence and arms control, it leads to disarmament.

## Safeguards and Sanctions

Discussions on disarmament suffer greatly from a confusion between the role of safeguards and that of sanctions. Safeguards protect the *complying* party from a violation that *might* occur; sanctions are applied to the *violating* party to prevent a repetition of violations that *did* occur. In a situation where one violation might be crucial, sanctions are of little importance compared with safeguards.[1] On the international scene, because of the inherent danger in any one violation and the inherent weakness of sanctions, compared to the possible advantage to be gained by a "crime," it is necessary to put much more stress on preventing a criminal from causing damage—that is, on safeguards rather than on sanctions after the act. A disarmament pact that has effective safeguards but no, or few, sanctions is definitely preferable to one that has no, or few, safeguards but very potent sanctions, since we may never live to see the sanctions applied.

### NUCLEAR SAFEGUARDS

The only feasible route to disarmament is a gradual one, in which the opponents disarm partially while they maintain potent safeguards. We have to learn to "climb off the precipice without jumping off." Safeguards are built into our arms reduction plan, in that weapons and strategic positions for protecting a complying party from a violator are given up in later stages, only after mutual trust, inspection systems, and international institutions have developed. *The only sequence of arms reduc-*

---

[1] This relative emphasis should be contrasted with the situation prevailing *within* each country. Within each country, the laws rely on safeguards (policeman on the beat, etc.) and on the deterring effect of sanctions, but chiefly on sanctions after the crime, to maintain law and order. The emphasis is on justice (punishing the violator), not on prevention.

*tion which supplies safeguards both sides are liable to view as adequate*—whether we like it or not—*is the one in which conventional arms are given up first, nuclear arms later,* and in which nuclear bombs serve as safeguards against violations, until a sociopolitical settlement is worked out and the need for such safeguards is no longer felt.

The grave danger of nuclear arms and the need to rid ourselves of them as soon as possible are very evident. But there is no way of abandoning nuclear weapons unless we first give up conventional arms, for *giving up one's nuclear arms first actually amounts to giving up all one's armed protection and might in one act!* Nuclear disarmament requires such extensive inspection that it makes much of conventional armaments useless, and conventional arms supply no safeguard against a nuclear violator. Hence, if we try to start with nuclear disarmament—as almost all supporters of disarmament advocate—efforts to disarm will continue to be deadlocked, as they have been in the past.

On the other hand, if we leave nuclear bombs to the second phase, and the most devastating bombs to the very last stage, violations of the arms reduction pact could not be crippling. Even if a violator turns out to have kept some extra machine guns, bombers, or even small atomic bombs, he will not dare to attack our heartland, for fear that we will unleash the big bombs in retaliation, in our frustration that the peace plan has been wrecked and in our fury at the cynical violation. (Measures to counter armed nibbling and unarmed subversion rather than outright attacks are discussed below.) There is no question of hiding "extra" superbombs, since these are to be controlled only when viable international institutions have developed sufficiently. Thus, their deterring effect is used to disarm, build a global community, and, ultimately, to remove the bombs themselves.

Nuclear safeguards ought to remove the fear of gross violations and, with it, many of our objections to conventional disarmament. Conventional disarmament will give us the atmosphere and the time needed to build the confidence, experience, and institutions nuclear disarmament requires; it will allow inspection to develop and sociopolitical processes to catch up. When finally the last weapons are to be abolished, we will be

143

insured both against violations and against rearmament by the global institutions. Nuclear bombs now used to deter major attacks may be used during the transition period to deter the violators of the arms reduction pact from exploiting their advantage. Instead of perpetuating war, the bombs will help to lay the foundation for peace. Man may yet turn the fission demon he has unleashed into his obedient servant.

## DESIGNED AND BUILT-IN SANCTIONS

There are only few and limited sanctions (or "punishments") that can be designed to support the enforcement of the arms reduction plan. Both sides could agree to deposit $5 billion dollars or rubles each year with the International Inspection Authority; minor violations could be penalized by forfeiture of these deposits. The interest on the funds deposited and those forfeited might serve to finance inspection. Thus, automatically, the more violations, the more funds would be available for inspection. The remaining funds might be used to finance mutually approved UNESCO activities. Having to destroy five extra weapons (above the regular arms reduction quota) of the type found unreported or secretly manufactured, in addition to all those so found, might be another form of sanction. But to a very large degree such sanctions can serve only to curb minor violations—such as bona-fide negligence or tardiness in the destruction or listing of some arms—but not to halt gross violations. Sanctions like these could, of course, be simply repudiated by any government deliberately bent on committing a gross violation. Thus their main role is that of insuring that the parties will be anxious to carry out their obligations to the letter, with great care; such compliance with the arms reduction pact will contribute to building up and maintaining the vital mutual trust, not to deterring a major attempt at violation.

Another type of sanction exists, which could be activated should any gross violation occur. This sanction is "built in," being part of the graduated arms reduction sequence itself. The failure of one side to carry out some important obligation would automatically halt the arms reduction of the other side; continued violation, discovery of large, hidden, or concealed production of significant weapons, would automatically trigger "regression"—that is, a return to an earlier stage of the plan

144

through some rearmament (such as recalling units into service or reopening some armament assembly lines)—to balance the violation. Any single violation of a critical nature (such as concealing missiles or atomic bombs) or a large accumulation of small violations (such as repeated discovery of concealed production of conventional arms) will signal the failure of the whole plan and invite its abandonment. Consequently, an even more bitter and aggressive arms race than the present one might ensue, as hope for a peaceful settlement became extremly slim. Hence, as long as both sides are committed to the basic goal of arms reduction and in agreement with its procedures, the threat of regression and possible abandonment of the plan—the threat of a no-holds-barred arms race—will serve as a potent sanction for the observation of various particulars of the arms reduction pact.

Nuclear bombs theoretically could serve not only as a safeguard but also to punish a gross violation, but no country would or should initiate a nuclear holocaust merely because the other side had violated some agreements, even if these concerned nuclear disarmament. Hence, the function of the temporary retention of nuclear arms is to insure that the disarming sides do not undergo undue risks in reducing their arms. They serve as safeguards, not sanctions.

*In toto,* our plan thus provides much more potent safeguards than sanctions; but this, we suggest, is the kind of plan needed. Surely the more potent the sanctions are, the more protected the treaty. But the essential quality of arms reductions pacts lies in the nature of their safeguards. Ours may be claimed to be too potent, but certainly not too weak.

## Working-Toward Effect

Arms reduction is a slow process because it attempts to tie the process of disarmament to the development of mutual trust and global institutions, in order to avoid premature disarmament, which leads to rearmament. To achieve this, arms reduction must occur step by slow step over time, and nuclear bombs must be retained temporarily as safeguards. This surely raises a central objection; since nuclear arms are the major threat, what does arms reduction as advocated here contribute to security? It should be pointed out first of all that to the best of

145

our judgment there is no other way to disarm; it is this sequence or none.

Second, there is a big difference between nuclear bombs under multideterrence and arms control, on the one hand, and the same bombs under arms reduction, on the other. Under the plan advanced here, bombs are held as a *temporary* safeguard, with the clear intention of ultimately abolishing them. This is a crucial difference, not only for the long run—the difference between a disarmed and an armed world—but also for the immediate and near future, since it changes the entire domestic and international psychological climate, through what might be referred to as the "working-toward" effect.

The chief danger from the bombs lies in the deliberate intention to use them. Undoubtedly there are the dangers of non-deliberate use, of accidental war. But some of these are eliminated in the first stage of arms reduction (we see below how the *n*th country problem will be tackled through nuclear embargo). Other dangers are direct consequences of the arms race and will disappear with it (when we remove our fingers from the triggers and reduce the hysteria, which encourages unauthorized behavior and mistaken judgments). Finally, some unilateral and multilateral arrangements to reduce the probability of accidents can be introduced as early as the initial tension-reduction phase. Hence, the danger of war by accident, which cannot be completely eliminated until arms reduction is completed, will be greatly reduced in its first stage, and will continue to decline as arms reduction evolves. For the first time since the invention of the atomic bomb, a decreasing column of probabilities will replace the heretofore ever increasing probability that a war by accident would erupt.

The chief danger, then, lies not in the bombs, but in man's intention to use them. The people of New Jersey do not worry about nuclear bombs in the hands of New Yorkers; the Southern states do not fear the atomic bombs in the North; and the Canadians do not expect an American nuclear attack. With the decline in international strains and suspicions as the first and second phases of Gradualism are completed and the third—that of arms reduction and political settlement—is agreed upon, along with the accelerated development of a global community, the urge to use the bombs will decline (though only gradually disappear), along with the fear of their use, though this fear will vanish only in the distant future.

Our attitude toward the bombs depends to a large degree on our orientation to the future. In a galloping arms race, we feel that bombs might at any time be dropped on us, and we see in our bombs a protection from attack. Under arms control, bombs are a permanent foundation that supports the balance of power that keeps each side from the other's throat. Under arms reduction, we see our archenemy slowly destroying his arms, and we gain confidence; our fear that the bombs will be used against us is reduced. We realize that bombs are not here to stay and will be demolished in the foreseeable future and that gradually we will have to learn not to count on them in our international give and take. Finally, as the global community matures, we will perceive them only as very dangerous devices without a function: relics of a barbarous era, capable at each moment of wrecking the peace we have built up over the years—instruments whose death grip upon the world we are anxious to loosen.

The most important source of arms reduction impact on our attitudes to the bombs (and other means of violence) is the orientation toward disarmament and stable peace as a future state of affairs toward which we work and progress—a prospect and vision which both multideterrence and arms control completely lack.

Our view of the future, by affecting our present anxieties, thoughts, and action, affects the future itself, since it is determined in part by what we believe it is going to be. This phenomenon has been referred to by the prominent sociologist Robert K. Merton as the self-fulfilling prophecy. This is a prophecy which, although false at the time it is pronounced, influences behavior to such an extent that the prophecy comes to pass. In short, the prophecy fulfills itself by virtue of its pronouncement.[2]

[2] Merton's classic illustration of this insight is derived from the Black Wednesday in 1932, when the belief that the banks would be unable to return cash to their depositors caused a panic and a "run on the banks," which is the only condition under which a normal banking system is unable to answer depositor demands. See his *Social Theory and Social Structure*, rev. ed. (New York, The Free Press of Glencoe, 1957).

If we believe that we are proceeding toward an armed show-down, we will multiply our arms, strengthen our fortresses, and put a finger on the trigger—all of which actions elicit a similar preparation from the other side, which still further intensifies our preparations in addition to justifying our earlier fear. One false move after that, and we produce the future we "antici-pated." If, on the other hand, we feel that we are working to-ward a world of peace, we are able to see ways of settling our disputes with the other bloc, as well as sources for safeguards, until we can overcome our remaining misgivings.

The feeling of progress, of advancing step by step according to a prearranged plan toward a set, concrete goal—a feeling that the implementation of arms reduction will generate—is especially constructive. As we give up one conventional arm after another, according to schedule, turning tanks into tractors, soldiers into workers, military appropriations into expenditures for research, development, and education, our belief in the eventual realization of what now seems a highly Utopian state increases. Moreover, as military researchers are transferred to peaceful work, as weapon factories begin to produce consumer goods, and as armament appropriations are used to build schools, we create a large variety of new interests vested in peace and we reduce the vested interests in the arms race. In addition, the more we progress toward this desired state, the larger the domestic and world public opinion pressure not to "regress," to maintain arms reduction obligations, to avoid violations.

In summary, our orientation to a state of complete disarma-ment helps to bring about the future we "anticipated." The very same weapons have a very different meaning according to our orientation. If we expect war, they are dangerous weapons; if we expect peace, they are temporary safeguards.

## Coextensive and Graded Inspection

The arms reduction sequence from conventional to nuclear weapons provides us not only with adequate safeguards but also with a foundation for an inspection system that appears to have none of the characteristics which either the Soviet Union or the United States finds objectionable. Two principles underlie the proposed system. First, inspection is *coextensive* with arms reduction, both expanding gradually. That is, all areas that are declared disarmed or arms that are declared destroyed, at any stage, are also covered by inspection, but no inspection takes place in other areas, nor are other arms controlled. This answers the American demand for inspected disarmament and the Soviet need for limiting the scope of inspection to that of disarmament.

Second, our inspection system gains from the fact that various inspection methods differ greatly, to the extent that they require penetration of the inspected country. We shall see that some methods require no such penetration at all and that others call only for penetration by radio waves and electronic beams. Even those methods that require the presence of aliens in the inspected countries differ in the degree of freedom needed by inspectors in order to perform effectively.

A central virtue of the arms reduction sequence advocated here is that it permits construction of an inspection structure layer by layer, *beginning with inspection methods that can effectively function from outside the country inspected, introducing only gradually and at later stages inspection that demands increasing penetration into the inspected territory.*

The secret lies in the nature of the arms reduction sequence advocated here. If we followed the opposite arms reduction sequence, from nuclear to conventional, extensive internal inspection, required by nuclear disarmament, would have to be introduced at the outset, before mutual trust is firmly grounded; such a plan would surely raise an insurmountable Soviet objection, for it would expose their conventional arms. On the other hand, if conventional disarmament is implemented first, it can proceed a long way while relying simply on external inspection. Once it is highly advanced, and nuclear disarmament and internal inspection begins, the main objection to internal inspection is removed—there are no more conventional arms to conceal (other than those of internal security forces). Thus, the scheme presented here should satisfy the vital interest of both parties.

Details of the arms reduction scheme and related inspection system would, of course, have to be worked out by teams of experts and around the international conference table. The following simply illustrates the two principles of coextensive and from-the-outside-to-the-inside inspection. Any details or all of them might be revised or adjusted, but the over-all plan would hold.[3] It is essential to remember that our plan would be initiated only after a successful completion of the tensions-reduction phase, and after agreement has been reached on the whole arms reduction scheme as well as on the political settlement, discussed below.

## PHASE ONE: CONVENTIONAL DISARMAMENT

*Cessation of Armament Accumulation.* To halt the arms race and set the stage for arms reduction, all participants in the pact will declare their intention to stop the production and development of all arms in the near future, according to an agreed-upon schedule. Exceptions might have to be made for countries which are particularly lagging in the development of weapons intended to serve as safeguards until later stages. For example, the continuation of the construction of early-warning radar networks could be allowed for a longer period.

No effective inspection can or need be introduced at this stage; but successive, more extensive, inspections, in addition to serving whatever specific arms reduction they are introduced to cover, will also serve to check abidance with earlier agreements. From the very beginning, intelligence work will provide a limited check. In addition, budget analysis can serve from the outset as a very crude, though by no means useless, method, for it checks what has been done with funds previously committed to armament. If claim is made that they are allocated to the production of consumer goods, we look for evidence of considerable increase in the standard of living; if they are to be used to develop backward nations, there should be evidence of new steel mills, highways, dams, and the like; reduction of taxes is easy to establish, as is every act that affects all citizens. While it is rather easy to hide up to 20 per cent of the armament budget by diverting funds declared for other purposes to armament, larger violations are difficult to conceal, even in closed

[3] For a list of publications that discuss various concrete disarmament proposals on which the following discussion draws, see Christopher Wright, "Selected Critical Bibliography," *Daedalus* (Fall, 1960), pp. 1055–1070.

societies. But, as we point out above, the main checks will come subsequently.

*Weapons Demolition and Alteration.* Reduction of conventional arms would follow. It might well start with demolition of some weapons which are few in number, big, and expensive, such as destruction of destroyers. Their small number and large size makes violations easy to detect; their price makes secret production to replace those destroyed rather unappealing, though by no means impossible.

Since the numbers of different weapons held by each country is not the same, and since reduction of arms is supposed to reduce equally the power of the two blocs, an exchange rate will have to be agreed upon, to determine what "contributions" of each side to the demolition fund will be considered "equal" to that of the other. (This problem requires more research and negotiations than may at first appear; the sides differ not only in the arms they possess but also in those they need to maintain equal military positions, chiefly because of the long Western seaways as compared to the East's greater land concentration.)

External inspection can be exercised, since the weapons would be sent to a place outside the territories of both sides (for example, the Solomon Islands), to be destroyed under joint supervision. The sight of an American destroyer tied to a Russian one, sinking together—with no one aboard—might serve as an effective symbol of the new international system. It surely sounds quite fantastic today, but not more fantastic than a suggestion twenty years ago that the two allies would become archenemies. Once big and highly expensive weapons are eliminated in this way, larger numbers of smaller items—such as submarines, bombers, supersonic fighters—are also to be destroyed.

One might suggest that most of these weapons can be disarmed and used for peaceful purposes. Destroyers might serve as merchant ships; bombers as civil airliners; and tanks as tractors. But since such disarmed vessels and vehicles might easily be rearmed, the sides will probably prefer in the first stage to destroy completely these instruments of violence. Or they might prefer to start weapons demolition with arms that can hardly be turned to peaceful use (each side might supply for

151

destruction one million rifles, machine guns, and hand grenades). Or the sides might favor conversion of arms which cannot easily be reconverted to military uses—they might wish to melt cannon into iron blocks. As the scope of inspection grows and confidence deepens, both sides might agree to bring ships, planes, and tanks to neutral lands to be stripped of all arms and electronic devices of direct military value and to be altered in such ways that rearmament would be highly expensive. Many engineers and technicians would take great delight in working out the details of such alteration. The very exposure of arms to the other side at the demilitarization post—at which free inspection of weapons disarmed should be permitted—would make their kind less effective even if rearmed, since their potentials as well as limitations would be known to the "enemy."

Some "cheating" might occur at this stage, by way of neglecting to report some conventional weapons, either in hand or under production. But, first, there is a more or less accurate knowledge of the number of the larger items (for example, destroyers); the time required for their construction is long, and their visibility is high. Second, since there will be no way of gaining a critical advantage through such violations, producing some arms secretly while destroying others publicly would be sheer economic waste; moreover, while such violations might gain a limited advantage, they would automatically cancel the arms reduction pact, a loss that few if any limited gains could offset. Finally, once all the weapons of a specific kind were destroyed, the mere sight of one—by tourists, intelligence agents, or, at a later inspection stage, by inspectors—would prove a violation of the arms reduction pact and would lead to its "regression" if not abolition.

*Base Demolition.* The next step might well be one in which military bases and air fields are closed or demolished, following an agreed-upon list and schedule. The nature of the inspection imposed will depend on the location of the bases. To the degree that they are in third countries (for example, in Morocco) and those countries are willing, free inspection of the sites might be allowed either through random checks ("Come look whenever you like") or by stationing inspectors on locations of former bases. In addition, whole areas might be declared demilitarized zones, open to inspection by both sides at any time, as the Antarctic is now.[4] The main burden may well be carried by electronic inspection or monitor devices and surveillance satellites, both extensively used already for intelligence work. From this viewpoint, the development of the American "spy in the sky," Midas satellite, is of special import. As their number increases, they will be able to determine with ease if a particular military base in any country is open or closed, its fortifications intact or leveled.

Aerial inspection of demilitarized areas could probably be agreed upon to supplement inspection by satellites.

The chief advantage of surveillance satellites is that, while they are highly effective in carrying out their job, they are blind to other military secrets (for example, nuclear caches, military research) and can hardly act as agents of subversion or social change; that is, they do not have the side effects that checking the same facts by inspectors would have. The same holds for aerial inspection.

*Demobilization.* Armies may be cut after, or concomitantly with, arms and base demolition. Fewer soldiers will be needed as the number of armed vessels, airplanes, and bases constantly declines. Agreement on the size of the cuts to be undergone by the sides simultaneously should not be too difficult to reach; actually, the United States and the Soviet Union came close to agreeing on such cuts in 1956. The Russians at that time even agreed to the principle that they ought to cut their army to a larger degree than the United States, in order to compensate for their larger army.

Demobilization inspection can be based in part on analysis of public documents, such as local newspapers, and intelligence work. There is nothing more difficult to hide than half a million soldiers. "Cheating" by 50,000 men would not make much difference at this stage, and it would be easily detected in the following stages, when internal inspection begins, long before nuclear safeguards are given up.

*Area Disarmament.* This step involves some internal inspection—that is, sending of inspectors into the disarming coun-

---

[4] The United States should have welcomed the suggestion to de-nuclearize Africa, demanding to set up a model inspection system on that continent. Such a model would facilitate working out many of the technical problems of an inspection system and would set precedents for de-nuclearization of other continents. France should have been encouraged to test its bombs elsewhere, if not to stop their production altogether.

153

tries—and hence prepares the ground for the next phase. By now the amount of conventional arms, armies, and installations has been greatly reduced. This stage further expands conventional disarmament and introduces additional checks on disarmament declared but only partially checked during earlier stages.

Both sides will agree to divide their territories into two kinds of areas: those in which missiles and nuclear warheads will be stationed (to be disarmed in the nuclear phase) and those in which no such weapons will be stationed. Territories will have to be fairly large—all of Southern California might be one armed territory—to insure that no side will be able to pinpoint or wipe out by large, indiscriminate bombing the other side's nuclear safeguards.

The areas to be disarmed in this stage might be divided into a large number of territories, let us say ten. Each year an additional one will be open to inspection. Thus, in ten years the whole country, with the exception of nuclearly armed areas, will be disarmed and inspected.

If there is reason to believe that at this stage the Russians still feel threatened by the de-Communization effects (real or imagined) of inspectors, such effects can easily be greatly reduced. Inspectors could be ordered to take their vacations outside the countries they supervise; they could complete their tours of duty unaccompanied by their families; they could be under orders not to fraternize; they could be made to live in isolated quarters or in big cities accustomed to aliens. Surely it would be better for all sides to open their homes to the inspectors; whatever effects they have would be extremely unlikely to undermine existing political structures and might somewhat increase international understanding. But it is essential for the success of the arms reduction plan that no side even attempt to use the inspection scheme for any purposes other than checking on arms reduction.

It should be noted, finally, that much inspection of conventional disarmament can be carried out by fixed inspection posts, without requiring free-roaming inspectors who can at will enter any facilities. Port inspection, for example, can be carried out by posting inspection ships at the entrances and an inspection tower equipped with searchlights at the center of the harbor, without having to let inspectors visit every storage house, nor, for that matter, having to let them spend their evenings in town.

At the end of this stage, the main areas of both countries will be free from nuclear arms (concentrated in limited, though large, areas) and from conventional arms (destroyed, converted, or dismantled). The major areas of both countries are under satellite, aerial, and manned inspection. If no gross violations have been reported for long periods, and international institutions have developed as expected, the sides would probably now be ready to begin nuclear disarmament.

## PHASE TWO: NUCLEAR DISARMAMENT

Cessation of the production and development of nuclear arms and such related "means of delivery" as missiles is to be declared as early as the parties can agree to it.

Disarmament of nuclear weapons may proceed from outside the country to within the country in a similar fashion to that of conventional disarmament. As a first step, each side will *declare his inventory* of nuclear bombs and remaining means of delivery, and *install consistent serial numbers on all weapons* (existing serial numbers of major weapons are deliberately inconsistent in order to mislead the "enemy"). The fulfilling of this obligation will be tested to a large degree in later stages; at this stage, it can be validated through intelligence work and citizen supervision (see below). To the degree that the sides feel free to permit it, it would be very helpful to introduce at this stage a limited number of random checks—not enough to establish the nature and position of nuclear weapons, and thus expose them, but sufficient to check on the serialization. All efforts are oriented to insuring that there will be no unnumbered items, or any two items with identical numbers, or weapons with numbers higher than those reported as the top limits. Violations of the inventory and numbering should be considered severe violations, because they would allow in later stages for the building up of caches of hidden nuclear arms.

Cessation of production will continue to be uninspected for some time by means other than inventory (serial number) inspection. Banning of tests may be monitored from stations outside the country and from some open, disarmed zones within the country.

Since so much attention has been paid in recent years to the banning of nuclear arms tests, we will briefly digress to explain why we consider such bans just one of many items in an arms reduction plan. First, testing is a supportive but not critical requirement for the production of weapons. Production without testing reduces the reliability of a weapon, but does not in any way eliminate it. Second, tests of new weapons can be made shortly before they are used, thus not allowing the other side (assuming that he realizes that a test has been made) time to catch up. Third, the most deadly weapons cannot be tested anyway, because of the damage they would cause to the testing party.

Banning the tests gained special emotional value when it was believed that fall-out (generated by testing) was the major source of danger to the existence of the human race. We have since learned that the immediate effects of the bombs are so much greater that fall-out casualties from testing seem *comparatively* low (for example, fall-out would generate serious defects in 4 per cent of all children for the next forty generations; the bombs could easily kill a third of all men, women, *and* children). The focus of various peace organizations on fighting fall-out proved unfortunate when "clean" bombs—those with very little fall-out—were developed, removing the major target of these organizations without bringing peace closer and when the American test-ban plan was formulated—a plan that ties banning of tests to what the Russians view as extensive inspection with practically no disarmament. Continued stress on achieving a permanent test ban serves only to prolong the present stalemate in disarmament negotiations.

For the present arms reduction plan, it is obviously desirable not to continue testing so long as Gradualism and arms reduction are tried, in order not to increase interbloc strains. But, inherently, the test ban is an item of limited disarmament value and one that is best inspected at a later stage, when monitors can be stationed in the disarming countries (though for tension-reduction purposes and fall-out prevention, it is desirable to initiate it at an early stage).

After a period of preliminary inventory validation by methods discussed above, missiles would be either *destroyed* in a neutral territory or used in a United Nations space exploration program.

This might be followed by turning over the *smaller atomic bombs* to an International Agency for Nuclear Energy, to be converted into sources of energy for underdeveloped countries. Larger hydrogen and neutron bombs will be gradually disarmed. Simultaneously the areas containing nuclear arms will be reduced one by one and opened to manned inspection, until finally each country will have only one such zone. The uncocking of the last nuclear bombs and the disarmament of the remaining armed area will be delayed until the day all sides feel that such safeguards are no longer necessary.

Complete disarmament will have to include also *the abolition of means of chemical and biological warfare*. Many people who gradually are informed about the horrors of nuclear war are still grossly unaware of the deadly nonnuclear weapons that governments prepare. In addition to the usual secrecy that surrounds arms and their usage, biological and chemical weapons are particularly concealed because governments do not want to increase further the anxiety of their people, at a high pitch already from the publication of information on the effects of nuclear bombs. To supply an illustration of the nature of the weapons involved, we can go back to a declassified document depicting a weapon which was available already in 1944.

> There was one biological [weapon] in particular of which we were afraid. It is so deadly that a dose in a microscopic quantity is fatal in six hours. If you could secure perfect distribution to all the world's people (which, of course, is impossible) you could kill everyone in the world with a quantity amounting to about eight ounces. This weapon has the further advantage that while it kills everybody in six hours, it is itself oxidized in twelve hours, leaving the ground perfectly safe to occupy, so that there is no danger that the troops of the Power which used it will be contaminated.[5]

These weapons have since then been "perfected" and mass produced, so that today a desperate party—if not some diabolic maniacs in cold blood—can attempt to lay low half of man-

[5] Philip Noel-Baker, *The Arms Race* (New York, Occeana, 1960), p. 352.

kind with anything from temporary paralysis to deadly cholera.

Such weapons are likely to be held by all sides until the last stage of arms reductions, since, like the largest nuclear bombs, they are most crippling and there are no safeguards against their illicit retention. Moreover, checking on their disarmament to any satisfactory degree will be possible only at the last stage, with the extension of manned inspection to all areas.

*Complete disarmament will require practically unlimited inspection privileges.* The main function of unlimited inspection will be to check that no new weapons are researched, developed, or produced, and that the development and production of all nuclear, chemical, and biological weapons has been completely stopped, their stock delivered to international agencies, destroyed, or converted for peaceful use, and their production installations altered.

One might expect that inspection of the fullfilment of the obligations undertaken by the sides under the arms reduction pact would require many hundreds of thousands, perhaps a million, inspectors. Actually, effective checks can be made without gigantic machinery if inspection is carried out on the basis of random spot checks. Statisticians can work out sampling procedures that would assure a high level of detection on the basis of a reasonable number of checks per year. In addition to random checks, special checks to examine "tips" received from various citizens will have to be investigated.

I say inspection "privileges" because, to the degree the sociopolitical processes will work adequately and sentiments will change as expected, there will be little interbloc suspicion and mistrust at this stage, especially if the many earlier inspections have revealed no violations or only trivial or technical ones. Granting unlimited inspection rights will reinforce the feeling of mutual confidence and reduce at the same time the urge to inspect. One of the major purposes of inspections at this stage will be, not so much to serve one superpower as a check on the other, but to allow the global institutions to safeguard against arming by various dissenting groups, such as a John Birch Society in the United States or a Stalinist cabal in China.

It should be emphasized again that the preceding discussion serves only as an illustration of the kind of conventional-arms-to-nuclear-arms reduction sequence which could be carried out. It exemplifies especially the gradual extension of disarmament and inspection, to cover more weapons and areas and to increase in effectiveness as the penetration into the inspected country increases. Any of the specific items may very well have to be changed as arms reduction is researched, negotiated, and implemented.

## Making Inspection Effective

The success of arms reduction depends to a large degree on the initial objective state of the parties entering it and their initial intentions. To the degree that all sides realize the dangers of the continued arms race and are able to rely on nonviolent means to secure and pursue their national objectives, to that degree are the basic conditions for effective arms reduction present. To the degree that the first two phases of Gradualism are carried out along the lines discussed earlier, the subjective psychological climate, too, will be ripe for arms reductions.

However, the successful implementation of the arms reduction pact will depend, not only on the predisposition of the sides signing the pact, but to a considerable degree also on their conformity with its clauses once implementation is initiated. This, in turn, is largely affected by the effectiveness of the inspection system. The more effective it is, the more violations will be found, sanctioned, and safeguarded against, but also the less likely are they to occur, because of the greater probability of detection.

There are three ways to enhance the effectiveness of inspection: by combining various inspection methods, by developing citizen supervision, and by largely expanding inspection technology.

### A Multimethod Inspection System

Each single inspection device—whether it be satellite, aerial, or manned inspection—is far from foolproof. But arms reductions does not require that any one device be foolproof. As inspection grows, as one layer is added onto the other, the total, accumulative effectiveness of inspection increases. This is especially the case where "holes" left open by one scheme are plugged by another.

The arms reduction and inspection proposal outlined above is designed to make later inspections close loopholes left by inspections introduced earlier, long before nuclear safeguards are given up. Thus, for instance, in the arms demolition stage a nation might conceal some war vessels, claiming it has no more. At this stage it may get away with the concealment because only external inspection is employed. But later, as satellite and aerial inspections are introduced and stationary, manned inspection in ports is added, such violations become almost impossible to hide. Similarly, it is easy not to number some weapons in the inventory reporting stage, but hiding these when the country is open for manned inspection is much more difficult.

The fact that the schedule for expansion and elaboration of the inspection system will be agreed upon in the initial arms reduction pact will encourage compliance with the pact even in the *early* stages. Realizing that the potential advantages to be gained through violations necessitate waiting for the lowering of the safeguards in the last stage, and knowing in advance that inspection will be tightened before this happens, a nation will regard the holding of illicit stocks as quite unadvisable. The chance to reap any benefits from them is small; the chance that one will sooner or later be caught red-handed and lose the advantages arms reduction offers is large.

Many nations signing the pact might secretly wish to be the only armed nation on earth, and they might be tempted to work toward this goal if there were a possibility of getting away with violations. But, since detection of violations is so likely, benefits from violations so few, and rewards for compliance so obvious, members of the pact will be encouraged to comply with its terms.

CITIZEN SUPERVISION

A rather unique inspection plan that would largely increase the effectiveness of the entire system is that of citizen supervision (or inspection by the people).[6] The central idea is that the people of each country will take it upon themselves to report violations to the International Inspection Agency. This idea

[6] See Seymour Melman, *The Peace Race* (New York, Ballantine Books, 1961), Chapter 11.

sounds quite fantastic at first, but a closer examination reveals that it is based on most solid sociological and psychological grounds. Citizen supervision in itself is highly unreliable, and hence of little value; but when combined with the other inspection schemes, it becomes a potent tool. It benefits from the other schemes and closes many of their loopholes.

Citizen supervision draws on the desire for peace of the average man and on the "working toward" effect. It rests on two valid facts: first, that violation of any significance will have to involve a large number of people (to hide the bombs and the means of delivery, to staff maintenance activities, to make and keep up to date attack plans, to launch a major attack); second, that in any large group of people, however carefully selected, there are bound to be some who, for moral or immoral reasons (because of their conscience or for a monetary reward), will report the violation to the International Inspection Agency or to the other side.

To increase the public acceptance of what under different circumstances might be thought of as "talebearing," the initial arms reduction agreement will include a commitment from each side to publicly direct *its* citizens, repeatedly and in unequivocal terms, to report violations to the International Inspection Agency. Various devices will be installed to guarantee communications possibilities for citizens wishing to report violations. Melman, for instance, suggested that ordinary mail service could be used for such reporting. To guarantee that the mail is delivered and not tampered with, the inspectors could, at random times and at random mail boxes, drop letters addressed to the Agency. If the mail were not delivered, that would be a clear sign of intention to violate the arms reduction pact.

To assess the chances for success of such a plan, it must be realized that in the post-cold war atmosphere, violations of the arms reduction pact would be considered the most contemptible international crime, and citizens would be encouraged by their own government to report them. The carrying out by governments of their duty to so instruct their citizens could be easily monitored. No secret instructions to the contrary could cancel the wide effect of a government's public commitment.

Citizen supervision alone is hardly a reliable instrument of inspection, but added to the others it markedly increases the safety of inspection. It largely reduces the confidence of those who consider a gross violation that it will go unnoticed, and thus it contributes to the deterrence of such an attempt.

## INSPECTION TECHNOLOGY

It is essential to put science to work for the success of the inspection system, especially for the control of nuclear disarmament. If we had taken only a small part, a fraction of 1 per cent, of the resources and ingenuity which have been spent on arms and had invested them in the construction of inspection instruments, if science had been devoted to peace as it has been to war, we would surely long ago have come up with instruments that would greatly increase the effectiveness of inspection and that require no penetration or only a limited penetration of the inspected country. Thus, for instance, one of the main difficulties in gaining an agreement with the Russians on the inspection of a nuclear test ban was over the number of inspection stations. These stations were to house various instruments to detect explosions of certain kinds and magnitudes. A large number of stations was needed, and they had to be located in Russia because the existing instruments could not reliably record such explosions from a great distance. If we could have increased their power ten times, we could have reduced the number of stations to a number the Russians considered acceptable; possibly we could even have monitored all such explosions from outside Russia.

It should not be impossible for scientists to build a kind of super-Geiger counter, which, while riding in a satellite, would be able to detect the existence of any processed radioactive ores. Then both sides would commit themselves (1) to list all places where such materials are used for peaceful purposes and to allow their continuous or random inspection, (2) to list all places where they are produced and to allow their inspection, and (3) to allow immediate inspections of those areas in which the Geiger counters—monitored by *both* sides—indicate the presence of radioactive materials other than those listed under (1) or (2). Such a Geiger counter would largely reduce the likelihood of hidden caches of nuclear arms, the most frightening disarmament violation.

162

But every instrument can be somehow deceived, and preparations for chemical and biological warfare, it seems, cannot be detected in this way. Hence, eventually manned inspection will still be necessary. But increased investment in inspection science and technology could greatly increase the effectiveness of inspection and could both reduce and delay the need for manned inspection—a fact which would make inspection more acceptable to the Soviet Union without foregoing the prime United States demand: no disarmament without inspection.

## Nuclear and Conventional Embargo

There are three major gaps not covered by the arms reduction scheme as presented so far: The $n$th country problem (that is, the dangerous consequences of the dispersion of nuclear arms to many countries), the danger of armed nibbling (that is, the use of conventional arms on a small scale in low-visibility military interventions, as in Greece and in Indochina), and the danger of subversion not supported by outside military force (the expansion of Communism as an ideological-political movement). The first two problems might be handled through certain interbloc and intrabloc agreements constituting a part of the arms reduction pact. The third problem is the true deficiency of arms reduction, and we will have to look beyond it for its solution.

Probably nothing demonstrates that the way to peace is hard indeed as much as the following analysis of additional requirement of arms reduction and settlement in general. An examination of what is required to solve these three problems indicates that there will be no disarmament of the Soviet Union and the United States without disarmament of their allies and their allies' allies, as well as potential allies—which, for all practical purposes, means disarmament of the whole world; this, in turn, means that a large host of political conflicts and problems will have to be settled in the process of negotiating and implementing the arms reduction plan.

### THE NTH COUNTRY PROBLEM AND NUCLEAR EMBARGO

It is widely agreed that unless some interbloc agreement is reached in the near future, nuclear weapons will spread to many countries, which will make war by accident or provocation more likely. It will also reduce markedly the control each superpower has over the members of its bloc, in particular that of the Soviet Union over Communist China and that of the United States over France and West Germany. There is therefore an urgent need for an agreement between the two superpowers not to supply nuclear arms, materials, or knowledge needed in their construction to any third country, as well as to do all they can to discourage other countries from producing nuclear weapons or to encourage them to give up such weapons if they are already in their possession. It would be best to include such an agreement in the initial arms reduction pact and to enforce it as soon as possible, since time is running out; it will be much more difficult to disarm nations once the weapons have spread than to convince them not to acquire them at all.

Such an agreement might readily gain the support of the United States and the Soviet Union, because both superpowers have much interest in such a pact. In addition to the growing recognition of the dangers in the spread of nuclear arms for all concerned, the two superpowers fear loss of much of their status and might once their monopolistic positions as nuclear powers is undermined. We must note that it takes more than the construction of a few nuclear bombs to become a nuclear power. Production of large amounts of bombs and "means of delivery" is needed. France, for instance, is a country with bombs, but is not yet a nuclear power. The main barrier to becoming a nuclear power, as England learned from bitter experience, is the high cost of research, development, and production of bombs and missiles. But with the invention of cheaper and simpler ways of producing nuclear bombs and missiles, many countries will be able to become, not just countries with bombs, but nuclear powers.

Efforts to limit the spread of nuclear arms have already been undertaken by both sides. The United States has enacted a law forbidding giving nuclear arms or know-how to other countries; the United States did not help France to construct its bombs, not even to the extent of sharing its scientific information; despite repeated "offers," the United States has not supplied NATO with nuclear weapons. The United States put much pressure on Israel to limit its atomic research. Similarly, despite repeated requests, Russia did not grant China either nuclear arms or missiles, nor did it do so for any other country in its bloc. It would seem that the United States and the Soviet Union would find an agreement on a nuclear embargo valuable in further justifying to their allies their nuclear monopoly.

In addition to a ban on the delivery of nuclear arms, the two superpowers would commit themselves to the use of all their powers of persuasion, as well as economic sanctions if necessary, to discourage members of their blocs from producing nuclear arms. At the same time, the superpowers would declare that every country foregoing nuclear arms would be protected —to the degree it so desires—by one superpower from nuclear attacks by the other.

The ban on nuclear production by third countries and the ban on the delivery of nuclear weapons to them is in line with the interests of these countries. Being without nuclear arms insures that, in the event of war, a country will not be a target of nuclear attack, at least not a prime one; further, were it to be attacked, it would be under the nuclear umbrella of "its" superpower—that is, its devastation could be retaliated. Hence, nations without nuclear arms could achieve whatever deterring effect nuclear retaliation has through a pact with "their" superpower. One might argue that having the bombs is a source of national pride and that for this reason countries will refuse to forego them; France is still trying to build up its grandeur in this way. But with the change in world public opinion that will precede arms reduction and be produced by it, giving up bombs rather than rattling them will surely be a major source of international prestige.

The question has been raised: can a country rely on the nuclear protection of a superpower? Would the United States enter a nuclear war for the sake of a smaller ally? It should first of all be emphasized that under the pact, nuclear retaliation will be forthcoming only if an ally is exposed to nuclear attack. Such an attack is not too likely, because it would immediately end the arms reduction agreement, would arouse enormous indignation, and—the crucial point—would not decrease the nuclear striking force of the other superpower. Since this *might* be used as justification for retaliation, a superpower exposing to nuclear attack a small country devoid of nuclear arms but leaving intact the other superpower, would not only invite the curse of history but would have chosen a poor military course.

Second, while the United States at the present time might well not engage in a nuclear war to defend a lesser ally, the interbloc embargo pact would make such engagement much more probable. The United States is at present not *committed* to defend with *nuclear* weapons any of its allies; under the nuclear ban pact, it would be.[7] While international agreements have only a limited binding force, in such a case the United States would not have much choice. It would either honor its obligations to protect those who gave up nuclear arms on the basis of its promise or—once an ally becomes the victim of nuclear attack while lacking nuclear protection—it would find all of its allies turning neutral, if not joining the other side, overnight. The same holds for the relationship between the Soviet Union and its allies. Some nonnuclear countries might prefer to seek protection in a position of neutrality in the interbloc strife, rather than in a pact with one of the superpowers, following the example of Sweden, Switzerland, and Austria. Actually, several Asian and African nations seem to be inclined to take such a course. These countries might even form an organization of their own (sometimes referred to as the nonnuclear club), to emphasize their determination not to produce, hold, or use these weapons. Such a club would make an attack on a member a major political blunder in a world where neutral countries carry more and more weight.

In short, nuclear embargo and the establishment of two pacts for allies devoid of nuclear arms, under the nuclear umbrella of the two superpowers (plus, possibly, one or more neutral clubs, for countries which forego nuclear arms but do not seek the protection of a superpower) as part of the arms reduction plan, is in line with the interests of the superpowers and their allies, as well as of neutral countries. This will probably be the least difficult part of our "riders" to the arms reduction pact.

Much more difficult is the problem of inspecting all the countries that claim not to hold nuclear arms, an inspection required if for no other reason than to insure that a superpower

[7] For details of such a pact and an analysis of its chances to work, see Thornton Read, *A Proposal to Neutralize Nuclear Weapons,* Policy Memorandum No. 22, Center of International Studies, Princeton University, 1961.

is not arming an ally while disarming itself. The West would hardly feel safe if it were only to inspect Russia and not Communist China, and the East would not be satisfied until France and West Germany were inspected. Hence, the arms reduction inspection system will have to cover the two blocs and all other nations, not just the two superpowers. This suggests that the various members of each bloc and the neutral countries should participate in all the phases of gradualism, in the arms reduction negotiations, and in the inspection agencies, so as to build up their support for the plan. Even if such global extension of arms reduction were not needed for nuclear disarmament, it would have to be introduced to allow for conventional disarmament.

## ARMED NIBBLING AND CONVENTIONAL DISARMAMENT

Ever since World War II ended in a mushroom cloud, the threat of a third world war has not stemmed from the fear of a direct, large-scale attack on the American mainland—which could perhaps be deterred by nuclear bombs—but from the armed nibbling across the rim that separates the Communist bloc from the Western bloc: Greece, Korea, Indochina, Laos, and Berlin are the major instances. Hence a central question for the advocate of our arms reduction plan is: what good are nuclear safeguards—maintained until a late stage—against invasions of third countries by conventional armies, or the taking over of third countries through outside military support to indigenous revolutionary forces? Does not our arms reduction scheme have the same flaws as Massive Retaliation? Let us assume that the sides are left with nuclear bombs only. Would not the United States hesitate to use nuclear bombs, fearing retaliation, if one of its allies, in particular a lesser one, were under attack by conventional arms? Would this not be so particularly in the case of an attack by proxy, in which local Communist forces, secretly supported from across the border, carried the burden of the attack?

As in other problems discussed above, here, too, there seems to be no simple or single solution; relying on a combination of partially satisfactory ones may provide our answer. The most important of these is conventional arms reduction as advocated here, since nuclear arms cannot be used for such nibbling. In view of the importance of conventional arms reduction in eliminating the threat of armed nibbling, it might be advisable to include in the initial pact a provision to the effect that the very first reductions of conventional arms would be comparatively large and rapid. Only their further reduction would be broken into many small steps. The speed with which conventional forces can be reduced was seen in the arms reduction the United States undertook after World War II, when in only about a year it sent more than three-fourths of the army home and dismantled most of the enormous military machine. Of course, under arms reduction as advocated here, both sides would cut their conventional forces, and the Communist countries—which have much larger conventional forces—would have to undergo larger cuts to maintain proportional strength on both sides. (The Russians have agreed to larger cuts in past disarmament negotiations.) Thus, both sides would reduce rapidly their ability to wage limited warfare and to support indigenous military forces.

Second, the two superpowers will, as part of the arms reduction plan, commit themselves not to supply arms of any sort or military personnel to any third country. Failure to live up to such a commitment will constitute a severe violation of the pact. Inspections will check on the fulfillment of this obligation. They might include inspections at points of entry to those countries, intelligence agents, aerial inspection, and the like. Since significant quantities of conventional arms, parts, and ammunition tend to be bulky, and their use often reveals their source, it is practically impossible to conceal significant violations of the conventional arms embargo. In the past, when the Soviet Union or the United States secretly supplied conventional arms to a third country, it was sooner or later found out. Nasser's arms deal with the Russians, Soviet armament shipments to Laos, CIA military support to the anti-Castro forces and to the antirevolutionary forces in Guatemala, Israel's arms purchases from France and its arms exports to West Europe, were all sooner or later revealed. It seems almost impossible to avoid detection. Moreover, since every major violation of the arms reduction pact would lead to its "regression," if not to its abolition, the two superpowers would be quite unlikely to risk "everything" in order to supply some conventional arms to any one country.

But embargo on shipment of arms is not enough. Unless bloc disarmament is accompanied by global disarmament, the new safe world will never emerge. Wars among small nations—using their own manufactured arms—will build up conflicts that might draw the support of other nations, possibly involving the superpowers themselves; the world would face new arms races with different rivals but similarly hazardous results. Moreover, if the United States and the Soviet Union disarmed and other countries did not, the superpowers of yesterday would be at the mercy of their smaller allies of today. Hence, as elusive, or even Utopian, as global disarmament might sound, there is no other way to eliminate the perils of armed conflict; world disarmament can be gradual, but it will have to be inclusive.

For this reason the political settlements (discussed in Part Three) will obviously not only have to cover interbloc conflicts but will also have to find a solution to, or establish nonviolent outlets and modes of settlement for, the differences among smaller nations, such as Israel and the Arabic nations, Communist and Nationalist China, India and Pakistan, Indonesia and the Netherlands, and so on, just as arms reduction by these countries will have to be part of the general arms reduction plan. Such a settlement might be somewhat easier to reach than it seems at the moment, because once the major interbloc strife is curbed, the ability of the smaller nations to use their conflicts to exact support from the superpowers will markedly decline; the United States and the Soviet Union might even cooperate in using their status and economic power to encourage local settlements or to keep conflicts nonviolent (somewhat in the way in which the two powers "cooperated" in stopping the invasion of Egypt in 1956).

The only bright element in this highly ambitious assignment is that many of the weapons and much of the money for their maintenance are provided by the two superpowers and a few of their major allies. If the United States, the Soviet Union, England, France, Czechoslovakia, and a few other countries wished to stop the arms race of the small countries, they could accomplish much by no longer supplying them with arms and

169

military aid. But since there is an international black market in arms, and since many small countries produce some arms themselves and even export them, disarmament will not be complete unless these countries are represented and participate in the arms reduction pact, both as suppliers of inspectors and as subjects for inspection. This is not to imply that every small country could, in effect, veto the arms reduction pact by refusing to join it and by maintaining an armed island in a disarming world, a constant source of danger. Undoubtedly, especially when East and West act in accord, the superpowers will, through recruitment of world public opinion, economic sanctions, and maybe even by employing a United Nations police force, be able to insure that no small country will upset the global settlement. At any rate, superpowers constantly interfere in the lives of smaller nations, using these same means to serve much less noble causes.

Arms reduction will at no stage remove those arms that neutral experts will agree are necessary to maintain a country's internal security. We are out to eliminate international violence and military establishments, not social order and police forces. Even when an international police force does develop, as a late stage in the establishment of new international institutions, its function will be to see to it that countries do not use their internal security forces to interfere in the affairs of other countries, but the international police will not serve to maintain the existing order in any specific country. It will then become more difficult to make revolutions, since revolutionary forces would not be able to obtain outside help, and might have to persuade the local police to join them, or at least not to block them. (Local police forces joined or supported rebels or revolutionaries in Algeria, Brazil, Congo and many other countries.) At the same time, revolutions will become easier to make, since the government threatened will not be able to obtain help from the outside, and will be deprived of heavy arms, nowadays often ostensibly maintained for external security but used to save oligarchic regimes from a fate they deserve. On the balance, revolutions will probably be neither much easier nor much more difficult to carry out than today. The main difference will be that they will be removed from the international armed struggle. Conflicts within one nation will no longer be transformed into regional or global wars, nor will they involve much bloodshed; either the internal security forces will join the revolutionaries, or—being with few or no arms—the revolutionaries will not have much of a chance.

## UNARMED EXPANSIONISM AND POLITICAL SETTLEMENT

Communism is spreading not only as a military bloc but also as an ideological-political movement; actually, in the last fourteen years the Communists have gained more as a movement— in Cuba, Syria, Iraq, Indonesia, Ghana, Guinea, and various Latin American republics—than as a military force. The United States, as a country determined to check the expansion of Communism because of its commitment to certain values, because it is the defender of the status quo in uncommitted nations, and because of concern with its own security, has resorted to force —in Guatemala and in Lebanon for instance—more often to stop this largely unarmed expansion of the Communist movement than to check the *military* expansion of the Communist bloc. The important question is: in a disarmed world, what would the United States substitute for arms in blocking Communism as a movement? If the farmers and workers of an Asian country, led by unarmed Communist agitators, were to go on a general strike, and the government were about to topple (assuming that the internal security force has also been won over by the Communist ideology), what would the United States do? In other words, what means would the United States apply to counter the continued appeal of Communism as an ideological-political movement? The arms reduction plan, as a strategy concerned with means of violence, cannot be expected to provide an answer. The import of this question cannot be overestimated; the United States can hardly be expected to agree even to multilateral, inspected, and safeguarded arms reductions if this would leave it without effective means to counter the nonmilitary expansion of Communism in the disarmed world. The major concern of the subsequent part of my analysis is to indicate the nature of a potent Western political strategy that answers exactly this need—it provides an effective, nonmilitary way to counter Communism.

This problem is closely related to another one that emerges from the preceding discussion—the need for political settlement

171

of the differences between smaller nations, so as to reduce pressures for secondary arms races and "private" wars and to enhance global disarmament.

Both problems are tied to the major problem of the progress of sociopolitical processes toward a global community. Arms reduction removes the instruments of violence, but not the urge to construct or use them. Actually, arms reduction will not be agreed upon—and if agreed upon, will not progress; and if progressing, certainly will not be completed—until a political settlement between East and West is worked out, and some global institutions for nonviolent settlement of conflicts are established. We discussed the armed part of the settlement; we turn now to the other, political part of it. Without solution of both of these in close articulation, there is no solution of either.

Chapter 8

## World Government and Supranationalism

A NUMBER of on-going historical processes will have to proceed a long way before the social and political prerequisites for world government can come into being. However, since international violence will not be eliminated until world government is established and since our short-run policies ought to support rather than to retard this long-run goal, an analysis of the ways to world government is an inevitable part of the study of the way to peace. Moreover, we might realize that we are somewhat closer to target than is often suggested and that we are able to accelerate these processes once we understand their nature. The emergence and consolidation of supranational communities is one such process; economic, social, and political development of unindustrialized countries is another. The first provides for part of the needed international integration by tying groups of nations to each other; the second, as we shall see, reduces the cleavages that separate nations. I discuss the first process in this chapter, the second one, in the two subsequent chapters. A number of other processes, each less important than supranationalism and development, but quite powerful in their cumulative effect, will also receive some attention.

### The Panacea of World Government

World government has been advocated as an immediate cureall for international violence at the rate of one book per three years for the last generation. Despite our historical experience of an impotent League of Nations and a feeble United Nations, the formation of such a government has not lost its appeal to human imagination. But, as political scientists often point out,

173

a world government, like other political institutions, will come into being and function effectively only after the required social foundations have been established. A government can force some of the people some of the time, but not most of the people most of the time; voluntary acceptance by the majority of the citizens who are politically conscious is a basic requirement of all governments.

This acceptance, in turn, is based on consensus—the sharing of ideas on what government should be like and what it should do. If half the people insist that they desire a Western form of government, and the other half insist equally strongly that they want a Communist form, then there can be none. If half the citizens were to direct their government to protect private property and political freedoms but otherwise to stay out of their lives as much as possible, and the other half were to direct it to nationalize property and to actively guide the citizen's life, there could be no shared government to do either. These differences of belief are reinforced and augmented by differences of self-interest. For instance, those who favor government regulation of the economy and social welfare tend to have less income than those who favor a system of pure free enterprise. Such differences of interest are often at least as much in the way of consensus formation as lack of shared beliefs.

The fact that the West has until now usually marshaled a majority of votes in the United Nations and other international organizations does not provide a solution. Within a nation, the majority has the moral right and the force needed to compel a minority to follow its decisions. But it does not follow that a "majority" of countries has either the moral right or the force to compel a "minority" of countries to comply with its decisions. The international "minority," the Communist countries, have never agreed to join with the Western "majority" in forming a world state, and all attempts to act as if world government existed have failed. All suggestions to eliminate international violence by creating a world government here and now will fail so long as a consensus on the nature and purpose of such a government has not been reached.

If, on the other hand, we view world government plans as depicting a future goal, one that mankind will have to reach before international violence is eliminated rather than as proposals applicable here and now, they deserve closest attention. They depict a desirable state of affairs toward which our long-run effort ought in part to be directed.

## WORLD GOVERNMENT DESIGNS

Recent world government proposals, by Cord Meyer, Jr., in 1947, Werner Levi in 1950, and by Grenville Clark and Louis B. Sohn in 1958, have much in common.[1] They all favor a world government having the essential features of a national government: an executive, a legislature, and a judicial authority. As a "practical" measure, they all suggest renovating the existing structure of the United Nations rather than starting from scratch.

The most elaborate is the 1958 proposal of Clark and Sohn, and it will serve to indicate for us the general nature of these proposals. Their New United Nations will legislate and enforce a world law under which all countries will disarm; it will have the necessary agencies to insure that disarmament is observed. To safeguard the new world order, all weapons will be destroyed or transferred to the hands of the world state. No nation will be allowed to remain armed, just as at present no group of citizens is allowed to maintain a private army in the nation state.

According to Clark and Sohn, the world government will not interfere in the internal economic and social affairs of any nation, not even in their immigration policy or matters concerning international trade. (Communists, socialists, and many liberals would surely expect the world government to have more functions; the limitation of the new United Nations to a minimal, peace-maintaining role is usually explained by American writers by the need to minimize the areas of possible disagreement between the blocs, so as to further the acceptance of the world government program.) The main agencies of the world government will be those needed for the fulfillment of its basic function of outlawing violence. These include an inspection commission, to insure that disarmament obligations are carried out; a nuclear energy authority, which will handle all

[1] *Peace or Anarchy* (Boston, Little, Brown, and Co.); *World Organization* (Minneapolis, The University of Minnesota Press); *World Peace Through World Law* (Cambridge, Harvard University Press).

fission and fusion materials to avoid that most dangerous of violations, the diversion of some nuclear material to clandestine production of nuclear bombs; and a world police force to enforce disarmament laws by punishing any violator.

In addition, there will be an outer space agency to guarantee that outer space research will be used only for peaceful purposes and that its products will benefit all mankind. A world development authority is considered desirable, to reduce the discrepancy between the have and have-not countries, but this is viewed as peripheral to the principal plan (actually Clark and Sohn added the proposal only in the second edition of their book). To insure that the whole operation will not be sabotaged or will fail because of insolvency, the world state is to have a worldwide revenue system to collect taxes from member states.

The General Assembly of the New United Nations will serve as the legislature of the world state. It will examine and approve the executive budget and formulate policies to implement the aims formulated in the New United Nations Charter—those of disarmament and lasting peace. The composition of the General Assembly is to be altered to grant fairer representation to various nations. Proportional representation will give larger nations more seats in the world legislature. This, in turn, will increase their impact on the decision made and readiness to comply with them.

The executive council of the New United Nations will serve as the world cabinet, to direct the United Nations inspection agency, the world police force, a global revenue system, and the other agencies of the world state. China, India, the United States and the Soviet Union (again according to Clark and Sohn) will be the permanent members of the executive council; other nations would either rotate or be elected at large to fill the remaining cabinet positions. No nation will have a right to veto any decisions, so that no state would be able to cripple world government.

To provide for peaceful settlement of conflicts that will surely occur, various forms of arbitration have been suggested by earlier students of world government. Clark and Sohn recommend a world equity tribunal, composed of fifteen persons of the highest prestige, each a citizen of a different nation, to help countries settle disputes, and an international court of justice

176

to determine the punishment due all parties that violate world law.

In hundreds of pages Clark and Sohn provide for multitudinous legal, technical, and institutional details, from the number of representatives allowed each country to the size of the world police force. When nations desire a world government, this plan will certainly not be overlooked. Meanwhile, its fate is the same as that of earlier proposals. The central question remains: what major historical processes point in this direction, and what can be done to accelerate them so that such proposals can be implemented? We shall see that the formation of supranational communities is one such process; economic and political development is another.

## Toward Supranationalism

We have all grown up in the period in which nationalism reached its peak. It still seems a potent historical factor, with new nations established by the month—seventeen in 1960 alone. We tend to forget that mankind was not always split into mutually exclusive and aggressive nations; the Roman Empire, for example, encompassed in a more or less peaceful unity for centuries most of the Occidental "world." We are likely not to notice that the heyday of nationalism is over; that most peoples desiring national status have already achieved it; and that many nations even now are engaged in the very processes that will overcome the severe handicaps nationalism imposes on their economic, military, political and even cultural well-being.

The trend of the future is toward establishment of supranational communities, whose nation members, like the members of smaller communities, are in general agreement on how their community ought to be run and what goals it ought to pursue and who share an effective supranational government. Most important of all: members of such communities give up the use of violence as a means for settling conflicts among themselves and establish political institutions to safeguard peaceful handling of conflicts that occur.

### WHAT IS A SUPRANATIONAL COMMUNITY?

A political community that encompasses nation states and has some sovereignty of its own is a supranational community (or nation-union). It is created either by one state's imposing itself on the others (the way Prussia unified Germany) or through a voluntary pooling of sovereignty (the way thirteen colonies established what later became known as the United States of America). The nations that form a union do not necessarily disappear in a supranational community; they might continue to fulfill many local roles and maintain a degree of political autonomy, the way the autonomy of the original American colonies is still reflected in some of the states that compose the American republic.

Supranational communities are often confused with international organizations and blocs. They differ from international organizations (such as the World Health Organization or International Labor Organization) in their more encompassing nature—they affect more spheres of life—and in their supranational sovereignty that allows these communities to make decisions binding upon member nations. The more intensive integration and the pooling of sovereignty characteristic of supranational communities explains in part why their membership tends to be considerably smaller than that of international organizations and, unlike them, includes members of either the East or West, but not both.

Blocs are typically political and militarily alliances, more integrated than international organizations but less so than most supranational communities, though this is a matter of degree. West, East, and to a degree the various neutral blocs, slowly evolve some supranational features, such as acquiring some ideological and symbolic value (for example, "Members of the Free World"). It appears that the blocs are gradually becoming a kind of supercommunity composed of smaller supranational communities.

SOME HISTORICAL PRECEDENTS

But have states ever really given up their sovereignty? Have people ever merged? Or are we back in the realm of Utopia? Nothing could be further from it. In one of the most important and exhaustive studies of this subject, Karl Deutsch, Yale Professor of Political Science, with the help of seven colleagues showed that such pooling of sovereignty has often occurred.[2]

[2] *Political Community and the North Atlantic Area* (Princeton, Princeton University Press, 1957).

Moreover, people living shortly before such unions took place, even while they were already developing, often were not only unaware of the process, but did not believe that unification can take place.

Every schoolboy knows the story of the thirteen colonies, all distinct societies, all separate political units, which slowly merged, not without pain, to become the United States of America; this process was not completed until almost the late nineteenth century, and the tenuousness of the association was clearly shown by the Civil War. Before the Civil War, the United States was referred to, in various documents, in the plural, as, the United States of America *are*. . . . Only in the 1890s did American official terminology shift to reflect the new sociopolitical reality, referring to the United States as a singular—the United States *is*. . . .

The unification of Germany out of more than 300 autonomous states—states which had often fought one another—completed in the nineteenth century, is almost as well known as that of the United States, and the same process can be seen in the unification of Italy. England and Scotland sealed their union in 1707, following an earlier unification of England with Wales in the sixteenth century. The emergence of the nation union now known as Switzerland, completed by the mid-nineteenth century, is made more remarkable by the large differences in the cultural, ethnic, and religious backgrounds of its people. Germans, Frenchmen, and Italians merged to constitute a highly integrated and peaceful society. Similarly, the Netherlands and Belgium emerged from the unification of highly heterogeneous groups. All these integrations, however, took place before nationalism had made the existing political units almost holy; often the integration itself was an expression of the new, nationalist spirit. Hence the question still remains: Will established *nations* merge?

## SOME CONTEMPORARY CASES

Our answer must be qualified for the present. We have no reports of complete merger of states after the advent of nationalism, but there is a large number of countries that seem to be in the *process* of unification, ranging from those which have only considered or declared union to those which have already partially merged. Obviously not all those nations that begin to unite will go the whole way; some unions will stagnate and some will fall back into groups of unrelated nations. But the majority, perhaps more than our nationalist vantage point will let us realize, are likely to establish firm communities of nations.

Among the relatively advanced contemporary unions is the European Economic Community, including France, West Germany, Italy, Belgium, the Netherlands, and Luxembourg. All these countries participate in a shared, though more encompassing, military organization (NATO), have a strong economic union, an expanding system of cultural and scientific exchange, a supranational atomic energy commission, and are working toward a political confederation. A United States of Europe has been turned from a Utopian dream into a distinct possibility.

The Scandinavian community—including Sweden, Norway, and Denmark and, to a lesser degree, Iceland and Finland—is another "advanced" case. Unlike the European community, these nations do not share a military organization (Sweden and Finland are not members of NATO), but they have established a system of close economic coordination and considerable cultural contact and exchange and, over and beyond the European union, they have removed limitations on immigration among these countries. From many practical viewpoints, a citizen of any Scandinavian country is also a citizen of the others. He can without red tape migrate, obtain work, bring in or take out his capital throughout these countries, and he enjoys practically the same social security benefits as the native citizens do. A committee composed of representatives of the various parliaments is working to "harmonize" the laws of these countries, so that a law breaker in one, who moves into another, will be unable to benefit from differences in their legal systems.

Much less well known are some African integrations, such as the reunification of Cyrennica, Ferran, and Tripolitania to form Libya in 1951; the Federation of Ethiopia with Eritrea in 1950; and the integration of two ex-colonies into Somalia. The cross-continent union of two countries lacking a common border—an African country, Egypt, and an Asian one, Syria—which together formed the United Arab Republic (1958–1961) might yet be revived.

180

Quite advanced, though we lack information on the exact degree, is the integration of Eastern Europe as part of the general integration of the Communist bloc. Sharing a military force (Warsaw Treaty Organization), an economic organization (Council for Economic Mutual Assistance), Communist indoctrination and party organization, and Russian domination, the integration seems to be destined to progress rather rapidly.

Less advanced, somewhere between merely being "talked about" and partially formed is the Central American economic union; the Latin American Free Trade Area which includes seven countries (Argentina, Brazil, Chile, Mexico, Paraguay, Peru, and Uruguay); and possibly the Eastern Caribbean Union. Other supranational unifications should be listed merely as potential or barely existing, including the plans of Tunisa, Algeria, and Morocco to form a union (referred to as Maghreb); the Central Treaty Organization (CENTO) countries (Turkey, Iran, and Pakistan), which at the moment form little more than a weak paper alliance but which are considering moving closer together; and various efforts to form West African unions, such as the loosely organized Conseil de l'Entent (including the Ivory Coast, Upper Volta, Niger, and Dahomey), and the somewhat more potent Union of Ghana, Guinea, and Mali.

There is hardly a day in which the newspapers do not carry an item about some step or effort at supranational integration; the long-run trend seems to be toward more and stronger unifications. Thus, the map of the twenty-first century is likely to show twelve to twenty-four supranational communities, plus a handful of nonjoiners, instead of the present hundred-odd autonomous nations.

What are the forces which underlie this process, and what effect does it have on international violence and the founding of a world government?

## Factors of Unification

The formation of supranational communities is not a consequence of deliberate decisions by the leaders of nations to enhance the political sociological conditions required for the evolution of a world government. Each country and the various

181

blocs, each pursuing its own interests and attempting to realize the values it believes in, contributes to supranationalism and thus, we shall see, furthers the achievement of lasting peace.

The basic drive behind the formation of supranational unions is the awareness that the typical nation is becoming obsolete. The nation-state, yesterday's latest model, is the Tin Lizzie of today's political driving. It is unsafe, uneconomical, too small, fast losing its sentimental value. The nation-state is no longer equipped to do the job it was created for. Many functions that were until recently carried out quite effectively by the nation-state now require more and more international cooperation. Cooperation is at first carried out on an intergovernment basis, each nation maintaining control over its part of the shared activity. But, as Ernst Haas has shown in a brilliant analysis,[3] as the scope and volume of cooperation grow, the pressure toward supranational control of the shared activities, grows too. With the increase in the power of, and commitment to, this new center of authority, supranational communities evolve.

## NATIONAL SECURITY: A CRACKED SHELL

Like turtles in their shells, human groups have shielded their members from outsiders since the beginning of history. But with time, these shells tend to expand to counter the increasing range of weapons outsiders employ.[4]

The medieval castle, for example, protected behind its walls the peasants of the surrounding estate from bandits and other lords' armies. (In exchange, the peasant supplied the lord and his knights with goods and services.) The cannon made the castle too small; it hopelessly cracked the "shell" of the medieval security unit.

The new protective shell was provided by the nation-state. Even the largest cannon could not reach its core unless the border fortifications were first cracked. Typically, World War I was fought along trenches that separated France and Germany, protecting the national borders and the populations behind them.

[3] Ernst B. Haas, *The Uniting of Europe* (Stanford, Calif., Stanford University Press, 1958).
[4] John Herz, *International Politics in the Atomic Age* (New York, Columbia University Press, 1959).

The introduction of the bomber in World War II made the national security unit too limited. The bomber could fly above the land-bound shell and hit the civilian population in the heart of the nation. But because of the limited range of bombers, an enlarged security unit could supply protection, if not to one country, then to the core of a group of them. Thus, for instance, even at the worst period of World War II, the United States— the industrial core of the allied forces—did not stand in serious danger of being bombed; most of the United States did not even experience a "black-out" in the midst of the most furious fighting.

The development of long-range bombers and missiles turned the whole globe into two security units organized on a bloc basis, each covering half the earth. The Western shell ranges over more than 20,000 miles, from Alaska to New Zealand, from Berlin to Tokyo, and from Hong Kong to Spitzbergen. It includes four military alliances interlocked by the leadership of the United States—NATO in Europe, CENTO in the Middle East, and SEATO and ANZUS in the Far East—as well as several two-country alliances. The Communists have a similar chain of alliances, centering around the Soviet Union.

All these military alliances started as strictly intergovernmental arrangements. War plans were coordinated, ammunition and weapons standardized, communication procedures formulated, and so on. But the tendency is to *merge* the national military organizations into a supranational military force (although it still might have national *units*). Thus a supranational commander-in-chief is appointed; a central, unified headquarters, to command the national units directly, is founded, and units of different nations are thrown together into shared military maneuvers. Thus, the problem of security calls for multination military cooperation, which in turn calls for a supranational military authority and organization.

It is questionable whether supranational military organizations grant security and whether the old conception of security through shells is still valid, in view of the range of the new weapons and their potency. Obviously, the author thinks that the days of man's security under a shell have passed, while most nations still act as if they can put their trust in their newly augmented shells. The main point about supranationalism, and the most widely accepted, is this: The days of *national* security have passed.

## The Payoff of Economic Union

There is only one way to eat your cake and have it too—and that is by increasing international trade. The increase in the volume of exchange generates an improved division of labor among the participating countries, each nation producing what it is best suited for rather than straining to supply by itself all or most of its manifold needs. The result is that *all* countries will have a larger national income without any increase in investment or effort. Hence, from a strictly economic viewpoint, removing all national restrictions on trade, so as to establish a free global market, would be the most desirable arrangement.

Actually, the removal of national trade barriers progresses gradually; sometimes it even goes one step backward before going two steps forward. There are no big jumps, such as the opening up of a continent to free trade. Like the expansion of the security unit from the castle to the nation-state, the free market expanded from the sphere of one feudal lord to that of the national market. Germany, the United States, Italy, and so on, became not only integral security units but also integral markets.

Now, with the formation of supranational security units, we find serious efforts to establish supranational markets, to co-ordinate and even integrate the economies of several nations, the way their militaries are integrated. The best-known supranational market was formed by six countries—France, West Germany, Italy, Belgium, the Netherlands, and Luxembourg—in 1957. It requires each member to reduce its tariff barriers against other members by 10 per cent each year. So far, not only have the tariffs been reduced ahead of schedule, but working conditions of the countries are also in the process of being made uniform: social security levies and working hours are matched, to create equal conditions for free competition; investment and monetary policies are coordinated; transportation and energy development plans are synchronized; and many other areas of economic activities are becoming truly supranational. England and six other countries (Sweden, Norway,

Denmark, Switzerland, Austria, and Portugal) formed their own "common market" in 1960. It is quite likely that the two groups will form a combined common market in the near future. Seven Latin American countries formed a common market in 1961. Attempts are also being made to put into effect two such unions in West Africa.

The Communist bloc's economic integration is also gradually advancing. There are no tariff barriers among Communist countries, and the five-year plans of various Eastern European countries are reported to be coordinated to develop a division of labor among them, to avoid duplication, and to encourage each to produce what it is best able to.

Like supranational security, supranational economies are first regulated by meetings of representatives of the various governments concerned. As the intercountry economic flow increases, statewide regulation of the economies is reduced. As the demand for a new regulatory agency is stepped up, the tendency is to pool some economic sovereignty and to establish a supranational authority that has some direct control over multinational economic processes. The European Coal and Steel Community, for instance, installed a High Authority that by-passes the six member governments and deals directly with management, unions, banks, and parties in the six nations, in order to regulate policies concerning investment, wages, working conditions, transporation, and other related matters. It can even impose fines on the corporations that do not observe the agreements and regulations, though in case of refusal to pay the fine, the police of the various states would have to collect it. Thus, supranational economies involve the gradual creation of supranational sovereignty the way supranational security does.

## POLITICAL INTEGRATION: POWER FOR PYGMIES

Though it receives little public attention, one of the strongest reasons for the pooling of national sovereignty is the desire of small nations to countervail bigger ones. Each small nation alone has little weight, but when a number of them act in unison, they are heard. Of the six European countries that are forming the supranational community, two—West Germany and France —are more powerful than the others. Hence we are not surprised to learn that the three smallest members have an additional strong integration of their own; Belgium, the Netherlands, and Luxembourg are integrated into Benelux. True, Benelux existed before the European community and has other reasons for its being, but since the European community developed, Benelux has found an additional reason for its integration, and the process has been accelerated.

Newly independent nations in Africa have been expected to be hypernationalistic (just as converts are often the most ardent supporters of a cause). Many otherwise acute political observers feared a Balkanization of Africa, the emergence of a continent full of many small, weak states, in continual conflict with each other. But the fact is that Africa has more planned, attempted, and budding nation unions than any other continent.

The underlying motive for political unification in Africa seems to be similar to that of smaller nations in Europe. African expert Immanuel Wallerstein points out that these nations seek independence not just to be free, but also to be equal.[5] As each realizes that it cannot gain such status alone, its supranational endeavors increase. Similarly, Latin American unification movements are encouraged in part by the desire of these countries to countervail the influence of the United States in the Western hemisphere. The Scandinavian unification movement has similar overtones, in its effort to balance the power of Great Britain. It is as if they all acted on the maxim: united we stand, divided we fall.

## CULTURAL BRIDGES

Many other less weighty factors operate in the same direction; each on its own would not move the mountain of nationalism, but as they are added to military, economic, and political efforts at unification, they ease, contribute to, and accelerate the process.

*Science* demands more and more manpower and becomes more and more expensive. Test tubes are still used, but much modern research requires a multimillion-dollar cyclotron. Binoculars are still of help, but important breakthroughs in astronomy are made with mammoth telescopes and highly expensive research rockets. Hence nations now tend, as do universities

[5] *Africa: The Politics of Independence* (New York, Vintage, 1961), Chapter 6.

within their respective countries, to specialize in some branches of science, leaving the other branches to other members of the international community, thus creating a scientific supranational division of labor. In addition, joint institutions are formed to serve the whole communities. UNESCO has established two centers for social studies—one in Brazil, the other in Chile— both serving all Latin America. The East European countries have a joint institute for nuclear research, located in Moscow. A joint school of journalism for the Scandinavian countries is attached to Arhus University in Denmark, and its board is elected by the press organizations in all Scandinavian countries.

The international flow of scientific information, the meetings with colleagues in other nations, and the shared projects, all strengthen the supranational community of scientists and scholars. These communities tend to be free from many of the nationalistic stereotypes and form a natural pro-supranationalism interest group. They also provide groups of experts who see matters in a comparatively objective light and are competent in cross-cultural and supranational communication.

A similar function is fulfilled by the increasing *"international civil service,"* composed of white-collar employees and professionals who find their career in the various supranational and international organizations. Geneva, Brussels, and Paris are full of thousands of such people, constituting an international community that meets at social parties, follows the careers of its members, and respects and encourages those who overcome national bias in their work. This provides for the necessary atmosphere for a neutral, supranational administration.

Of special interest are regional *educational* institutions, where young intellectuals and political leaders of various nations gain a similar outlook and come to know each other intimately and which train an increasing number of the members of the "international civil service." The College de Europe in Brussels, the International Seminar in Salzburg, Austria, and the European University in Florence, Italy, play this role. Such institutions will eventually supply more supranationally-minded leaders and more supranational ties among the elites of the various countries.

More common are the many educational exchange programs that bring students, professors, businessmen, and leaders from various countries into close contact. Supranational summer camps, work camps, and song, dance, and sports festivals lend some support to the formation of supranational sentiments.

The revolutionary advances in *transportation* of goods and people have shrunk the earth. The airplane reduces the social size of a supranational community to that of a large city. This makes cross-national contact easier and more common, and this in turn supports a feeling of community.

Revolutionary progress in *communication* further shrinks the globe. Regional networks of radio and television are well underway. Eurovision carries television programs from a large number of Western European countries into the homes of millions of citizens of this supranational community. East Europe and Scandinavia have their own supranational networks of television and radio. Such communication networks make foreigners less alien and allows nation-communities to share events that range from the opening of a supranational research institute to a multination festival.

While these factors are often viewed as "international," affecting members of all nations, they are actually "supranational," affecting chiefly smaller nation-communities. While interbloc cultural, scientific, and educational exchange programs gain much public attention, such exchanges among the members of the same nation-community are much more common. Moreover, interbloc exchanges not only are less frequent but also have much less effect on international relations, because, while such exchanges can accelerate and support an ongoing process of unification, carried by more weighty factors in the military, economic, and political spheres, they can neither initiate nor carry on a unification process, as some enthusiasts of interbloc organiations and exchange programs believe.

## The Expansion of the Moral Community

The existence of an effective government on the local, state, or national level is predicated on the citizens' not using violence against each other. To some degree the government can force observation of the law, but if the citizens are basically wolves, no government will have enough force to control them. Hence, a moral commitment by the citizens not to exercise violence toward each other is an essential requirement for the existence

188

of a shared viable government. It is this moral community—the communities of those to whom we do not apply violence even when differences of interests and opinions are large, and whom we expect not to use violence toward us—that provides the moral foundations for peace.

The scope of this no-violence community has gradually expanded throughout history. It included only a few hundred people in man's primitive stage; outsiders were literally free game. The Greek polis extended the no-violence status to all its citizens, but "barbarians" and slaves were at best partially covered. With the emergence of the nation-state, the no-violence moral community expanded greatly—though, again, not all social groups were included.

Over the last hundred years, the moral community has gradually expanded to include all groups within one nation: first, women and children, then the laboring classes; most recently, racial minorities are gaining their place. The redefinition of the insane and the criminal as not morally bad but as mentally ill, hence as entitled to treatment and rehabilitation, rather than segregation behind bars, is an expression of the same basic trend. We are close to the day when all those who live within the boundaries of a nation-state will be treated as members of its moral community, entitled to the basic human rights and freedom from violence that such membership involves.

Many religions have declared the moral community to be universal, to encompass all created in the image of God. But until recently, such pronouncements had only a limited effect on the behavior of mortals. While many subscribe in principle to universal expansion of the moral community, they rarely act accordingly. The best way to become a national hero is still by killing as many citizens of another nation as possible.

But in recent years there has been a growing tendency to truly extend the moral community beyond national boundaries. More and more neighboring nations are included, especially when other supranational ties are already shared. A simple but central indicator is that we find war with those nations "inconceivable" (so long as they do not apply violence to us, which we believe they will not). An interesting case is the slow evolution of a European no-violence community whose members include Germany and its arch enemies of yesterday. France and

Germany fought each other, with much bloodshed and abuse, three times in less than a century. Between the wars, the level of animosity was high, both on the national and interpersonal levels. The idea of revenge, of redeeming the national pride from the last defeat, was a conception on which the post-1871 and post-World War I generations were nourished. Not so after World War II. West Germany and France are now intimate allies, supporting each other's demands in the political arena; West German and French towns declare themselves "sister" cities; children of the two nations spend time together in summer resorts, and German soldiers could recently use French soil for their military exercises, with next to no protest.[6] It seems that in the near future Frenchman and German will find war with each other, as well as with other members of the European community, "inconceivable." This provides the moral fiber for the evolving supranational community.

Similarly, the Scandinavian countries, which used to fight each other bitterly, now not only constitute a peaceful community, but they also delete past bloody incidents from their history textbooks, so that the younger generation will grow up on brotherhood, not hatred.

Supranational expansion of the no-violence community often follows the formation of other supranational ties, such as those of the economic, political, and military spheres. It benefits from the expansion of communication networks, tourism, cultural exchanges, and shared educational institutions, which add their

[6] Even England, which is at best on the verge of joining the European community, is already changing its attitude to West Germany, and not only on the official level. The *Guardian* (Manchester) of August 15, 1961, reports:

"The commanding officer of the 84th Panzer Battalion, West German tank battalion, that will train on the firing range at Castlemartin, Pembrokeshire, next month, flew back to Germany from Wales delighted with the facilities at the camp and with the way he was received.

"Lieutenant-Colonel von Kleist said: 'My reception was much better than I expected.' There had been no hostility towards him during his two-day visit to Pembroke, where he paid a courtesy call on the Mayor, Alderman J. Sidney Rees.

"Colonel von Kleist, who did not wear his war decorations, which include the Iron Cross, at a press conference, placed some emphasis on the greeting that is already being extended to his men.

"Several British girls wanted to strike up pen friendships. There had also been several offers to spend weekends in British homes.

"Colonel von Kleist, a relative of the wartime Panzer general, was asked how he felt in bringing uniformed Germans to Britain, where he was a war captive for two-and-a-half years. 'We feel guilty for the last war, but we are now integrated fully in NATO,' he said."

The British labour party, however, passed a resolution in October, 1961 to deny British training facilities to West German troops.

influence to the more basic bonds. While the extension of economic, military, and political ties often precedes the expansion of the moral community, these ties are greatly strengthened once the moral community catches up with them. Violence among the member nations is now considered not only against the interests of each nation, but also immoral.

## From Nation-Union to Global Society

One or two generations from now, the earth will probably be populated with a score or two of supranational communities, instead of the present multitude of nations. Many of the supranational communities will be united in supercommunities, or blocs. How much closer will this bring us, though, to a global society and a stable peace? Will not these supranational communities be nations writ large, fighting each other with the same venom but with more strength than the nation-states? While this possibility cannot be excluded, it seems to me that nation-unions both in the long and short run brighten the outlook for evolving a stable peace.

### NATION-UNIONS AND NONWAR

Most contemporary supranational communities are less than ten years old. Many, in fact, are only at the beginning stage, and only a few of the new nation-unions have developed to the point where strong loyalties to the nation-community have been firmly established. But even in this short period, some not insignificant contributions to peace have been made.

The most immediately apparent one is the absence of wars among member nations *within* supranational communities. Archenemies of yesterday are now sharing a union and are extremely unlikely to fight one another again. Not only have all border fortifications and troop positioning been abolished, but their military organizations are also gradually integrating into one supranational organization and their citizens are beginning to include each other in a moral community.

On the bloc level, the West encourages peace in its sphere of influence, and the tightly integrated Communist camp has until now excluded war from its boundaries. Turkey and Greece, archenemies of yesterday, are now sharing NATO membership; much pressure was put on India and Pakistan to contain their conflicts. In 1948, when both Israel and the Arab nations were still in the Western sphere, the United States used its influence to terminate the war. In 1955, the United States did much to stop an invasion of Costa Rica by troops from Nicaragua.

Second, the creation of supranational communities has many of the attractions colonization once had but without many of its bad effects. Supranational unification allows countries to improve their standard of living, but not at the expense of other nations; it provides the outlets for ambitious, imaginative entrepreneurs once supplied by colonies and open frontiers, but does not involve exploitation of native peoples. Thus, the motivations and energies that once sowed seeds of deprivation, envy, and future unrest over much of the world, can now be channeled into constructive ends—toward the gradual development of nation-unions who know no war.

Finally, nation-unions have a moderating influence on more aggressive members, in their relations with members of the *other* blocs. Russian restraint of Communist China is much commented upon. Less often noted is the fact that the United States prevented Nationalist China from engaging in large-scale aggressive acts against the Chinese mainland. England often has a moderating role in the Western camp; it helped to keep the Berlin crisis from deepening and it is easing the way for the acceptance of Communist China into the United Nations; however, in at least one case—the 1956 Suez crisis— England was the nation that needed "moderating," and it received it from the United States. The Latin American republics had a moderating effect on the United States response to Castro; out of respect to their feeling, United States Air Force did not participate in the first invasion of Cuba, and a second one was prevented or at least postponed.

One might wonder if a supranational community is not just as likely to have the opposite effect, to build up the aggressive orientation of its members to outsiders, rather than to moderate it. While this undoubtedly does occur, it is of interest to note that moderation is attained much more frequently than the opposite effect. The chief reason for this lies in the fact that most international setbacks affect the interest and prestige of one member of the community much more than those of the others. Thus, for instance, nationalization of the sugar industry in Cuba was of more direct concern to the United States than to any of its allies, and the Congo crisis hurt Belgium much more than it did the other five members of the European Economic Community taken together. Assuming that those who are relatively uneffected can view the situation more calmly, we often find that most of the members of a supranational community (or a bloc) take a more moderate view of the situation than the country directly involved and tend to influence it toward moderation, rather than in the opposite direction.

These are the immediate contributions of present nation-unions, at a time when supranationalism is just budding and still quite weak. We can expect in the near future, as such unions expand and strengthen, complete elimination of wars among nations within the various unions, and possibly, within the blocs, an increasing sensitivity to the public opinion of other nations in one's own bloc concerning relations to the other bloc. But all this is largely a soothing medicine, because while it somewhat reduces, it does not even come close to eliminating the dangers of a war between the two blocs. What long-run role will supranationalism play here?

## THE TWO-STEP PROCESS

Seemingly, from a long-run viewpoint, supranational communities are a complete waste, even retarding the evolution of a global society. By transferring the national sentiments from "We French" and "We Germans" to "We West Europeans," and from "We Bulgarians" and "We Hungarians" to "We East European Communists," mankind seems to be simply building new partitions, which will prevent evolution of the sentiment to "We Human Beings." Similarly, by integrating the economies of six or seven countries, new barriers are erected in the way of global international trade; and by integrating some nations, the exclusions of others becomes emphasized.

Surely, if we could jump from a national society to the world state, we would all be better off, saving much frustration, energy, resources, and time. The trouble is that social and political process rarely proceed by jumps. If we view history and contemporary trends with open eyes, we cannot but realize that, regardless of our desires, that while mankind is not ready here and now to form a universal community, mankind *can and is*

193

*suppressing national boundaries as the first step in a two-step process toward a global community.* The supranational communities provide a middle layer between the ground floor of nations and the roof of a world state. Why is this grouping of nations a necessity before the universal community can be established?

The secret lies in the dynamics of consensus-formation—that is, the process by which people or groups that differ in beliefs and interests establish an agreement about the nature of the government they will share. One essential prerequisite for successful formation of consensus is that the number of people or groups be small. If the number is large, consensus will not be forthcoming. *Consensus among a large number of units can, however, be reached by breaking the participants into groups, each group working out an agreement among its members, with the group's representatives working out a general consensus.* (This can then be approved by a general meeting of all members.) Thus, by breaking consensus formation into two or more steps, the large number of participants is broken down first into groups of a small number of members each; then consensus formation continues in a small group of representatives, one for each first-level group. Thus, effective consensus formation among a large number of nations is possible. Let us note that whatever *agreed upon* decisions the United Nations and other international organizations are reaching these days (chiefly on nonpolitical matters, such as those concerning the various UNESCO activities) are actually gained in such a two-level process: first, each "bloc" works out its position—the West, the East, and the Afro-Asian blocs "caucus" separately; then their "representatives" negotiate, and an ultimate all-encompassing policy is worked out.

Consensus formation on the national level is a much easier job than on the international one, because there are already established shared bonds among citizens, and differences of interests and opinions are less manifold. Still, all effective national governments find it necessary to have at least a two-level consensus-formation structure. Political parties serve as the first level, helping to produce compromises and consensus among the various groups represented by *each* party; interaction in the Congress and between the Congress and the Administration (or the give and take among parties that form a coalition government) serves as the second level, producing compromises and consensus on national policy and action. One of the sources of the failures of the Third and the Fourth French Republic was the representation of a large number of interest groups directly at the top political level, without provision for lower-level consensus formation among them.

In the global society, supranational communities will serve as the first level of global consensus formation. Since their members tend to be countries that are comparatively similar to each other, sharing many interests because of their similar geographical position, consensus formation on this level will be less difficult, and the existence of a sovereign supranational government will supply the mechanism for carrying it out. The representatives of the supranational communities will bring their positions to the world government (or a revised United Nations) for final bargaining and worldwide policy formation. Thus, supranational communities will be both a stage in the development of the global society and a permanent part of its structure.

## The Final Unification

Economic and political development, as we shall see, will put the national layer on solid grounds and reduce cleavages in the ground floor of the global house; the supranational communities will provide the second floor. But the global roof will still have to be laid. It is almost impossible at this stage to depict with any detail or clarity how this last step will come about. A few comments can be made on factors that will probably influence the ultimate formation of a world government.

### UNIVERSALIZATION OF INTEGRATION FACTORS

Many of the factors that press now for supranational unification will at a later stage greatly press for universal integration. Once the benefits of regional international trade are exhausted, the demand for global free trade is likely to mount. Once the expansion of the moral community to the supranational level is firmly established, the world brotherhood called for by religious dogma and secular ideology will seem more attainable. The ever increasing potency of weapons might finally

195

make men realize that they share the fate of a small planet in the age of big bombs.

## INTERNATIONAL "FLOATING VOTE"

A particularly important role might be played in the formation of a viable world government by an increase in the size of the international "floating vote"—that is, the interbloc shifting of the political support and economic, military, and cultural ties of the various countries often referred to as the "uncommitted" nations. This is actually an unfortunate designation, for it implies that there is a limited pool of countries that have not yet made up their mind, but that once they are "committed," the struggle for their support is over. Actually, countries are constantly shifting sides, becoming committed to one bloc, uncommitted, committed to the other bloc, and recommitted to the original one. The countries that join a bloc cannot, therefore, by any means be written off as lost to the other bloc and as reducing the size of the floating vote. Further, one has to realize that shifts are more subtle than simply joining and leaving a bloc. For instance, Egypt and Iraq were once "safely" in the Western camp; internal revolutions took them out of it, but not quite into the Communist camp; in recent years, they have shifted Westward, though only to a limited degree. Similarly, Brazil, Ghana, Guinea, and Cambodia moved in the opposite direction without becoming Communist countries or allies. Shifting is sometimes expressed through votes in the United Nations General Assembly, but of much more importance are changes in the membership of military alliances (for example, Iraq's leaving the Baghdad Pact), in trade agreements (for example, Russian influence in Guinea was thus initiated), in cultural exchanges, as well as in related changes in the domestic political composition (for example, left-wing revolutions).

The importance of floating votes is well illustrated on the national level, where it takes the form of voters who shift their party support from one election to the next. This shifting plays a major role in keeping the democratic process democratic and effective, because the floating vote provides a constant chance for the minority to become the majority. Without a floating vote, a minority would be likely to become desperate and try to get its way by the use of force. The floating vote also helps to keep the system effective by siding with the party which serves broad, not just partisan, interests; this penalizes the less effective, more partisan, parties and encourages them to "improve."

Similarly on the international level: as long as countries keep shifting sides in part according to contributions the superpowers make to supranationalism, development, and peace—whatever their motives—service of both superpowers to the potential world community is rewarded. Moreover, both blocs will neither feel pushed into the corner ("We make no progress," "All leave us," "Nobody joins") nor will they despair and turn away from nonviolent means of competition; finally, moderation in international behavior is often rewarded in this way, since the "floating vote" is "between" the sides, and extreme partisan positions are unlikely to appeal to it.

Because of the central importance of the international "floating vote," every factor that supports it should be encouraged. The recent increase in American tolerance for shifting (mainly for limited shifts from rigid Western commitment to pro Western neutrality or neutral neutrality) is valuable from this viewpoint. Under the foreign policy of John Foster Dulles, neutrality was not recognized; a country was either for the United States or against it. Under the Kennedy administration, departures from the Western position are not equated with joining the Communist bloc. Though Cuba was still defined as having "gone Communist" long before the Communists were entrenched there (thus their entrenchment was directly helped by the United States), shift to more neutral positions by Cambodia, Thailand, and Brazil in 1961 did not elicit symbolic or economic sanctions by the United States.

Russia has frequently granted economic aid to non-Communist countries and has not demanded joining its military alliance or bloc as a prerequisite for foreign aid. Among the countries that have received Soviet aid are Guinea, Cambodia, Ethiopia, and India. On the other hand, ever since the "mistake" of Yugoslavia—which left the Communist bloc—the Soviet Union has seen to it that a country that does join its bloc (as distinct from a country which merely declares affinity) is unable to leave; this is accomplished by stationing Red Army units in or near such countries. Thus, the Soviet Union is both more and less tolerant than the United States—more so to sympathizers; less so to joiners.

The international "floating vote" not only directly supports nonviolent interbloc competition, but also forwards the foundation of a world government.[7] By providing both blocs with the hope that under such a government they might not be a permanent minority, and might have the predominant influence in directing the world state, it makes the acceptance of a world government by both sides more likely. Once such a government is established, even in a partial way, the very existence of the international floating vote, and in particular further increases in its scope and potency, will channel support and commitment to the world government, by rewarding nonpartisanship, service to the global community, and tolerance of the opposition and to the floating vote itself. Hence, both in order to support peace in the short run and enhance world government in the long run, all available encouragement should be given to the shifting process. A great virtue of the arms reduction plan advocated above (from conventional to nuclear disarmament) and of the new development strategy to be introduced below is that these will reopen the bloc boundaries and allow countries to shift more freely between the blocs.

## THE ROLE OF THE UNITED NATIONS AND INTERBLOC ORGANIZATIONS

The fact that the United Nations exists already might provide a framework for world unification and the formation of a viable world government. At present, the United Nations serves chiefly as a place where the blocs can communicate with each other, as a platform from which to appeal to the public opinion of other nations and of their own, and as an agency for a host of nonpolitical activities that have little effect on international relations, such as providing milk to needy children or circulating information on how to produce educational television programs. (The United Nations acts directly relevant to international violence, such as its intervention in Korea and the Congo, are Western, and not shared interbloc, acts.)

[7] See Talcott Parsons, "Polarization and the Problem of International Order," *Berkeley Journal of Sociology*, Vol. VI (1961), pp. 115–139.

These severe limitations on the effectiveness of the United Nations are chiefly due to the lack of a sociopolitical basis for world government, and not to the organization's structure; hence, restructuring it will be of little value. The big power veto, for instance, is simply an instrument used to prevent decisions that a major bloc finds objectionable. If a different procedure were established, one to which a bloc took major exception, the objecting bloc would either ignore United Nations decisions or simply walk out of the organization—and this would be the end of its limited usefulness. After all, even now more United Nation resolutions are ignored than vetoed.

The United Nations is destined to play a larger role in the future if its legitimation is not undermined now; it is therefore from a long-run viewpoint desirable not to act as if the United Nations were already a world government, whose majority decisions are binding on all members and whose "minority" is to be morally condemned when it does not abide by a majority decision. The emphasis in the United Nations for the near future should be on interbloc communication, on the working out of agreements in those limited areas in which they are possible (chiefly nonpolitical ones) and on the addition—wherever possible—of new positive functions, such as an interbloc exploration agency to study outer space and an organization to study the granting of additional kinds of technical assistance to developing countries. As the prerequisites for world government are developed, the United Nations will be able to increase gradually the scope and importance of decisions made and to insure their realization. At some time along the way a major procedural reorganization will be called for to express the changing sociopolitical reality, to give a more adequate representation to power differences among the members, to recognize supranational communities and governments, and eventually to form a United Nations Police Force, to gain exclusive control over whatever international means of violence may be left.

Other international organizations, from the World Meteorological Organization to the Universal Postal Union, from the International Civil Aviation Organization to the Frequency Registration Board, might eventually serve as agencies of the world government, but even if their number is increased many

199

times, they cannot in themselves bring about world government because of the narrow range of responsibilities they subsume and the limited weight of the factors they tackle. Countries might share a postal service, an antimalaria campaign, a milk-for-children agency, and fifty other such activities and still go to war the next day. To the degree that these interbloc organizations are not abused, so that the belief in their international impartiality is not undermined, they might contribute to global unification by supplying ready-made formats, when finally the prerequisites for world government are provided.

## A COMMON ENEMY

One major barrier to the unification of human society is listed again and again: the lack of a common threat. Groups give up their identity and sovereignty, it is said, only to unite against an outside enemy. Who will serve in this capacity for the global society? Against whom will East and West unite?

It should first be stressed that many of the present unions are only in part or indirectly formed against a common enemy. It is true that military alliances, by definition, are alliances against someone; and certainly the United States would hardly pick up the tab of India's irrigation system nor would Russia build a dam in Egypt, if there were no global strife. But other factors loom large in encouraging unification. The benefits from economic integration do not require any "enemies," nor even economic rivalry. All nations would benefit from a universal market, none would lose. The same holds for global division of scientific labor, unlimited cultural exchanges, and so on. Actually, only military alliances and, to a degree, political ones are formed against someone. Thus the theory that an outside threat is *necessary* for unification is not valid. While such an outside challenge might advance unification, the global society is not lacking in challenges.

The world is threatened with a rapidly increasing population on a planet with a limited and declining amount of natural resources. Coal, oil, and perhaps the supply of drinking water will be exhausted before the year 2062. Food scarcity will mount as population continues to "explode." New sources of energy and calories must be found; oceans must be desalted; nuclear energy must be harnessed for peaceful use; the bottoms of the seas, heart of the earth, and outer reaches of space must be combed for new resources, if the children of our grand-children are not to go hungry. This requires the shifting of an ever increasing amount of funds and talent now wasted on arms and duplication (or multiplicity) of national efforts to shared worldwide endeavors to solve these problems.

But if these challenges lack the kind of desperate urgency the threat of an enemy poses, the human race now faces the most cruel and devastating enemy it has ever known—the danger of nuclear bombs. If what the world needs for unification is a common enemy, these superbombs certainly provide one.

If we understand the process of history, and acccelerate instead of hinder it, the historian of the twenty-second century may review with surprise our biggest misconception: the nuclear bombs, he will know, were a major source not of disaster but of consolidation, not of war to the finish but the finish of wars.

## CONSENSUS FORMATION AND REDUCTION OF CLEAVAGES

The increasing need for global security, trade, scientific di-vision of labor, and cultural exchange seem in the long run to support the formation of a world government; shared challenges and perils might encourage it; the existence of interbloc organi-zations, in particular that of the United Nations—if not abused and if reorganized—might ease the last stage of the process. An increase in tolerance toward the shifting allegiances and com-mitments of "neutral" nations might play an important role in the process, although the international floating vote will be guaranteed only when reduction of conventional arms makes it impractical to prevent changes in bloc affiliation. A central contribution to world government is made by the evolution of supranational communities, which carry out the first step of global integration by forming multination economic, political, military, and other unions, and by providing the necessary in-termediary consensus-formation level for the edifices of the world government.

The supranational layer of consensus formation, however, will hardly be constructed and, if constructed, will be unable to fulfill its function, unless the cleavages among nations are greatly reduced. Consensus cannot be formed among nations, *or among supranational communities,* that are worlds apart, especially not so long as most of the global world's income, power, and prestige are concentrated in the hands of a few "have" nations, and misery, poverty, lack of a voice, and inferior status are the fate of the large number of "have-not" nations. Development of the nonindustrialized societies is the major social process that will reduce these cleavages. How precisely will development contribute to the formation of world government? What does it take to develop half the world? How can this process be accelerated?

## Chapter 9

### Development, Democratization, and Peace

East and West, pursuing their interests and expressing the values they believe in, pour millions of rubles and dollars into the modernization of underdeveloped countries. Yet this interbloc rivalry helps to preserve the armed truce and, more important, advances the formation of a world government. Some questions are thus raised: How exactly does development contribute to peace? And if it does, how long and how much does it take to industrialize four scores of countries, on three continents? Does the West command the means to develop all the countries in its sphere of influence? And what political changes are necessary before economic modernization can progress?

The Western growing investments in foreign economic aid, as well as that of the East, do not indicate that the two powers have decided to engage in a crash program to create the social prerequisites of world government. The East sees in development a way to expand its influence and to bring the Communist way of life to "uncommitted" nations. The West endeavors to check the spread of Communism and to bring to unindustrialized countries a high standard of living and political freedom. But whatever the motivations that drive the sides to develop the poorer countries, and as unintended as such contribution might be, the fact is that development contributes greatly to the historical evolution of world government and to the preservation of peace.

## Development and Investment in Peace

The basic idea is rather evident: the larger the differences among nations, the less likely they are to agree on the nature and the purposes of the government to which they are willing to be subordinated. Development of the "have-not" countries will bring them closer to the "have" countries, not only in economic terms, but also in their social, cultural, and political structure, since economic development both requires and effects modernization in all these spheres. Thus differences of interest and viewpoint among countries will be reduced, and a major barrier to international concensus formation will be removed. Second, when persons, groups, or nations have little, they have little to lose, and have thus only a weak stake in law and order. They are willing to engage in violent action to improve their lot. When the needs of all people are at least partially satisfied, their interest in order increases. Sharing with the poor, therefore, is the best policy the rich can follow. It allows them to keep part of their wealth rather than risking, and sooner or later losing, all. Sharp cleavages undermine not only law and order but also the position of the "have" social groups that are protected by law and order.

It is essential to recognize that the recommended reallocation of assets encompasses much more than wealth and income. Those who "have not" economically are frequently rejected socially and deprived of political representation; the greater the redistribution of one kind of asset, the more conspicuous becomes the inequality in the monopolization of other assets, and the more intense the demand for reallocation of these assets as well.

An historic illustration of this relationship between preservation of law and order and the voluntary sharing of economic, social, and political assets with rising groups is provided by the comparison of the response of England and France to industrialization.[1] One country read the course of history correctly and was spared turmoil; the other ignored the warning signs

For a fine analysis, see David Thomson, *The Democratic Ideal in France and England* (Cambridge, Cambridge University Press, 1940).

and ran into the arms of violence. In both countries during the Middle Ages a sharp cleavage separated an aristocratic leisure class from the impoverished peasantry, unaware of its deprived status because of the tradition and the belief that the existing social order was God-given. This medieval structure was undermined with the increase of commerce, reaching a peak in the seventeenth century, and vastly increasing the size and power of the merchant groups. In both countries, landed aristocracy first rejected the *nouveau riche* and their business activities. But as the bourgeoisie grew in power, the response on the two banks of the channel differed greatly. In England, the aristocracy opened its ranks. It allowed the *nouveau riche* to share its lands and its titles, and some aristocrats engaged in agricultural modernization, commerce, and manufacturing. As the aristocracy gained wealth and the wealthy middle classes acquired social status, the economic-social discrepancies between the two groups declined. Soon the newcomers also gained representation in Parliament and a share of governmental power. As their place in society was assured, their stake in it was established. In the process, without bloodshed and without the uprooting of any social class, England changed from a feudal, agricultural society to one with a large industrial middle class.

On the other hand, the French aristocracy refused both to initiate and introduce industrialization and to share its power and status with the rising bourgeoisie. With the French Revolution, the bourgeoisie forced its way in, sending the aristocracy to the guillotine. The cleavage between the two classes never healed, and a tradition glorifying change by force was established. France never completely recovered from its revolution.

The rise of the merchant classes in both societies was shortly followed by the industrial revolution. The increased exchange of goods made machine manufacturing the order of the day. The operation of factories required the recruitment of uneducated farm hands and the concentration in overcrowded cities of large groups of workers. The industrial proletariat was created. Soon it presented the bourgeoisie with much the same dilemma that the latter had presented to the aristocracy in the days of their ascendancy.

In England, again after some initial resistance, the doors were opened. Labor gained an increased share in the national income through higher wages, improved working conditions, social legislation, and welfare measures. Social acceptance came about through the knighting of labor leaders, and opening of the formerly exclusive Oxford and Cambridge. Political representation in Parliament and government was gradually attained and England changed from an early industrial society to one of "mature capitalism" (or a welfare state), without any major outbreak of violence. In the process, the commitment of the new social class to law and order was insured; no class was either dispossessed or beheaded.

The French bourgeoisie was about as receptive to the pressure of the ascending labor class as the aristocracy had been to its demands. French labor remained for a long period less well paid than workers in England, with few social rights and little political representation. While the unbridged gap never led to a full-fledged revolution, it certainly was one of the major reasons why France has never attained a stable political government and was and is a torn, violent society. Moreover, unlike England, it has a strong Communist movement, which continues to have much influence over its labor class and commands up to 25 per cent of all French votes.

The lesson of this historical comparison, applied to the development of a global society, is multifold; the "have-not" countries—Communist China is a prime example—have little stake in world order and, unless their lot is improved, they will be willing to apply violence against the "have" countries. Industrialization is the only way to significantly improve the standard of living in these countries. Economic and technical aid thus not only serve basic human values, but also, by reducing the gap between the rich and the poor countries, support the world order and a reduced though newly secure place of the "have" countries in it.

The global redistribution of noneconomic assets has already progressed a long way. Nationalism and related independence movements have transformed the colonies of yesterday into the proud nations of today, commanding all the national status symbols, from a flag to a seat in the United Nations.

Changes in social status are also evident in new attitudes toward the colored nations. In the world of yesterday, the white nations made up the global "upper class"; now the trend is toward granting social acceptance to the nonwhite nations. This is reflected in the increasing pressure of world public opinion on the United States and South Africa to grant full rights to their nonwhite groups, in the acceptance of Hawaii— one of the most socially mixed, nonwhite melting pots of the world—as a full member of the American federation, and in particular in the interbloc courting of nonwhite nations. The Communist bloc boosted the nonwhite social ego by its alliance with powerful, nonwhite China.

Thus, with political and social assets well on the way of redistribution, the economic gap is becoming even more conspicuous. Few people are aware that this gap does not decrease but, on the contrary, is constantly increasing. For roughly the last 100 years the industrialized countries have doubled their standard of living every generation, while the unindustrialized countries have remained chained to the same mere subsistence level. The rich countries are becoming richer, while the poor nations remain in their poverty-stricken misery.

The economic gap has now become a subject of interbloc strife similar to that between the Whigs and the Tories who, trying to gain the political support of the English lower classes, competed over who aided them most. Ideologically, the East represents itself as the champion of anticolonialism, as the bloc that offers economic aid without political strings, and as a model for rapid industrialization. The West counters by pointing to its way of industrializing as yielding a higher standard of living, to its superior technology, and to the price of industrialization in the Eastern way—the lack of political freedom.

Viewed in terms of a power struggle, the East wishes to expand, the West to check this expansion. The East furthers its aims by supporting elites and groups pressing for development, the likely rulers of tomorrow. The West's best chance—slowly being recognized—lies in eliminating the sociological conditions under which Communism is most successful: sharp social and economic discrepancies, a high rate of illiteracy, a low standard of living, and masses oppressed by traditional elites, such as landed oligarchies and military dictators.[2]

[2] For a potent analysis of these factors, see Seymour M. Lipset, *The Political Man* (New York, Doubleday & Co., 1960).

Thus both blocs find moral and political satisfaction in supporting a process that coincidentally, by reducing the political, social, and economic cleavages within and among nations, gradually creates one of the basic prerequisites of world government.

## The Price and Pace of Development

The use of development as a strategic tool in the interbloc rivalry, as well as to forward world government, however, confronts us with a dangerous illusion, that of underestimating the amount of resources and length of time required by economic, social, and political changes. We might become disillusioned and reject development, not because it is incapable of bringing about the desired state of affairs, but because it does not live up to our too demanding delivery schedule. A realistic assessment of the price and pace of development is crucial to its continued support and success. Moreover, only a full knowledge of the obstacles it will meet can direct our search for means to accelerate the process.

By most standards, only about a third of the world is "developed." Scores of countries have an annual average income per capita that approaches half of the American monthly average income, and 80 per cent of the population can neither read nor write.[3] Practically all of Asia, Africa, Latin America, and parts of southern Europe remain to be developed, though of course there are significant differences in degree within and between the continents. Some people still live in the Stone Age, as the Papuan tribes in New Guinea; some countries—Yemen, for instance—are as "advanced" as early medieval societies; while others, such as North Africa, are well on their way to becoming modern societies.

Despite the large differences among countries on each continent, important for our subsequent analysis are some systematic differences between the continents themselves. In general, Latin America has more natural resources than Africa or Asia and is less overpopulated; it has, for example, three times more land per capita suitable for cultivation than Asia. Africa is probably poorer in natural resources than Latin America, but it is neither as poor nor as overpopulated as Asia. Asia is the

[3] The "money" GNP per capita in dollars in 1961 was 187 for the Middle East, 100 for Africa, 84 for Latin America, and 2,790 for the United States (figures calculated by Professor P. N. Rosentein-Rodan).

least blessed with resources and the most "blessed" with population.

Capital is obviously the most essential and immediate requirement for the industrialization of many of these countries. Without a large increase in the means of production, transportation, and communication, industrialization will never progress. Without industrialization, the aspirations of these nations for a large and rapid increase in their standard of living will never be satisfied.

Estimates of the amount of capital that has to be provided through outside aid or through outside investment vary. MIT economist W. W. Rostow now estimates that "with current levels of both domestic capital formation and external aid, an increase of the order of some $4 billion in annual external aid would be required to lift all of Asia, the Middle East, Africa, and Latin America into regular growth, at an increase of per capita income of, say, 1.5% per annum."[4] British economist Barbara Ward estimates that $6 billion of annual investments are needed in the next twenty years. Figures by other economists vary between $3 to $8 billion. It is my contention that these figures are far too low, because they do not take sufficiently into account the increasing consumption demand that siphons off much, if not all, of the increased output and because they do not give due allowance to unavoidable waste. To counter the wide-spread illusions about the costs and pace at which development can be achieved, it seems necessary to spell out somewhat more fully what development requires. Only a recognition of the magnitude of the problem will prepare us for drastic steps that need to be taken to make development feasible and accelerate its pace. The remainder of this chapter is devoted to underscoring the problems of development; the subsequent one, to a new approach to the solution of the problems.

One central factor that retards development is the continuing *population explosion*. While transferral of most achievements of modern civilization to backward countries is highly difficult, some of the major benefits of medicine can be provided rapidly at little cost and without any cooperation by the native popu-

---

[4] W. W. Rostow, *The Stages of Economic Growth* (Cambridge, Cambridge University Press, 1960), p. 143.

lation. Spraying the countryside with DDT from a World Health Organization plane flown by an American pilot, throwing some chemical in the water mains, and taking other similar measures results in a sharp decline of the death rate caused by mass diseases like malaria, yellow fever, cholera, plague, smallpox, and typhoid. A 50 per cent decline in the first decade is by no means unusual, though the record is probably held by Ceylon which, after a DDT spray in 1946, showed a decline of 43 per cent in one year! Since the birth rate scarcely lessens in so short a time, the population increase is incredibly rapid. The world population increased from two billion in 1930 to three billion in 1961—that is 50 per cent in only 31 years. The rate of population growth is still rising; according to United Nations estimates, it will soon reach 2 per cent a year. At this rate, the world will have four billion people by 1980. Much of this growth is concentrated in the "have-not" countries. Expert Kingsley Davis calculated that, at present growth rates, the population of some of underdeveloped countries will *double* in approximately twenty-five years and will multiply *ten* times in seventy-five years. Indeed, in some of these countries, such as Egypt, the population has already grown three times faster than has the increasing area under cultivation.

Not only is there an ever increasing number of mouths to be fed, but the appetite—and not just for food—greatly expands. Impoverished people are experiencing what Adlai Stevenson termed the "revolution of rising expectations." The radio (one in each village square), visits to the big city, and movies bring to the masses an increasing awareness of their poverty. Education further whets the appetites and fires ambitions. Thus, much if not all of the output of additional investment, if not the investments themselves, disappears in greater consumption by the growing number of consumers. The product is eaten up instead of being partly reinvested to build up the producing capacity of the economy. It follows that, even if all economic aid were wisely used, no corruption existed, and the population were willing to work as hard and efficiently as American workers, building up investments for further industrialization might still be rather difficult. But, of course, none of these preconditions exist.

Many of underprivileged countries are run by highly corrupt

oligarchies that succeed in spending astronomical sums on harems, the French Riviera, golden air-conditioned Cadillacs, and private Swiss bank accounts. Most Latin American presidents in the past, even if they remained in office only a few years, have accumulated multimillion-dollar fortunes while in office. Oil-rich countries, such as Saudi Arabia, have a multimillion annual income, and yet these countries are not simply underdeveloped, they are undeveloped. A Brazilian proverb suggests, "Our country grows by night, when the politicians sleep."

In addition to conspicuous consumption by corrupt rulers, their courts, relatives, and selected loyal supporters, waste occurs because workers, management, government clerks, and others have not yet adopted modern administrative patterns and work habits. The elimination of this waste requires changing the culture, social structure, traditions, beliefs, and mental outlook of these people. Workers have to learn to report for work at 6:30 A.M., not "sometime after the sun rises"; they must come to work every day, not just when they are short of money. Business owners must learn to reinvest some of their profits in their enterprises. Government clerks must be disciplined to grant licenses, concessions, and precious foreign exchange, not to their first and second cousins, but to imports which contribute most to the growing economy. Politicians have to become interested in tedious details of administration and economy. Millions must be trained as skilled workers and professionals by thousands of teachers, who have to be educated at hundreds of colleges and universities which do not exist.

The list could be easily extended, but the point should be clear: to create the basic conditions for economic development, many habits have to be uprooted and new ways must be learned. Gigantic funds are required to finance education to introduce the new ways and to make up for waste due to mistakes, inefficiency, corruption, nepotism, and the general persistence of the old ways. This waste can be somewhat trimmed through improvements in the administration of economic and technical assistance, but since the more basic roots of these phenomena lie in the very social and cultural structure of the countries involved and in the attitude of their people, these "diseconomies" will markedly decline only as modernization markedly progresses. Meanwhile, although waste must be constantly countered, assessing the cost of development requires taking into account the enormous magnitude of the funds that are and will be lost due to it. Nobody should be surprised if the actual sums required for industrialization run between ten and twenty times more than often suggested.[5]

Finally, it is crucial to realize that capital allocated to these countries not only is in part wasted, or completely lost, but can and does *actually make their condition worse!* In order for these countries to reach a level from which they will be able to proceed with their industrialization without continued foreign aid, they have to "take off."

The image of "taking off," suggested by Rostow, refers to an airplane, accumulating speed as it rolls down a runway until it has built up enough momentum to "take off" from the ground, to continue in its movement without the support of the runway. If the speed accumulated is not sufficient, the plane will not leave the ground; the whole effort will be wasted. With economics, the problem is analogous: the initial investment for industrializing must be sufficiently large for the nation to build up its production means to a level that output will satisfy its current needs, as well as enable the country to save some to continue to build and extend its production means from its own, now greater, output.

Even if aid is granted continuously year after year, if the economic aid given does not suffice for take-off, the situation might easily get worse instead of better. As the population continues to grow and aspirations are built up—in part due to very activities generated by economic aid—the demand for consumer goods increases rapidly. To the degree that output builds up more slowly than the population and consumption demand, consumer goods available for each person of the now larger multitudes will be smaller, and their frustration larger.[6] To the degree that output just catches up with the increased

[5] Recently the Venezuelan government moved 17,000 families as part of a resettlement plan of 350,000 rural families. Though the plan was carried out on a higher level of efficiency than is standard in underdeveloped countries, the cost was so large that had all the families been resettled in this manner, the process would have taken fifteen years and cost $6.7 billion. Even then, of course, only a quite minor part of the agricultural development of one country would have been achieved.
[6] According to *The Economist* (April 22, 1961), after two decades of development, 10 per cent of the Mexican people were better off, 70 per cent, about the same, and 20 per cent, worse than ever.

demand, still all the aid given disappears in increased consumption without allowing direction of some of the output to increase the production capacities of the country. The crucial point for the West is that under these conditions these countries do not gradually attain a state of self-sustained growth and can be weaned off aid; they become more and more dependent on it.

But even if the sums provided were large enough to take into account the various kinds of waste and the need to grant an originally large enough amount to bring the countries to the "take-off" stage, even if due attention were paid to the need to change work and administration habits—still the whole endeavor might be impossible unless efforts to initiate economic development were accompanied by deep political changes.

## Political Development

### THE OPPOSITION

At one stage or another, all underdeveloped countries are confronted with strong resistance to industrialization and related social changes by power elites and social groups that benefit largely from the existing social structure.

The landed aristocracy is the major group opposing modernization in many countries, and its reaction to development typifies that of other groups—the church, the king's court, and the tribal chiefs. The landlord—controlling both the government and the major source of wealth, the land—is the most powerful figure in the feudal society. Often a very few lords hold a vast proportion of the country's land; in 1961, 1.5 per cent of the land holders owned 50 per cent of all the arable land in seven Latin American countries. Similar figures are reported for Asia. Many hundreds, sometimes thousands, work on these estates for "room and board" or supply up to two-thirds of their crops to the landlord in exchange for the privilege of working his land. The landlord's power over the peasantry is practically absolute. He often has his own police force or controls the local one, appoints the local judge, and frequently influences the selection of the priest. Keeping the peasants in perpetual debt to the landowner is a favorite device to keep them legally bound to the estate.

Industrialization would spell ruin for the landed aristocracy.

It would supply the peasants with an alternative source of liveli-hood and thus break their virtual enslavement. The spread of education and information undermines the belief of the peasants that their miserable fate is God-given. The growth of the cities and the industrial middle class establishes a rival political power that often works against the interests of the landlord. The urban dweller, for instance, is interested in low prices for agricultural products and presses for the removal of import duties on such products from other countries. By supporting land reforms, industrialists sometimes even deliberately seek to undermine the landlord's wealth and political power. The gov-ernment might go as far as to expropriate the land, or buy it, and distribute it to the peasants. Land, however, is for the lords more than a source of income and power. Running an estate is their only skill; owning land is their major source of prestige. The estate is the base of their social, cultural, and leisure activities. In short, giving up the land is like giving up everything. No wonder that landlords, and other groups that have similar stakes in the traditional society, fight change in every conceivable way.

Those who support change are less clearly distinguishable; as a rule they form a highly varied coalition. Often it includes some of the younger lords, court princes, and tribal chiefs, who are expressing both their position in a typical intergeneration conflict and their growing identification with the fate of their country in an awakening world. Merchants, who exist as second-class citizens in most traditional societies, support changes that will increase their wealth, power, and social status. To the degree that there are some professionals and students, often educated abroad, they tend to support modernization. The awakening peasants and labor force accumulating in the growing cities supply potential mass support for these pro-change groups.

The speed, expense, and eventual outcome of development efforts are largely affected by the power struggle between these pro- and antidevelopment forces. Wherever the resistance of antidevelopment elites is not overcome, development is ex-tremely difficult, slow, and expensive, if not impossible. The vast power of landlords in most Latin American republics, for instance, largely accounts for unsuccessful attempts to modern-ize agriculture in these countries. Similarly, tribal chiefs in

Africa and shieks in the Middle East often block industrialization in order to protect their near-absolute power, status, way of life, and economic privileges.

In view of the strong vested interest that traditional elites have in the existing structure and their control of the centers of power in these societies, no one can expect distribution of pamphlets or pep talks by Point Four experts to overcome their resistance. As a rule, even painting the Communist devil on the wall does not move them, and often when they finally concede some reforms, it is too little and too late. The miserable share-croppers, serfs, workers, and frequently the frustrated professionals and the unemployed intelligentsia, have already given up their hope for gradual evolution and have turned to the support of revolutionary forces. By the time the Communists took over China, Chiang Kai-shek was rejected by the professionals and businessmen as well as the more traditionally "left" groups. Thus, in sum, to gain economic development, political changes have to be introduced. To assure that those are introduced in due time and scope, now social forces, we shall see, have often to be supported.

## DEMOCRATIZATION: FIRST OR LATER?

Assuming that the antidevelopment elites have been removed or their opposition has been overcome, a question still remains: what political framework is to be established. Is democracy needed for development, or development for democracy?

The advocates of the development-first-democratization-later school insist that rapid industrialization and modernization require a tough, totalitarian regime. Germany, Japan, and Russia —all developed in a generation and all under totalitarian (or authoritarian) regimes—are cited again and again as supporting cases. Although modernization in England and the United States was carried out under democratic rule, circumstances were especially favorable, and the process took two generations, not one.

The totalitarian organization of society is credited with a number of advantages for socioeconomic modernization. Centralized control can accelerate take-off greatly by regulating prices and wages, forcing saving, and thus keeping consumption down and investment up. Second, such control can be used to order labor to move where it is needed and can establish discipline. Third, the state's power can be exercised to reallocate land and other capital goods without much attention to property and individual rights but in accordance with master plans and economic needs. Fourth, much corruption and conspicuous consumption by a small minority can be eliminated by a combination of ideological indoctrination and stiff punishment.

For these reasons, it is claimed, totalitarian regimes can rapidly develop a country even with comparatively little outside capital investment; force greatly reduces the price and greatly increases the pace of social change. Advocates of this method point to the fact that Communist countries "take off" in rapid succession.

No Western experts would suggest introducing a totalitarian regime where none exists. But the question is raised in connection with those non-Communist countries that are not democratic. Should they be encouraged to put effort first into development, or first into constructing a democracy?

The democracy-later school claims that to undergo two revolutions simultaneously—one of development and one of democratization—is to experience one too many; that unless force is used, development will proceed at a snail's pace, and take-off will be greatly delayed if it is ever attained at all. The slow pre-take-off development of democratic India is their favorite example. (Claims of democratic development in Puerto Rico and the Philippines are written off; they counter that Puerto Rico is not democratic and the Philippines are not developed.) It is also argued that for a hungry peasant or unemployed worker, the right to vote is largely meaningless. Democracy is an abstract luxury, appreciated by those who are fed, clad, and sheltered; when 70 to 90 per cent of the population are illiterate, their information on national policies is nil, their ability to judge them minimal. Hence democratic conduct of nationwide politics is impossible. Democratization ought to come later, when a higher standard of living, mass education, and increasing pluralism have established the sociological conditions under which democracy can flourish.

On the other hand, the democracy-first school claims that the regime that effectively carries off industrialization, whether that regime is democratic or not, will be endorsed by its people;

those who benefit from such a success are unlikely to demand a different political system. Although Japan and Germany became industrialized and their people educated, they democratized only after a defeat in war and under pressure from occupying powers. It is asserted that no country has become democratic *after* industrialization. Democracy-first advocates also deny the superior efficiency of totalitarian regimes, depicting them full of bureaucratic handicaps, such as red tape and the shirking of individual initiative and responsibility, especially among the individualistic peasants. Finally, democracy is declared to be the most effective political framework for economic development, since it removes arbitrary state intervention on both the local and national levels, thus establishing the free interplay of economic forces necessary for successful industrialization. Thus, democracy-first is claimed to be not only a moral and political necessity, but also the superior sequence economically.

## GRADED DEMOCRATIZATION

One cannot escape the fact that rapid industrialization of undeveloped countries has occurred only under right- or left-wing dictatorships (of either authoritarian or totalitarian type). Some degree of force seems to be needed in most countries to remove the antichange elements, to hold down consumption, to reduce waste, and to enforce discipline. Surely not all diseconomies can be so eliminated, and some new ones are produced by the very use of force. Still, the balance is on the side of force. Development can probably be attained with little or no force if *much* more time and resources are available. Then consumer *and* producer goods can be purchased, waste can continue and still leave some funds for investment, and perhaps the antichange elites can be won over to the cause of development. But the resources needed under these conditions are astronomical, and the time required is extensive indeed. To attain low-cost rapid industrialization, force may well have to substitute to a degree for both resources and time.

This is not to imply that democratization must be completely deferred until industrialization has been completed. Democratization should be broken into stages and introduced concomitantly with economic development. Political development should be advanced in a sequence that minimizes the economic liabilities of democratization and maximizes the support for democratization derived from the progressing industrialization.

The first stage of political development—abolition of terror—should be introduced at the very beginning and supported without compromise by whatever nonviolent power other nations have over the developing one and by social groups in the country that seek the best for their nation. Terror regimes should not be supported under any circumstances. The value of development is high, but not high enough to justify police brutalities, firing squads, and concentration camps. Hence, even if it would increase the expense and time development required, "minimum democratization" (or rather "detotalitarization") should be introduced.

On the other hand, there might be less objection at the initial development stage to a "tight" control by those in power. One has to distinguish between a bloody whip and a tight rein. After all, even established democracies suspend freedoms and introduce tight controls in wartime; development is the war of survival of the new countries. Its first stage often requires much central control in appropriation of properties (such as land), nationalization (for example, of oil), regulation of prices and wages, and forced saving. That is, steps must be taken to speed take-off and to keep the development elite in power, despite the antagonism of traditional groups.

After a country has taken off and its economic growth is insured, additional democratization should be encouraged. The second stage might be, for instance, an increase in local democracy (assuming that the economy will continue to be controlled to a large degree from a national center). The third stage might bring evolution of democracy on a national level, activization of national political parties, labor unions, and chambers of commerce. How to plan a democracy, however, and introduce it gradually, and how to synchronize it with economic development, is still a practically unstudied problem.

While it is true that in itself development does not guarantee democratization, it certainly makes it much easier by establishing many of the economic, educational, sociological, and psychological prerequisites of democracy. Those who have learned

217

to read blueprints and technical manuals can also read newspapers and campaign pamphlets; those whose minds are not totally absorbed by their effort to subsist can turn to matters of state; and those united in an economic effort, whether factory workers or corporation executives or university professors, might form the base of political units.

Western public opinion, advice, and possible nonviolent sanctions that affects these societies should be used to stress both the immediate abolition of terror practices and further democratization after take-off; they should be used to encourage the gradual loosening of political controls as the prerequisites for democracy are provided by economic development and the economic need for them declines. Such pressures will encourage turning democratization potentials into realities.

The same distinction between terror and tight regimes ought to be applied to the Communist countries. Khrushchev's Russia, for instance, is less totalitarian than that of Stalin. Fewer police brutalities seem to exist in the contemporary Soviet Union; people get fired from their jobs instead of being hanged; some cultural and political liberalization has taken place. Russia will probably continue to move somewhat more in this direction. Communist China, now in the Stalinist stage, might move in the same direction after its economic development progresses.

A decline in the use of force is to be expected in Communist countries as they complete their basic industrialization and are able to improve their standard of living. After all, unlike the Nazis, Communists are not force-crazed. Holding down the standard of living of the masses might prove dangerous in the long run. After all, there is a bloc that might one day support their rebellion. Thus detotalitarization is in part due to and encouraged by the very existence of the West.

In short, we must realize that democracy and dictatorships are not two neatly separate categories but form a continuum. There are many differences of degree. De Gaulle's France is by no means as democratic as the United States or England; Mexico at best qualifies as a semi-democracy; and Poland is less totalitarian than Rumania, and present-day Russia less than Communist China. Somewhere along this line must be a point where we are willing to say: I do not approve of this form of government, but this is their business. We certainly view France and Mexico in this light. I would draw the line for countries in the pre-take-off stage between terror regime and the tight-control regime, and I would expect all countries to untighten as their development progresses.

## Limping Development

We have to preserve the nonwar state and strengthen the factors that prevent war, until the prerequisites of world government evolve. Economic and political development contribute directly to both needs. In the short run, the interbloc rivalry over who helps most underdeveloped countries, provides a nonviolent outlet for the clash of East and West. In the long run, this might prove to be a dangerous outlet; the development race could rather easily heat up tempers to the boiling point. Meanwhile, however, it limits the East-West conflict to the rather useful competition over who gives more, best, and with least strings attached. The development race also serves the long-run goal of building up the stakes of poorer countries in world order and of reducing the cleavages between "have" and "have-not" countries—a necessary condition for the formation of agreed-upon global policies and procedures: in short, world government.

Development, in the long run, supports the values the West stands for. It increases the standard of living, spreads education, and provides the economic and social foundations for political freedoms. By the same token, it eliminates the sociological conditions under which Communism thrives.

But it is most essential to understand fully the enormous effort development of a country necessitates. Much of the political, social, and economic fabric of a society has to be redone before it can continue to modernize on its own. Politically speaking, there is no take-off without overcoming or removing the resistance of the traditional elites. While the need to support pro-development elites is clear, implementing a full democratic rule before industrialization is launched might be detrimental to industrialization, if not simply impossible. It seems that after abolishing terror practices—a minimum of democratization without which no human being should have to live—democratization will have to progress slowly and gradually, hand in hand with economic development.

Economic development requires gigantic amounts of resources; in part because the assignment is simply so large; in part because the growing population, and its growing demand, siphons large amounts of investment funds; and in part because of the large quantities and varieties of waste in the use of the economic aid. Any policy that does not take all these difficulties fully into account is bound to fail. But probably the chief drawback of the present Western modernization strategy is that available foreign-aid grants have been spread so thin that no country obtains enough resources to take off; thus, in a sense, *all* the aid given is wasted.

Whatever position one wishes to take on these highly complex and controversial matters, one point must be stressed and belongs to the category of fact, not opinions or moral judgments: *while the Communist countries take off, those in the Western sphere of influence do not.* A continuation of the present Western strategy will at best keep development highly expensive and slow, possibly altogether stalemated. Such limping development not only retards the establishment of world government, but directly undermines the international position of the West and the present armed truce. Realization of the grave dangers involved in half-hearted development underscores the need for a new strategy.

## Chapter 10

## A New Development Strategy

### Leapfrogging and World War III

THE COMBINATION of a limping development policy and a rigid military strategy has brought about one of the most dangerous situations since World War II, a situation that undermines both the position of the West and the state of armed truce. The inability of the Western development policy to bring non-Communist countries to take-off has been pointed out. The related rigidity in the military strategy of the West needs to be briefly indicated. The discussion will be followed by a presentation of a new development strategy and an examination of its military correlates.

## HOLDING THE RIM

All the American armed-deterrence strategies, whether Containment, Massive Retaliation, or Multideterrence, are based on two assumptions: (1) that the military power will deter a Communist nuclear attack on the heart of the Western bloc and will check Communist military expansion by a military rim, a 20,000-mile line established by the Truman Doctrine in 1947; (2) that the ideological expansion of Communism into the countries behind the rim will be checked through development of these countries, eliminating the sociological foundations of Communism.

Thus, fifteen years after it was formulated, after two changes' of administration and after a period in which the Soviet Union moved from a weak, inferior power to one with nuclear parity and possible space and air superiority, the United States is still holding the same Maginot Line around the Communist bloc, still has no realistic plans to bring political freedoms to the people under Communist rule, and still considers every country that happens to be on this side of the rim part of the Free World and the Western protectorate. The Western strategic perspective has remained essentially the same in spite of tremendous changes in the international power situation. Thus, a cardinal sin of policy making has been committed: flexibility and adaptability have been almost completely lost. The West continues to hold a line nailed to a global map as if the East-West conflict were a trench war over territories.

On the face of it, rim holding has been and is much more successful than one would assume from listening to the spokesmen of the opposition and the administration. It can claim to its credit holding the Communist military bloc to its previous territorial boundaries for fifteen years on every single front from Greece to Korea, and from Iran to Berlin, with the single exception of Southeast Asia.

Nor is there a very great danger of an all-out attack in the near future on the Western heartland. America's improvement of the ability to strike back, in particular the development of the Polaris submarines and the Minuteman missiles, does not grant security, but it makes a direct attack unlikely for a while. More important, it would be more than foolish for the Communists to risk all their achievements as long as their "leapfrogging" continues to work so well. Here lies the major short-run danger to the United States, the West, and peace. It is Communist "leapfrogging" that makes rim holding less than useless.

## THE THREAT OF LEAPFROGGING

The expansion of the Communist movement into the huge areas that lie *between* the rim and the Western heartland is the major short-run threat. Communism is not just a military bloc, it is also an ideological and political force; it has and will in the future leap over the rim held by Western forces, to claim more and more of the large number of underdeveloped countries in Latin America, Africa, and Asia. If the West follows its present policy, it might one day find that while its soldiers are patrolling the North-South Korean borders, Communism is taking Indonesia; while the West holds the rim in Iran, Communism is claiming West and Central Africa; and while NATO busily protects the rim in West Berlin, Communism is making inroads into South America.

The essence of leapfrogging is that it is not checked by a military rim, nor is it stopped by geographical distances or lack of supply and reinforcement lines. It operates in two ways: by supporting overdue social changes in underdeveloped and oppressed countries, introducing Communist or left-wing governments; and by dislodging countries from the Western bloc or pro-Western orientation and trying to elicit a pro-Communist foreign policy in these countries. The two processes clearly reinforce one another (as in Cuba, Egypt, Iraq, and Guatemala), though by no means all countries that shift away from the West or toward the East also experience an internal revolution, nor do all those that have a left-wing or even Communist government necessarily belong to the Communist bloc: Brazil moved away from the West in 1961 without a left revolution, and Yugoslavia is not part of the Communist bloc.

The most spectacular leapfrogging to date is the Communist success in Cuba. The Communists sent no military force or arms to overthrow Batista; since they initially considered Castro an amateur, they did not even support his revolutionary effort financially or morally. Only after the revolution was carried out and Castro was holding the reins did the Communists join the bandwagon. This Communist success, thousands of miles from the closest Communist country and only ninety miles from the United States, underscores the point that ideology and political movements know no distance and are not "deterred" by Maginot Lines or SAC bombers.

Much less complete and quite different in nature is the success of Communism in the Middle East. The Communist movement still has only little influence over the internal affairs of Egypt, somewhat less influence in Syria, and is a far from decisive power in Iraq. Its chief success here is in dislodging these countries from the Western camp. Although these Arab countries have not been integrated into the Communist bloc, and have recently even moved ever so slightly away from it, they are definitely outside the Western sphere of influence. This is reflected, for instance, in their support of Lumumba in the Congo and in their position in the 1961 Belgrade Conference of neutral countries.

Even less complete but still rather impressive are the fruits of leapfrogging in Indonesia, in West Africa (particularly in Guinea and Ghana), and in the Congo, where the strongest leader is the Communist-supported heir of Lumumba, Antoine Gizenga. In none of these countries has Communism penetrated very deeply or consolidated its gains, but it has succeeded in neutralizing much of the Western influence without resorting to armed intervention.

The potentials of leapfrogging may well be even larger than its achievement to date. After all, Communism's rising power, especially in space technology and related military rocketry, became evident only late in 1957. Moreover, the Communist success might well turn out to have a snowballing nature; though starting slowly, it might build up momentum as it accumulates weight. Thus Nasser's power has increased since his rapprochement with the North African leader who resisted his influence, Bourguiba; Nasser will be many times more powerful if he succeeds in his efforts to firmly establish an all-Arab nation, which would require first of all his regaining control of Syria, the former partner of the United Arab Republic, and coming to terms with Jordan and Iraq. Cuba's influence would grow greatly if *Fidelismo* would spread to just one more American republic. Ghana and Guinea already reinforce each other's non-Western tendencies and those of their neighboring countries. Thus it is quite within the realm of possibility that in Asia, Africa, or Latin America—behind the rim—anti-Western or even pro-Eastern blocs will be formed, gradually expanding to include many of the underdeveloped countries, especially if leftist revolutions occur in them.

The final consolidation of these gains by the East, if they continue to occur and accumulate, will necessitate a crack in the West's rim to integrate these countries into the major Communist bloc. In the past, at any rate, the Soviets found it necessary to station the Red Army in satellite countires in order to insure their continuous membership in the Communist bloc, and the Soviet Union, because of difficulties in supply and reinforcement, is reluctant to send military forces to countries not adjacent to its major land bloc. But *the Western rim,* which currently separates the Communist bloc from pro-Communist nations, *might be cracked by a combination of pressure by pro-Communist rearlands and social revolutions in the rimlands.* For example, the Communist gains in the Middle East (especially if Egypt, Syria and Iraq come to terms) might be consolidated by a breakthrough in Iran. Iran separates Russia from Iraq and the Northern part of Syria by no more than 200 miles. Iran itself, after $1.1 billion American military and economic aid, is still economically underdeveloped, ruled by an oligarchic landed aristocracy and a tyrannical Shah, widely penetrated by Communists and quite ready for a revolution. Similarly the breakthrough of the rim in Southeast Asia may come after pro-Communist revolutions in Indonesia and/or Cambodia, which might then be consolidated by a social revolution in rimland South Vietnam or in the Western part of Laos.

If the Communists continue to avoid committing themselves militarily in nonadjacent countries, consolidation of their gains in Africa depends on a successful consolidation in the Middle East; those in Latin America, upon Africa. With the increasing power of the Communist bloc, however, and improvements in aerial and space transportation, the Soviet Union might position the Red Army in pro-Communist countries behind the Western rim, not so much to gain bases closer to the West than to keep these countries under its control and to use them for further expansion.

The dangers of a hold-the-rim, expose-the-rear policy are illustrated by the fate of the notorious Maginot Line, on which the Western rim is actually modeled: it did not fail under a frontal attack, but rather through a combination of "leapfrogging" (that is, conquest of the rear lands by paratroops) and an attack on the rim from the rear to integrate captured rearland with the main bloc.

## THE PRESENT COUNTER STRATEGY

To counter Communist leapfrogging, the United States used its military force in the rearlands. Since stationing forces in all the rearlands is neither militarily nor politically feasible, a variety of mobile units and tactics was used to counter leapfrogging. The anti-United States left revolution in Guatemala was unseated by forces armed by the CIA in 1956; the United States marines interfered in Lebanon in 1958 when it was believed to be going Communist, and—more subtly—Western and some neutral forces, under the United Nations flag, tried to restore "order" in the Congo when a leftist government seemed to be emerging from the chaos created by recently acquired independence. On several other occasions, such as the crises in Jordan and the Dominican Republic, the United States Navy and Marines were sent to the vicinity to counter potential leapfrogging.

With the exception of the attempted invasion of Cuba, these rear-guard actions were successful in checking Communist gains; in the long run, however, they assist Communist leapfrogging. In the interbloc strife, the United States wishes to gain the voluntary support and cooperation of the people of the underdeveloped countries. The United States goes to great pains to abolish the imperialist image created by its association with colonial allies, its past gunboat diplomacy, and by Communist propaganda. Every time the United States (or the West) uses force to restore order in an area, especially to keep in power some right-wing, antidevelopment, oppressive elite, the action both reinforces its imperialistic image and alienates the large number of people who suffer under, and will eventually overthrow, those regimes. It leads the advocates of social, economic, and political development to seek aid in the West, which successfully represents itself as the anti-imperialistic, pro-development power.

While the Communist bloc has not yet taken over any of the countries in which the United States militarily interfered (directly or indirectly), ruling elites of these countries have not changed their antidevelopment oppressive rule. In most of these countries, the Communist movement makes headway locally, and sooner or later a new revolutionary attempt is sure to be made. Even now constant reports of social unrest, riots, and revolutionary attempts come from these countries. Revolution is reported to be brewing again in Guatemala; the Congo is moving left as these lines go to press; all is quiet at the moment in Lebanon, Jordan, and the Dominican Republic, but those familiar with the situation in these states would agree that this is the quiet before the storm. Military forces have often before delayed social changes, but rarely did they prevent the eventual outbreak of revolutions. The damage done to the United States and the West by these measures in countries other than those directly affected should also not be overlooked. The double standards uncommitted countries apply to the United States and to the Soviet Union on matters such as Hungary and Suez (in 1956) and resumption of testing (in 1961) are explained away in American newspapers as revealing the moral weakness of these countries and their succumbing to fear of Russian bombing. All this may be true, but this unsympathetic attitude to the United States also reflects the reaction of uncommitted countries to what they consider unjustified United States intervention, and to United States use of *military* force to counter Communist *ideological* expansion and *other* leftist revolutionary movements in the rearlands. The fact that the Communists use force to hold their bloc together does not whitewash the use of such force by the West, in the eyes of these nations.

## THE BASES OF LEAPFROGGING

Communist leapfrogging benefits from two Western—in particular, American—mistakes that have often been pointed out but have yet to be remedied. First, Western support is given to status-quo governments that delay necessary social reforms until only a revolutionary outlet is possible, and the revolutionary forces, seeking international support and rejected by the West, necessarily turn to the East. Second, identification of every shift away from the West as equivalent to joining the Communist bloc helps the East to convert a mere pro-neutral shift into a gain for the East.

But even if these two mistakes are removed, as there is much reason to believe the Kennedy administration is attempting, some rather basic factors supporting Communist leapfrogging yet remain. The lack of take-off in the underdeveloped countries supported by the West while there is rapid industrialization in the East increases the appeal of Communism; the constant increase in power of the Communist bloc makes shifting away from the West or even joining the East seem a "wise" policy. In addition, the continued success of leapfrogging in itself, as the influence of *Fidelismo* on Latin America and Nasserism in Asia and Africa would indicate, has a bandwagon effect.

Losses to leapfrogging, we shall see below, actually weaken the Western military, economic, and political power much less than is often claimed. Leapfrogging, however, brings about three dangers. First, it makes a farce of the whole notion of holding the rim. What good does the rim do if, while it stands, the countries it "shields" leave the West and lean toward, if not join, the East? Second, as long as holding all the countries behind the rim serves as a measure of Western power and status, continuous loss to Communism—of another half dozen Cubas, say—cannot but generate highly dangerous frustration in the West. Finally, the focusing of resources in military development of rim countries greatly reduces the means available for economic development of rim and nonrim nations necessary to counter leapfrogging. Thus not only is the West losing by leapfrogging, but the present state of armed truce is also endangered and means are wasted that could aid in establishing the prerequisites of stable peace.

## Accelerating Development

Recognizing the limitations of using force to prevent the expansion of Communism into underdeveloped countries, the United States at present is engaged in a development strategy to eliminate the sociological bases of leapfrogging. The basic idea underlying this strategy is valid: only to the degree that the elementary needs and aspirations of the people of these countries are satisfied through industrialization, ignorance eliminated through mass education, and oppression is reduced by democratization will expansion of Communism be checked. The way development has been conducted so far, however, hardly brings about either economic or political progress, and hence does not fulfill its counter-leapfrogging functions. *For the Western development strategy to be effective, the gap between the means provided and those required must be greatly reduced, both to make for more development and to prevent the frustration of unmet expectations.*

Economists estimate that about $3 to $8 billion of foreign economic aid is needed per year for the next twenty years to bring the non-Communist underdeveloped countries to take-off. For reasons discussed above, I think that the sums needed are much larger. But whatever the sums required, they are not available, nor are those available effectively used. As a consequence, the non-Communist countries do not take off. Theoretically, the problem could be solved by increasing the funds appropriated to economic aid by the "have" countries. This is, by far, the most frequently advocated solution. While I fully agree that investment in development should be immediately increased, I cannot escape the conclusion that whatever increases—if any—are forthcoming, they will not come close to answering the need. The citizens of the "have" countries are strongly opposed to paying considerably higher taxes or allowing their national debts to increase to the degree needed to finance multicontinent development. There is little reason to believe that the Western democracies will take a cut in their standard of living large enough to raise significantly that of the underdeveloped countries. We must look for a new approach to development, not to substitute for an increased contribution to economic aid but to add to it.

Several changes in the development strategy that would multiply the effectiveness of the means available are suggested below. Some have already been partially and slowly introduced by the Kennedy administration; some—of much more radical nature—have yet to be tried. We begin with the less controversial and less radical ones. It is only after we realize that even those will not do that we will be willing to consider the needed drastic measures.

## MILITARY OR ECONOMIC AID?

In the past, American foreign aid appropriations gave priority to military aid and to economic support of rim lands that share the West's military effort to hold the line (for example, South Korea, South Vietnam). Only the remaining funds were directed to bona fide development. Obviously more aid, especially if additional funds are to be available, ought to be concentrated on building up an economic take-off base, since armies may hold the rim, but not—as we have seen—check Communism. The recent focus on the economic development of Latin America, Kennedy's Alliance for Progress, is certainly a desirable change from this viewpoint.

## PRIVATE OR STATE ENTERPRISE?

In the past, the selection of projects to which American aid was granted was influenced by American ideology, not simply by the needs of the developing countries. "Free enterprise" and "no state intervention" are still semi-holy institutions in the United States, despite the fact that in practice the nation has a large state welfare and social-security program, six regulatory commissions that "interfere" in many major aspects of the economy, and wide support among its manufacturers for "fair trade" (that is, state limitation on market competition). Moreover, few Americans know that their country, as well as every one that has ever industrialized, benefited heavily from state finance and enterprise in the first stage of industrialization.

In the underdeveloped countries many investments are urgently needed to create the conditions under which private enterprise can do its share of the development job. Schools, hospitals, and means of transportation and communication, for instance, must be established—all ventures that reap too little profit to attract private enterprise. Instead of blessing government expenditure that opens the road to private enterprise, the United States long refused to support any state enterprise. This rigid belief in private enterprise was another factor that reduced the effectiveness of the limited economic aid that the United States did grant. Some first cracks in this wall of ideological influence on what ought to be strictly economic considerations are seen in the Kennedy administration's support to the nationalized oil industry of Venezuela. Projects should in the future be judged in terms of their contribution to the evolving economies, not by American philosophies.

## ADMINISTRATIVE IMPROVEMENTS

Part of the limited economic aid given is wasted through poor administration, inadequate planning, corruption, and so on. (A House investigating team recently found that 25 per cent of emergency food shipments to Peru, under a $14 million famine relief program, never even reached the drought area; and that not all the food that did arrive was distributed to the needy.) Much of this lies so deep in the social structure of the receiving countries that there is little hope of reducing waste significantly, but this is not to imply that it cannot be cut at all. Bakeries need not be built in rice-eating countries, nor need villages be constructed in valleys about to be used for rainwater storage. Some improvements can be made effective without social change in the aid-receiving countries, but rather by changes in the granting agencies. The accumulation of failures and the ill reputation of the present American aid-administering departments would suggest, drawing on administrative research, that establishing a completely new development agency might be preferable to trying to improve the existing ones.

## NEW SOURCES OF FUNDS

Increase in development funds from private sources might be achieved through government encouragement. The American tradition of *voluntary giving* has hardly been tapped for this purpose. Issuing development bonds, or stamps, or buttons, as part of a campaign of a voluntary development association could help not only to gain more funds but also to educate citizens to the importance of development. To come to know underdeveloped countries and to help them in whatever way possible, from technical assistance to short-term loans in an emergency through funds voluntarily collected, every one of the fifty American states might adopt one underdeveloped country (according to its size, Texas-Brazil, Rhode Island-Ceylon), and each American town might aid a village or town in the underdeveloped country with which its state has formed "sister" relations; thus Austin would be the sister-city of Brasilia; Providence, of Colombo, etc.

Second, the West might establish under the United Nations or some other international agency an insurance fund that would compensate investors in underdeveloped countries in case of nationalization. The fund would be financed by a small levy on the dividends of the corporations investing in underdeveloped countries (which often return high profits to their Western investors) and by contributions of the development governments. Such insurance might, through the lever of small sums, insure large investments of private firms. It would also deprive nationalization of much of its emotional nature. Nationalization would no longer serve as an anti-American, anti-French, or anti-Belgian act, because the loss would be that of the international insurance fund, not of any particular country. This might influence underdeveloped countries not to nationalize as a demonstration of anti-Western feeling, but only when they are able to handle these industries.[1] Such an insurance fund would also modify the reaction of Western business groups to nationalization of their investments, a reaction that sometimes seems to have a distorting effect on the foreign policy of their countries.

Finally, aid should not be made in grants. Development funds should be given as loans with little or no interest, for a set period, at least until take-off has taken place. All repaid loans should be directed toward the development of other countries, first of all toward the other members of the supranational community of the repaying nations. This will provide the newly

[1] See Gunnar Myrdal, *An International Economy* (New York, Harper & Brothers, 1956), pp. 123–125.

developed country with additional motives for reaching the stage at which it can graduate from aid and turn from receiver to grantor (as Israel, with great pride, became in Africa). It will also supply, in the long run, an ever-increasing flow of development funds when repaid loans are added to the "have" countries' continued contributions.

## DEVELOPMENT SCIENCE

Major scientific breakthroughs, especially the combination of two or more of these, could change the whole desperate development picture; it could make industrialization much less expensive and less demanding in terms of social changes required in the modernizing societies.

Natural scientists expect that in about twenty years they will be able to command the release of nuclear energy so that we will have a *cheap source of energy,* based on a raw material found in abundance. This breakthrough would be the equivalent of supplying all underdeveloped countries with rich coal mines or large hydraulic plans. Could we bring this breakthrough ten years closer, development would receive a major boost. Moreover, cheap electricity would permit maintaining machines in small villages, thus greatly reducing the time and social cost of industrialization.

We are on the verge of finding a way to turn the *salt water of the oceans into fresh water* for irrigation at a low price; ultrasonic energy might allow desalting at less than $.20 per 1000 gallons, as opposed to the present cost of $.50 to $1.10. An even larger reduction of the price of water could turn deserts into blooming gardens, triple the harvest of many areas, and save enormous crops in periods of drought. The need for land reforms would decline if abundance of water could be combined with pumps run by cheap nuclear energy; deserts would be opened to the landless peasants without removing any landlords.

Finding a safe, effective, and cheap *oral contraceptive,* which science is on the verge of doing, and asking anthropologists, sociologists, psychologists, and theologians to search for a way to make it acceptable to those who object to its use, could shorten considerably the road to development.

Another major task for social scientists is to study such areas as work habits and managerial practices, to see if learning and change of patterns can be *accelerated*. Without some major new insights here, economic development may well founder on the rock of social traditionalism.

One could easily extend the list, but the very nature of science is that it is unpredictable; thus, while searching for ways to produce cheap calories, it might come up with an inexpensive fertilizer that can double a crop. Hence what is needed urgently is not a list of specific problems science ought to be able to solve but a vast increase in the means granted to development research; once these are provided, science will do the rest.

At present, when research funds and scientific talent are parceled out, development is a poor relation compared to the rich uncles of basic and military science, civilian space exploration, and private industry's applied research on consumer goods. Following the practices of private corporations, the new Development Agency ought to appropriate 5 to 10 per cent of its budget for research on problems related to development. An enormous army of the highest-paid researchers work for American private industry, spending their efforts on making cocktails salable in plastic bags, designing machines that open tin cans automatically, and making compact cars look big. Public interest in the progress of development science—evident in newspaper reporting, Congressional Medals, and other forms of community recognition—in addition to increased salaries and funds available for development research, might bring about a shift of scientists from consumption to development research, similar to the one created in favor of space research.

But the problem is too large to be solved by these methods alone. Western contribution to development funds might be at best doubled in the next ten years, a period in which a tenfold increase might well be the minimum needed; the military establishments in the rim countries are unlikely to lose their appropriations in favor of economic development, even if some funds are reallocated. More rational, less ideological appropriation of funds and more efficient administration might increase the effectiveness of the given funds by 10 to 20 per cent but would not close the gap between the given and the needed.

A large immediate spurt in development research might pay off dramatically in roughly ten years, the period it probably would take to make major breakthroughs and learn to exploit them. What is therefore needed for the immediate future is some radical change in the whole development strategy.

## Focused Development

The strategy I propose would remove a number of difficulties that plague the West's present strategy. It would bring the West's aid commitments into balance with the resources available, eliminate the exposed rearland, and substitute for the present rigid, untenable rim a dynamic frontier. The strategy suggested involves certain limited risks, to be spelled out below; it might well force the West to take some losses in the short run in order to maximize the long-run gains. Surely the West would prefer not to take any losses, but this is not given; the choice is between keeping up the present streak of small setbacks, not leading to any improvement in posture, and a new approach that cuts losses once and for all, in a meaningful pattern, to establish a winning posture.

The new strategy requires *focusing of development* (to be discussed in the remainder of this chapter) and a *new political orientation* (the subject of the subsequent chapter). The relationship among focused development, political reorientation, and arms reduction is raised last. It should be pointed out here that while the new strategy would operate most effectively under arms reductions, it is still the best available for the West if arms reduction is not agreed upon. The strategy is first presented under the most adverse conditions, assuming no arms reduction.

### MATCHING COMMITMENTS AND MEANS

The West, in particular the United States, has made so many explicit and implicit commitments in fifty-odd countries on three continents that the aid it can give is spread dangerously thin. Development commitments alone cover much of Asia, Africa, and Latin America (as well as some European countries and Micronesia in the Western Pacific). The means available, even if the present economic-aid budgets are to be doubled and their effectiveness increased, do not come even close to backing all these commitments. The American promise of development followed by a frustrated take-off softens the ground for Communist take-over. Thus the first principle ought to be the *adjustment of all Western commitments to the level of resources available* (after these have been increased and their use made more effective). Such a reduction of commitment would obviously lose all its effect if the commitments to each country were reduced in the same degree, since no country would ever reach take-off if its now inadequate aid would be further cut. Commitments and resources must be *focused* on a limited number of countries at a time.

## THE NEIGHBORS-FIRST CRITERION

While the West has a general moral obligation to share its wealth with the less fortunate people of the world, this does not mean that it can undertake to better the welfare of all peoples, everywhere, at once. The means for this, we have seen, are simply not available. It should also be frankly admitted that the United States has different degrees of moral and political commitments to various countries, stemming from historical and cultural ties as well as the United States various legitimate interests, including safeguarding the rear of the rim from leapfrogging. On these counts the United States deepest obligations are to its close neighbors. Ever since the Monroe Doctrine, the United States has taken upon itself the responsibility for the well-being of the Western hemisphere; its citizens have more investment in this continent than in any other; and Communist take-over in the Caribbean, Central or South America would threaten United States security more directly than would comparable events in Africa or Asia. Thus, under the new strategy, economic aid would be focused on these countries. To the extent that resources will be sufficient for aiding more countries, African countries will be next on the list, the Middle East follows, then Central Asia, and finally, Southeast Asia. (We will discuss below why India might prove to be an exception.) The underlying principle is first to cover the rearlands closer to the United States, then to re-extend the development frontier from neighbors to neighbors' neighbors and to more remote countries. Priority lists for countries in each region have to be worked out, also taking this criterion into account.

The other Western powers would have different priorities, according to their locations, interests, and historic ties. Quite possibly, France and West Germany will put some African countries at the top of their lists; England might be more concerned with the Middle East and some other African countries; and Japan, New Zealand, and Australia might devote their attention to the Far East. All Western countries are expected to help *their* neighbors and traditional allies.

The United States list of priorities has one major advantage: it gives higher priority to a group of countries that are, on the average, closer to take-off and easier to develop. As we have seen, Latin America is abundant with natural resources and is least overpopulated; Africa seems second, and Asia third in these respects. This means that *the United States will be able with the funds available to bring a comparatively large number of countries to the take-off point* in a comparatively short period, and it will soon be able to re-extend its development commitments.

## A Dynamic Development Frontier

As the United States checks off the "aid" list those countries that have graduated to self-supporting economic growth, it would *re-extend its commitment to more remote countries and continents,* always guaranteeing that the countries within the development frontier have already passed take-off. Once the Western hemisphere is developed, the United States would probably help its allies to develop first Africa, then Asia. For some countries not included in the first development round, the knowledge that they are next in line will somewhat alleviate the strain of the no-aid period. Similarly effective will be the recognition that when help comes this time it will be adequate for take-off, will take them off the aid receivers' list forever. In general, though, the initial reaction to focusing of Western aid is likely to be negative by those countries not immediately included. But the United States is not running in a one-shot popularity contest; for its own good and for that of the underdeveloped countries, it may well have to take some steps that will prove to be temporarily rather unpopular. The test of the new development strategy will be in the more lasting reactions and effects.

## CONSEQUENCES OF FOCUSED DEVELOPMENT

To the degree that other Western nations do not fill in the gaps left by the United States, the focusing of development on particular continents and countries is likely to have some *short-run* effects similar to leapfrogging. Countries where Western aid now maintains a precarious antidevelopment tyranny, as in South Korea and South Vietnam, might undergo a left-wing or even Communist revolution; some countries in Asia and Africa, such as Cambodia and Indonesia, might shift their votes in the United Nations to the East; and some other countries might declare an alliance with the East in hope of increasing their share of aid from this source. Should the Communists respond by granting aid to all or most of these countries, they would soon face the danger that now traps the West, that of spreading their resources too thin, gaining neither development nor political appreciation of their effort. Moreover, most uncommitted nations would soon realize that it is to their interest to wait for the full-sized Western aid, which will carry them to self-sustained economic growth, rather than to receive the below-take-off aid that keeps them in perpetual need for more aid and hence in dependency. If, on the other hand, the East will also focus its development aid to uncommitted nations, being much less wealthy than the West, with less to give and more in need itself, it could hardly grant full-sized aid to more than a very few countries. Again, after a short while, most nations will realize that it is to their interest to wait for the re-extension of the Western development frontier, which is likely to come much sooner than that of the East, both because the West commands more resources and because it starts at the comparatively easiest end (Latin America), while the Communists work on the most difficult one (Asia). Moreover, it has to be emphasized that the more developed a country is, whoever developed it, the less open it is to Communism (if it has not been taken over), and the more likely it is to undermine Communism (if it has fallen for it).

The largest difference between the present limping development strategy and the new one advocated here is in their political-psychological effect on the West. Under the present strategy, losses to leapfrogging will continue until the whole Western position collapses, or until the fear of such collapse pushes the West into uncautious, even irresponsible, acts. Under the new strategy, losses will be cut once and for all, a new line will be drawn, a development frontier will be erected that from then on will move forward, not backward.

Nevertheless, focused development raises three questions that must be faced. Would not the United States security be threatened by even such temporary losses? Would the United States business interests jeopardized in these countries block the acceptance of the new development strategy? What about the United States moral commitments to the people of these countries?

*Military "Losses."* The loss to Communism of more of Asia or Africa is often pronounced fatal to American security. Many discussions of American strategy close with the dogmatic statement that this or that policy cannot be followed because it opens another country to Communism. It is precisely because of the rigid notion that the West must maintain every piece of the multicontinent periphery that United States foreign policy has lost so much of its flexibility and effectiveness. Moreover, the military value of all these territories is never demonstrated, it is simply asserted.

Just to underscore the point, let us consider for a moment what, *on strictly military grounds,* the United States would lose if—in the worst possible case—the Communists held two more continents by 1970. The East would have more bases from which to attack the United States and the latter would have fewer bases among which to spread its might. But even now the Communists have springboards over a third of the globe, in the seven seas, in air, and in space. And once "enough" bases are available, additional ones do not add much more than expense. Moreover, the addition of static land bases is of little value; they are the most exposed to nuclear bombing and are widely considered obsolete. (Actually, the United States plans to close several of its overseas bases in the next few years, and it will keep many of the remaining ones for nonmilitary reasons.) Modern military bases are nuclear submarines, airborne bombers, satellites, and mobile missile launchers that need not more than at the most one continent to move around in. In short, little security would be gained by the Soviet Union or lost by the United States if two continents were to go Red. The United States would still have the Western hemisphere, sea, air, and space in which to spread its striking force.

Many people, and it seems even many generals (who are often oriented to the last war, in which their old strategies were successful), seem to view the interbloc conflict as a World War I or II battle over territories, in which breaking into the enemy's country requires breaking his land-bound shell, his Maginot Line. Actually, territories today do not make much difference. Nuclear warfare will jump above land-bound defenses and continents as if they did not exist. In earlier wars keeping the enemy far away saved the United States from attack. The strategic perspective was that the further out a nation's outposts, the greater its security. From the United States point of view, World War I, World War II, and the Korean War were fought in other people's backyards, but in a nuclear war the United States is as shielded without these lands as with them. In fifteen minutes enemy bombs can cover the United States—unless the Russians launch their missiles from submarines, to bomb the United States within sixty seconds. Territories no longer offer protection. The United States could hold all the land from here to Moscow, and yet Khrushchev, sitting on his balcony, could shoot into every American window without so much as getting up.

Finally, the territory behind the defense lines is said to provide the economic basis for a country's might. This was of crucial importance in previous wars; the countries with the larger industrial potential eventually won, whatever their original setbacks. But the territories that might be temporarily "lost" under the new development strategy are not a source of economic might. These are underdeveloped countries and are economic liabilities, not assets. In the event of war, they will have to be supplied, and will not be able to serve as bases of industrial production. While these countries hold some raw materials, many materials needed by the United States are abundant in Latin America, and therefore development here would easily compensate for losses elsewhere. Many of these materials are in any case gradually being replaced by man-made products, such as synthetic rubber and electrical energy. Blockaded Germany showed how a country can go on for years, even under the most adverse conditions, without the "essential" raw materials. An even more crucial fact is that nuclear war, experts judge, will last from two to a maximum of thirty days. In such a short period, the economic potential of the fighting countries will be of little importance, while the military strength they command on the day bombs are first dropped will be crucial. Thus, even if one could eventually develop these countries, they would be of little economic-military value in a nuclear war. At most, they would serve as a distraction for a few of the enemy's megaton bombs.

*Business Interests.* It is often suggested, especially by radical writers, that the United States will not reduce its commitments in foreign countries because of billion-dollar investments of American oil companies, fruit concerns, and other business groups. American history offers well-documented incidents in which first the State Department and then the Marines have protected the interests of American corporations in one Latin American republic or another. A radical weekly suggested that the United States invasion of Cuba came only after Castro nationalized the American-owned sugar industry.

Actually, such statements are largely exaggerated. Although in the late nineteenth and early twentieth centuries the United States supported its companies rather aggressively, since the introduction of the Good Neighbor Policy in the 1930s the United States has rarely interfered when other nations have nationalized its citizens' property. The United States Marines did not step in when the Standard Oil Company holdings were expropriated in Bolivia in 1936 and those of other oil companies in Mexico in 1938. While it is true that Castro nationalized the relatively small American investments in Cuba, he committed many other acts that infuriated the American government before an invasion was attempted, and there is no evidence whatsoever that the nationalization of the sugar or refinery industries caused the invasion. It is true that American business interests affect United States foreign policy and might well wield more power than do other interest groups. Nevertheless, other groups do influence policy making and can push through a policy business does not support. Nor is the national interest ignored by business itself. After all, a nuclear war will not distinguish between shareholders and wage earners.

Moreover, sooner or later those business groups that do influence the American government to maintain commitments on far continents will realize, unless they lose the ability to do bookkeeping, that it is exactly this multicontinent commitment that endangers all their investments as well as the very survival of their businesses and their lives. They must choose between sacrificing some foreign investment in order to keep the rest and endangering all they have abroad and at home. The fact that the largest American investments are in Latin America and that England and Western Europe are likely to support focused development in the Middle East, the second American investment center, should keep the losses due to focused development fairly small. In addition, the compensation for investment loss by an international agency should further reduce the resistance of business groups to the new development strategy.

*Moral Commitments.* Public opinion is another source of American pursuit of a rigid and antiquated strategy. The public has been led to believe that every piece of land behind the rim in part of the "free world" and thus, as a matter of principle, must be defended. Whether or not these areas have military value, are defendable, or strategically important, Americans insist that the Communists must be prevented from taking them to prevent these people from being enslaved. Otherwise, the integrity and moral foundations of the Free World are undermined; otherwise we are soft, spineless, Munich-type appeasers.

Undoubtedly, the West, and the United States as its leader, has the historical mission to protect political freedom, to bring it to all who lack it, and to help all people reach a decent standard of living, both as a value in itself and to provide the social foundation of democracy. But under the *present* strategy, the United States does not carry out these moral obligations. In order to protect the free world from Communism, it holds the rim and controls the rearlands; in turn, to achieve these goals, it supports nondemocratic and antidevelopment governments in many countries. Actually, there are more dictatorships in the "free world" than there are in the Communist bloc. The Communists hold twelve totalitarian countries. Directly supported

241

by the West are at least the following tyrannies, authoritarian oligarchies, and military dictatorships: Yemen, Saudi Arabia, Iran, Haiti, the Dominican Republic, Spain, Portugal, Turkey, South Korea, South Vietnam, Taiwan, Pakistan, Paraguay, Nicaragua, and Honduras. Many other countries are semi-democracies at best. If the number of people under the Communist dictatorship amounts to about a third of the earth's population, the number in the "free world" nondemocracies is not much smaller.

The claim that these people are better off than they would be under Communism has little moral validity. A dictatorship—red, blue, or green—is a dictatorship. If it is ethically wrong to hang people without trial, it does not matter if it is done by Khrushchev or by United States allies Franco, Salazar, or Park (the recent military dictator of South Korea). If it is morally repulsive to torture people, it does not matter if it is done in Hungary or Haiti. Dictatorships of both left and right violate our conception of freedom. Moreover, while left-wing dictatorships develop the economies—often at a high human price—the right-wing dictatorships, as a rule, do not develop their countries, though they often charge a similar human price.

It is crucial to realize that the United States is involved indirectly in keeping many of these no-freedoms no-development regimes in office. Even according to *Time* magazine, hardly suspected of left-wing bias, Haiti dictator Francois Duvalier would topple overnight if United States economic aid to his government were stopped. United States help to Chiang Kai-shek shields him not only from a Communist attack but also from opposing Taiwanese politicians, who would probably win if elections on the island were freely conducted. (A Taiwanese government is believed to be less inclined to keep a return to China's mainland as Taiwan's principal ambition.) In the Shah autocracy of Iran, in the military dictatorship of General Cemel Gursel of Turkey, and in the military autocracy of Field Marshall Mohammed Ayub Khan in Pakistan, United States experts on "subversion"—members of a CENTO commission—help local security forces control not only the Communists but also other left-wing and even liberal groups. The United States kept Ngo Dinh Diem in control of South Vietnam not only against the Communist and the pro-French Binh Xuyen, but also against a rebellion of his own army. United States tolerance of Castro was rapidly exhausted, but not that of archtyrants Batista or Trujillo. Few Americans remember now that the United States military mission in Cuba trained Batista soldiers and gave arms to those who were fighting Castro *before* Castro turned against the United States. Peruvian dictator Odria was awarded the Order of Merit by the United States. The citation accompanying the Order included a line praising Odria for his "fight against the Communists and other subversive elements." This phrase, "other subversive elements," was widely interpreted in Peru to mean the Aprista party, the majority political organization in the country, until recently the only organized democratic party in Peru, and a party with a thirty-five-year history of fighting the Communists on their own ground, among the workers, the peasants, and the intellectuals.[2] The argument that blocking Communism is of such great importance that it justifies compromising other values, that the goal justifies the means, is a strictly Communist argument. The essence of the Western tradition is that unless the means too are legitimate, they vilify the goal.

Nor is blocking Communism in this way the wisest policy politically. Certainly these regimes temporarily keep their countries in the Western camp, but by delaying partial and gradual reforms until they are long overdue by blocking development, and by depriving the people of the freedoms we advocate, the United States is employing the most effective way to prepare a country for Communist take-over. Batista is the example closest to home. For years he was the friend of the United States and was supported by it, while he stuffed his jails with socialists and liberals, not just Communists. Farouk of Egypt, Nuri Said of Iraq, and Chiang Kai-shek of China all fall in the same category. Support of right-wing dictatorships that oppose change and stifle left-wing opposition barters the future of the West in return for short-run, temporary security. It is both morally wrong and politically inept.

Focused development, on the other hand, guarantees that we will honestly discharge one of our first duties: raise the standard of living of some of these people, both to provide for

[2] Charles O. Porter and Robert J. Alexander, *The Struggle for Democracy in Latin America* (New York, The Macmillan Company, 1961), p. 192.

their most elementary material needs and to supply the social foundation for stable democracy. In the countries to be developed by Communist aid, while the people will continue to be deprived of political freedoms, development will occur, preparing the ground for abolition of Communism and democratization. But, one must ask, how can we be sure that once these countries are developed, in the East or by it, they will be free to realign themselves with the West, to gain the essential political freedoms? The answer to this question lies in the synchronization of focused development with arms reduction, discussed below (see pp. 254–256).

In sum, no real military loss is involved in applying the new development strategy; the losses to American capital would be smaller than under other strategies, and various arrangements might well limit and soften those losses that do occur; furthermore, on moral grounds this strategy is certainly superior to the present one. Thus, whatever virtue the rim-holding policy might have had fifteen years ago, under the present international circumstances it ought to be abandoned immediately, in one big sweep—not simply piece by piece, for this would really smack of Munich.

To satisfy the West's strategic needs for countering Communist leapfrogging and the strategic needs of peace, we need in addition to an increase in development means and pace, in addition to the new development strategy, a political reorientation. The new political strategy will both assist the evolution of the political framework that economic development requires and hasten the evolution of democratization. Thus it will forward social justice and political freedom, which must be within the reach of people of all countries before stable peace can be safely established.

# Chapter 11

## A Political Breakthrough

AMERICAN political strategy in its orientation to political relations in and among other countries has been geared until recently more to immediate or short-run checking of Communism than to the long-run aspects of this challenge. Countering Communism has been understood as requiring four principles, all of which paid off on the short run but steadily worsened the long run prospects: supporting local power elites that are "safely" anti-Communist, even if it meant blocking both economic and political development; supporting major allies even if this meant toleration of their continued colonial policies; making membership in military alliances rather than in nation-unions the basis on which to judge regional coalitions; and holding rigidly to the military rim around the 1947 line. While maintaining this political perspective, the West seemed to be barely holding its position but was actually living on borrowed time. But time is almost up, as we are about to witness, chiefly through accelerated Communist gains through leapfrogging, unless a new strategy is implemented.

It is necessary to devise a short-run political policy that will support rather than undermine the long-run needs of the West and of the world; its implementation requires the quality of leadership rather than of mere political skill—the leadership of the West must have courage to take some short-run losses if these are required to maximize long-run gains.

This political reorientation will have to take into account four sets of relationships: those among various political forces in each country, those between the imperial powers and their colonies, those among nations in the same region, and those between the two major blocs. Although some reorientation concerning the first two sets of relations is already taking place, little or none has touched on the other two. It is crucial therefore to point out that unless all four are reconsidered, and in more than a limited, half-hearted way, the new political strategy will be at best partially effective and will lose much of the dramatic impact of a sharp, all-encompassing reorientation. The international political struggle, it must be emphasized, is to some extent a struggle over public opinion, which bows to sweeping, imaginative changes but is grossly unimpressed by piecemeal adjustments.

## For Political Development

The new political strategy's first principle concerning rival powers within the various countries will be to support democratization in the West, in developing countries, and in the East.

Although the strategy will recognize that tyrannies, of the right or the left, cannot overnight become towers of democracy, steady evolution will be urged. Immediate abolition of terrorist practices and police brutalities should be expected as a minimum entrance card into the community of nations, and further democratization will be encouraged by all but violent means, as progress in the economic sphere will both allow and support it.

Extent of democratization attained ought to be *one* of the criteria determining the West's general attitude toward a country, including the dispensing of economic aid. Military force should never be used to impose a political regime on a country, because it is both morally objectionable and sociologically impractical, but full expression of the West's approval or disapproval ought to be given through symbolic and economic means. Thus, while the United States should recognize and maintain diplomatic relations with *all* nations, it must make a clear distinction between warm relations and cool ones. No tyrants, for instance, should be invited to visit the United States, especially not to come to the White House or to address Congress. The warm reception in Washington of Pedro Estrada, head of the terrorist police of Perez Jimenez, Venezuelan dictator, is a good example of the kind of gesture that should be avoided. No American representative should pay any visit to countries governed by tyranny. If the United States has to grant any sign of recognition to a dictator, it should certainly not be the Order of Merit, awarded to dictators Manual Odria of Peru and Perez Jimenez of Venezuela in 1954. Personal friendships, as existed between Batista and the American ambassador to

Cuba, should be strictly taboo. The United States approval of progress in democratization could be expressed by the same means.

With regard to economic sanctions, the principal criterion that determines the selection of development regions must be a neighbor-first policy; degree of democratization, however, should serve as the criterion for selecting nations within each development region to determine in which order their industrialization will be supported (to the degree that resources available will not suffice to develop a whole region simultaneously). A country consistently refusing to democratize might even be left undeveloped, when the development frontier extends to more remote countries, as long as the surrounding region is safely developed.

It might be to the interest of the West, and in line with its basic values, if other "exceptions" were made as a way of emphasizing the significance of democratization. Granting support to a country far from the developing area because it is highly democratic or actively democratizing would stress the importance the West attaches to this form of government. India is a natural candidate for such an "exception." Making a few exceptions is by no means the same as continuing the present policy; granting some aids to a country that will not increase the security of the Western bloc in the near future is not the same as wasting most or all development funds by spreading them over scores of countries.

The United States should not have any qualms about making democratization, and for that matter other development endeavors, a condition for its moral approval and economic support; this is far from the often denounced "intervention" in the internal affairs of another country. The "no-intervention" concept applies to one nation using violence against another, making it subservient to foreign interests, or forcing aid rather than granting it. Political and economic development, under the new strategy, would be backed only by nonviolent means oriented to the benefit of the country supported, and aid would be granted only if the country in question desires it. But if aid is desired, the whole package must be accepted; a nation should not be allowed to take the candy while refusing the medicine.

Communist countries should not be excluded from the moral

demand to democratize, and the West should express its approval of changes toward less totalitarian practices and of comparatively less totalitarian Communist countries (for example, Poland as compared to Czechoslovakia). In the first stages of the new development strategy, the expression of such approval would probably be chiefly in symbolic and not economic terms; in later stages—as more means are available for more remote countries and especially if the military interbloc barrier will be removed by arms reduction to allow free association of countries—economic aid could be extended to Communist countries. It is essential to remember that not only does development check the expansion of Communism into non-Communist countries but it also undermines Communism where it is already established.

The complete withdrawal of Western support for elites opposing development and democratization is necessary for bloc interests as well as world interests. In countries where overdue social changes are blocked by right-wing tyrannical elites, the support of left-wing, non-Communist forces is the best political strategy for the West for two reasons. First, the right-wing groups are frequently the antidevelopment elites (or supporters of limited reforms, such as cleaning the streets and making trains run on schedule, which please many tourists but have little relevance to the more basic needs of abolishing corruption, spreading mass education, and introducing land reform). Second, Social Democrats and other non-Communist forces of change are most likely to take the wind out of the Communist sails and still loyally support democracy and the West. Confusing Communists with Social Democrats reveals a fantastic political ignorance; supporting right-wing groups over Social Democrats reveals lack of political insight and foresight.

Withdrawing support from right-wing elites might often require support of revolutionary forces, since the traditional oligarchies are unlikely to give way by other methods. Such support has been withheld in the past because of the fear that supporting revolutionary forces means enhancing Communism. Moreover, right-wing dictators have learned from extremists in the United States to call all their opponents, especially all liberal and left-wing ones, Communists. But this is too transparent a trick to fool any nation. To put it in a nutshell, right-wing power elites that do not develop or democratize are moral and political liabilities; they undermine the West's claim to represent freedom and justice, and they are the surest way to introduce Communism into any country. Liberal, even left-wing, non-Communist forces are the best guarantee for economic and political development and hence for Western values and, in the long run, a pro-Western orientation of developing countries.

The time is short; the job to be done is large. All forces that encourage modernization work for the West, and for peace, even if this is not evident in the short run; all those who block modernization, at least in the long run, work against both.

## The End of Colonialism

The success of leapfrogging and that of efforts to block it are directly affected by the interbloc strife of ideas and ideologies. The nonmilitary expansion of Communism largely benefits from its ideological potency. Here lies one of the gravest shortcomings of the West.

Americans who travel abroad for the first time are often extremely surprised at how "misunderstood" their country is. They cannot understand how any people can *prefer* the Communist viewpoint. The fact that this occurs, and that more and more people in uncommitted nations are attracted by Communism, is often ignored or explained away. Since Communism is defined as immoral, its danger as an ideological force, as an instrument of leapfrogging, is underestimated. Communist successes are frequently accounted for as brought about by an "armed minority," "supported by outside military force," subordinating an unwilling and ignorant majority.

This might be true in some instances, such as Communist occupation of East Germany, but in the majority of underdeveloped countries, the Communists have many voluntary sympathizers and their take-over, when it occurs, has a wide popular base. Anti-Western and pro-Communist feelings are a major source of the success of Communist leapfrogging. These feelings, in part due to the people's lack of education and in part an expression of their pressing needs, are evidence of their willingness to forego freedoms they have never had in order to gain more rapid improvement in their standard of living. Their reaction can partially be explained by the greater effectiveness of Communist development methods and their economic aid, frequently invested in highly visible projects, such as steel mills and dams, granted without any open political strings attached (for example, no demands are made to join Communist military alliances; India, for instance, is a recipient of Soviet aid). *But no less important is the failure of the West, and especially the United States, to make its ideological case. The West still has the imperialist image.* Moreover, it is true and not merely an "image" or a Communist invention that England, France, Belgium, and the Netherlands, all respected United States allies, oppressed for centuries—and in some instances still oppress—the very countries whose alliance the West is now seeking. Western countries exploited the colonies' natural resources, retarded their industrialization, and resisted their fight for independence. Many of the premiers of these countries were in Western, not Communist, exile and jails, from Cyprus's Archbishop Makarios to India's Nehru, from Tunis' Bourguiba to Kenya's Kenyata. It is true that they might have fared less well under Communism, but these countries did not experience Stalin's rule and did undergo that of Western colonial powers.

By now the empires have crumbled and most of the colonies have become the independent, much courted, nations of today, although some powers still hold fast to "left-overs" in yesterday's colonies. Yet instead of treating these few "left-overs" in a way that would allow the ex-colonies to forget the West's past, every month or so some Western power does something to remind all these newly independent nations of their former imperial oppression. Thus, in 1961 alone, the Dutch just about fought Indonesia over the remaining part of their colony, West New Guinea (sending their aircraft carrier for a "visit" in the area); Portugal savagely suppressed an uprising in Angola; the French acted in the worst gunboat tradition toward their most loyal ally, Tunisia; and Belgium played a major role in the secession of the rich province of Katanga from their ex-colony, the Congo, and helped to fight its legitimate government. Britain continued to force an unwanted, white-dominated "federation" on the Africans of Nyasaland and Northern Rhodesia. The United States criticized Portugal on Angola, did not support the Netherlands on New Guinea, and tactfully kept out of the French-Tunisia conflict. But much of the credit these reactions tended to build in the eyes of neutral and uncommitted countries was lost when the United States reminds them of its Marine-supported foreign policy and CIA interventions with the attempted invasion of Cuba. The United States holds no colonies but has one rather small (population 76,000) United Nations trusteeship—the modern equivalent of colonial title—in Micronesia. Instead of making this set of islands, in the Western Pacific, a show case of Western development (which would not even have cost much), the United States not only used the area for nuclear tests (at Eniwetok and Bikini) but also neglected the administration of the area. In 1961 a four-nation (Bolivia, Belgium, Britain, India) committee, appointed by the United Nations, charged the United States with the traditional imperialistic charges: not developing the country, keeping its industrialization on the pre-World War II level, not placing Micronesians in top administrative positions, and neglecting to encourage evolution of self-government and independence on the islands.

The new development and political strategy would provide an opportunity for the West to write "finis" on the book of colonial history and, following Roosevelt's successful declaration of the Good Neighbor policy for Latin America, declare that colonialism has ended once and for all. All colonies the West holds—there are only a few left—should be declared independent at the same time (the United Nations could provide whatever experts are needed to avoid chaos due to the sudden withdrawal of the West). Such an act would involve some losses, but these are nothing compared to what the colonies have cost and will cost the West by sustaining its imperialist image. Once colonialism is abolished, the West can point to its clean slate.

In the past, the losses such a policy would inflict might have seemed too great for it to be advocated, and the resistance of some groups in the United States too powerful. It seems now, since the remaining colonies are so few and small, that it could hardly be worth the damage that holding on to them inflicts. (Actually, the losses might be smaller than expected. The British have proven in India and Burma that voluntary withdrawal leaves behind many more economic and political ties than does forced departure.) All that most imperial governments may need now is the support and pressure of a collective Western decision to bury colonialism to overcome the resistance of those at home who find it hard to accept the inevitable.

## For Nation-Unions

The importance of supranationalism in preserving the present armed truce and in facilitating the long-run formation of world government has been pointed out above. These reasons alone should compel the West to support all nation-unions, East, West, and neutral, but still other reasons exist.

The West, we have seen, has much interest in accelerating development; thus, it benefits greatly from the formation of common markets. Democratization is also advanced by nation-unions to the degree that it makes member nations more sensitive to the public opinion and moral approval of other democratic or democratizing members. Peace benefits from the prevalence of the moderates in most nation-unions.

While in general nation-unions ought thus to be encouraged and even advanced by the United States, it does not follow that the more nations included in each single union, the better it is for the nations concerned or for the West. In order for unification to extend to the deeper levels of society, beyond customs unions and military sectors, especially for political integration to take place, it is necessary to let small groups of nations consolidate their communities before additional members are introduced.

The evolution of nation-unions under Western leadership would be a powerful force preventing one or another country from shifting to the East, though forming and joining neutral blocs might be equally effective as far as the West is concerned, and even more desirable from the viewpoint of a world government. The main concern, however, ought not to be with the initial bloc affiliation of a nation or nation-community, but with its freedom to change sides, to keep the international "floating vote" floating. This is closely related to the question of removing the military rim.

## Removing the Military Barriers

In the past, the West used military forces to (1) restore the previous government in a country that has undergone a left-wing revolution (as in Guatemala); (2) protect rim-countries from outright attacks by Communist-bloc countries (as in South Korea); (3) prevent the Communist bloc from giving military support to indigenous Communist forces attempting to complete a revolution (as in Greece); (4) prevent the Red Army from advancing into countries that experienced an anti-Western revolution, making them captive members of the Communist bloc (as in Iran); and (5) maintain bases in rimlands (Turkey, for instance) and rearlands (Morocco, for instance) in order to deter Soviet attacks by protecting the heartland and holding the club of retaliation. Some of these functions of Western military forces are becoming obsolete, some are politically unsound, and some are nevertheless unavoidable, it seems, unless arms reduction is advanced.

*Holding bases* in countries around Russia to keep a potential war away from the United States, to be in striking distance of Russia, and to protect United States forces through dispersion were all once military necessities. But with the production of long-range bombers and missiles and with the positioning of Polaris submarines and mobile missile launchers, these land bases are rapidly losing their military values and becoming an economic and propaganda liability. Whether or not there is arms reduction, their gradual abolition is probably in the best interest of the United States. (Of course, such closing of bases could be effectively used for the tension-reduction phase of Gradualism and as one of the first steps of arms reduction.)

Using military power to *prevent what are strictly internal revolutions,* in rimlands and especially in rearlands is a poor strategy on many grounds. As we have seen, it is morally invalid; it enforces some of the most tyrannical regimes on earth without keeping Communists out. Also it is politically unwise; it furthers Communist take-over by strengthening the imperialist image of the West and by delaying political and economic change. Finally, it is unnecessary, since supporting the non-Communist revolutionary forces can bring about both modernization and confidence in the West.

This leaves the military functions of *protecting the rimlands and rearlands* from an outright Communist military invasion, from Communist support of a revolution initiated from within, and from the stationing of the Red Army in a country that has

253

completed an anti-West revolution on its own. On strictly military grounds, as we have seen, no solid argument can be made to justify countering even this type of Communist expansion. In cases in which the Communists use military forces to advance their expansion against the wish of the people of the countries occupied, or bar their free choice of blocs, the West is morally called upon to maintain its rim. This single justification for the rim-holding strategy would disappear with arms reduction, an integral part of the Gradualist strategy.

## Arms Reduction and Interbloc Shuttling

The elimination of international violence requires the foundation of a world government, which in turn will be delayed until the global income and political rights are more evenly distributed within and among countries. If the West commanded sufficient means and power to develop and democratize all countries, there would be neither an objective need for interbloc shifting of countries and hardly a subjective desire to do so. But since scarcity of means imposes sharp limitations on the number of countries the West is able to develop, modernization of the rest will have to be in part based on "shuttling" of countries, in terms both of their internal political structure and of the international bloc affiliation.

In the first stage of development many countries will experience a left-wing, some even a Communist, revolution, to remove the barriers to development. Some of these countries, especially those geographically close to the Communist bloc, which will not be included in the first or the second round of Western focused development, and which might attain Soviet economic aid, are likely initially to reorient their foreign policy toward the East. Both processes look like setbacks to the West but are not *as long as the freedom of interbloc association is maintained* because then, as industrialization progresses, the people of the countries that first turn left will put an ever-increasing pressure on their governments, to add political freedoms to their newly gained improved standard of living. Countries that initially shifted Eastward will seek to realign themselves with the West, especially to the degree that the steps advocated above will make it clear to them that the West really supports political freedoms (not oppressive elites), economic modernization (not antidevelopment groups), national independence (not imperial powers), and freedom in interbloc affiliation (so that commitment to the West would not be irrevocable). The long-run trend of history favors the West, if the international situation does not become frozen so that the short-run gains of the East become permanent ones. The East should have to continue to compete with the West, once the latter's major advantage looms large, once the demand for political freedoms command the center of the scene, as industrialization does now. The freedom of interbloc affiliation will insure that countries can turn back to the West. This freedom, in turn, can be guaranteed in the same way the more immediate problem of the arms race can be overcome, through arms reduction. Only conventional disarmament will eliminate the means by which blocs can hold nations in their camp despite their wish and force on them governments the people do not desire.

Arms reduction provides the essential guarantee for free interbloc shuttling. A declaration of the freedoms of countries to realign themselves should be part of the arms reduction pact. The right of each nation to move in and out of blocs, to remain neutral, or to unite to create a new bloc, should be most explicitly recognized. With conventional disarmament, both the Western rim and the Communist parallel military barrier will be resolved. The removal of interbloc barriers will take the form of closing Soviet and United States bases abroad; returning home of all armies to their countries, including that of the Red Army to Russia; and complete conventional, later nuclear, disarmament.

With the abolition of conventional arms, all legitimate reasons for holding the Western rim will disappear. There will no longer be an exportable Communist army that could help internal revolutions (which in themselves should be tolerated), invade countries, or nail nations to the Communist bloc. Countries that move Eastward will be free to move back again. If the Communists are willing to change the interbloc rivalry to one of ideas and economic development, we should certainly be willing. If we lose in these competitions, we hardly deserve to win. Moreover, the West has no right to impose its way of life on other countries; if in a disarmed world they freely choose to become or remain Communists, Buddhists, or sun worshippers, as long as no force is used to keep them so, it is none of our business.

It may be suggested that the Communist bloc will never agree to such a raising of the military "curtain," because all the Eastern European countries would join the West. But why not offer the Soviet Union our plan and see? If they accept it, the Eastern European countries will get their first chance to break away. If the Soviet Union does not accept it, the Communist bloc will be put into the position of rejecting a disarmament proposal, a role in the past often forced on the West.

Actually, I see many reasons why the Communists should and would accept the removal of the interbloc military barriers. First, not all the "satellite" countries will leave the Communist bloc, for in many of them Communism is rather well-rooted. Second, the Communists ought to be willing to risk losing some countries (probably not more than three) for a chance to increase their influence on three continents. Third, in a disarming world, military blocs are meaningless and alliances will be only political and ideological. There is no reason to believe that the countries that have been in the Communist bloc for a long period, unlike recent joiners, will necessarily abolish Communism as their internal structure. Certainly Yugoslavia did nothing of the kind after breaking away from the Soviet bloc; most anti-Stalinist and anti-Russian leaders in Poland intend to maintain a Communist form of economy and society if and when they break away. What is much more important than our assessment of these historical processes is the fact that the Communists certainly believe they will do best in a disarmed world.

## Interbloc Shuttling and Focused Development

The development strategy, military strategy, and political strategy advocated here all support each other. Arms reduction is the best guarantee for the freedom of bloc association. The freedom of bloc association, in turn, is the best condition under which focused development can be applied. Focused development is necessary in order both to bring countries to take-off and to counter Communist expansion into the countries adjacent to the West, either under a system of arms reduction or if the arms race continues. But arms reduction is the best way to insure that the West could re-extend its development frontier once the neighboring countries have been developed, and that the uncommitted countries are free to seek Western aid after they have tried to obtain Soviet aid and were rejected (if the Soviets will also focus their development) or have realized that the thinned-out Soviet aid will get them nowhere (if the Soviets will not focus). Above all, freedom of the bloc associations provides the best way for the distribution of political freedoms as development provides the social foundations for democratization. Removing the interbloc armed barriers gives the Communists a chance to bring their case to all the people, unhampered; but it also gives the people of East Germany, East Europe, China, and Russia the chance to decide to what bloc they wish to belong, and, what is even more important to all concerned, what way of life they wish to pursue.

## Peace, Freedom, and Social Justice

Gradualism offers the world a slow, hard but safe way—I believe the only feasible one—out of the continuous slide into the thermonuclear furnace. I kept referring to "a settlement" in the first part of this volume, to be attained in the interbloc negotiations, to follow reduction of tensions through psychological Gradualism. The settlement I envision is not one in which all interbloc conflicts are resolved, but one that creates the condition under which this conflict can continue in a nonviolent way. This is the "settlement" that has to be reached: to "fight" it out, to test whose ideas, economic systems, and political structure are more effective and satisfying to mankind—without arms. This might even require the West to let some countries have a taste of what communism is like; and for the East to allow countries of its bloc to see how they feel under capitalism. Both sides should see no long-run harm in such experimentation as long as they believe in the virtue of their system, and the freedom to change one's political structure and bloc affiliation is maintained. Arms reduction, as discussed in detail above, is the only way to safeguard these freedoms. No verbal agreement, summit conference declaration, or change in the charter of the United Nations will provide the guarantees for such a new approach to the international life. Thus, arms reduction, which is vital for our very survival on this planet (or any other one), is also the best—probably the only—way to safeguard our evolution toward a better world. For the inter-bloc competition, whatever its dangerous side effects at the moment, has one great virtue. It brings political freedoms to those who lack it, and it makes for a redistribution of the global wealth and income in favor of the "have-not" countries, both processes of the highest human value in themselves, and at the same time it directly enhances the establishment of a global community and a viable, new United Nations. Thus, continuation of the interbloc competition is highly desirable as long as it can be safely curbed. Arms reduction will thus not only save our generation and our children from dying a horrible, unnatural death, but it also opens the way toward a better world, a world in which all men will be free, equal, and living in peace.

## Chapter 12

## Epilogue: Nuclear War II?

> *Who is the slayer, who the victim? Speak.*
>
> SOPHOCLES

### The Probability of Nuclear War

IF A COURSE like the one suggested here is not followed, the arms race will continue, and sooner or later a thermonuclear war will erupt. It could come about in several ways. First, the side losing in a limited war, fought with conventional arms, might pull the nuclear trigger. The West, which has fewer conventional arms and armies than the East, might lose a limited war, anywhere from South Vietnam to Iran, from West Berlin to Taiwan. Such a loss might generate strong pressure to use tactical atomic bombs the way they were almost used in Korea, and the way now recommended by various American military experts. The East might come under similar pressure if an advance of Western troops initiated extensive rebellions in the Soviet bloc that would seem to threaten its existence.

The expansion or "escalation" of limited war, although not a negligible threat, is also not the most likely cause of World

War III. Both sides might succeed in keeping limited wars under control, as they have done in interbloc skirmishes until now. It should also be pointed out that even if bombs are dropped, "only" the countries that participated in the limited war might suffer. It would not necessarily mean an all-out nuclear war.

More dangerous than the pressures to use atomic bombs to prevent or reverse a loss in a limited war are those that advocate changing the situation altogether by an all-out strike, attempting to annihilate America (or Russia) once and for all. The instruments for such a blow are being steadily perfected. The most likely direct cause for their use seems to be the accumulation of frustration caused by a sequence of setbacks by one side. We must remember how World War II started: the Germans were successful in one "limited" conquest after another, until finally another small conquest started the war.

In recent years, the American public and its leaders have felt an increasing sense of annoyance and frustration over growing Communist might—losses in Korea (which were actually rather small), Soviet leadership in space explorations, and leapfrogging. Each successive setback looks worse, and the feeling grows that "we must not let them do it again," that unless we "do something," the West will be nibbled to death. Another series of Communist successes might intensify the efforts of those who advocate a preventive war. The expectation of such a preventive strike—whether it is based on fact or on misinformation—is one possible cause for a Russian all-out pre-emptive attack. In turn, the possibility of such a Russian strike further strengthens the hand of the American advocates of preventive war.

Two major factors halt an all-out war at the moment. First, in the present situation, a preventive war is unlikely to succeed. To the best of our knowledge, an all-out attack at present would leave enough nuclear striking power in the East to cripple the United States, and vice versa. Second, the consideration of how many millions of men, women, and children would be killed in one blow certainly has an inhibiting effect.

There are conditions, however, under which both of these "brakes" might be released, and then *it will happen*. For one thing, a major technological breakthrough by one side will make a preventive blow rather certain, for it will be extremely unlikely that the other side will have a ready-made countermeasure. A device that would halt missiles in mid-air could serve this end. Such a technological breakthrough would leave between the finger and the trigger only the feeble, unreliable international conscience of political leaders—a conscience that, if not muffled enough as things are, would certainly be silenced, if only temporarily, by an increase in inter-bloc tension. Although an American might be sure that his president will never dare, he would agree that a Russian or Chinese might. And a Communist, of course, believes that America might initiate the attack.

## The Strategic Futility

Unless a strategy of the general nature of Gradualism is adopted, a nuclear war cannot be prevented; this raises a question that lies beyond the scope of this book: What comes after? We are still too frightened to look history in the eye and consider this question. We feel that if man is so low as to commit "nucleocide," he might as well perish, and that a thermonuclear war is so horrible that we should devote all our energy to preventing it. Thinking about what will come after is almost like accepting a nuclear war.

The fact is, however, that whether or not we "accept" it has little effect on the probability that nuclear war will erupt. Thus we cannot escape our responsibility as thinking human beings. What comes after?

The nuclear war will be a horrible, repulsive experience for mankind, in particular for the societies directly hit and their surviving neighbors. In its wake will come wide demands "to do something" to prevent "this" from happening again—a wave of sentiment of the kind that gave us the League of Nations after World War I and the United Nations after World War II. It is vital that this moment of sanity not be missed or misused, that we know how to act; if this chance is wasted again, a new arms race will follow the nuclear war just as it followed earlier wars. The result will be a new war, in which the large missiles and megaton nuclear bombs will be considered "conventional" arms. Eventually one giant war or the accumulation of small nuclear wars will actually put an end to the human race.

Much of what is to be done after Nuclear War I depends

upon the nature and outcome of Nuclear War I. The belief that we will all vanish if there is a nuclear war—and that we thus need not be concerned about the future—is as untrue as the often repeated statement that neither side will win. Although a total-annihilation war is, or is becoming, a possibility, Nuclear War I might have several other outcomes that must be considered.

1. If the war results from escalation of a limited conventional war and is limited to the countries in which conventional conflict has occurred, these nations and their neighbors may be devastated, but the superpowers will remain intact. (Both sides have shown a strong tendency to fight limited wars in other people's homelands.) An armistice after such hostilities would leave about the same barriers to lasting peace that we face today. For since mankind did not benefit from the experience of Hiroshima, it seems quite possible that a "small" nuclear war would not frighten the two sides enough to work out a settlement. Aside from the loss of a few countries, we would soon return to an interbloc arms race much like the present one.

2. A war that started as a consequence of accumulated frustration and a technological breakthrough, where an attempt is made to wipe out the enemy, or a war to prevent such an all-out attack, would directly involve the superpower homelands and is more likely to be "decisive." Unless complete annihilation results, which hardly requires consideration of the "after," such a war would lead to one of the following situations.

(a) *The heartlands of both sides might be devastated,* after which the international positions of the United States and the Soviet Union would be reduced to those of an Iceland and an Albania. The other nations, some undamaged, others partially devastated, might learn the lesson and establish a world government. Another possible outcome is the revival of an arms race between new partners—perhaps Communist China and a United States of Europe—and the repetition of "nucleocide." The second course seems more likely, since the prerequisites for world government would still be nonexistent after such a war, and the trauma of a nuclear war might not suffice to compensate for their absence.

(b) *Russia might succeed in crushing the United States without suffering more than limited damage itself* by halting

United States retaliation. This would probably lead to world occupation by the Red Army. The Communists have a rather clear image of world order; they have established one that covers a quarter of the world's area and a third of its population. Subordination to the Red Army in all countries would prevent them from fighting among themselves and from attacking Russia. In addition, the Red Army's presence would enforce general conformity to the World Communist Government.

It does not follow, however, that peace will reign forever in the Red world. Countries that have experienced a high standard of living, political freedoms, and strong anti-Communist values, like Canada and Western Europe, are likely to put up an intense guerrilla fight with conventional arms. With the population on their sides, and nuclear bombs particularly ineffective against this kind of warfare, these struggles might continue for a long time. The conquered nations will surely also prove highly resistant to control by indoctrination. Moreover, a war between Communist China and Russia over world leadership is far from inconceivable. If, however, Russia has the foresight to disarm all countries, including Communist China, immediately after such a war, to impose extensive inspection, and to grant relatively larger autonomy to the ex-democratic societies, the world might face a long period of no war and global integration under Communist domination.

(c) On the other hand, *the United States might wipe out the Soviet Union and halt much of its retaliation.*[1] Should this happen, an unanticipated peril might then present itself: that United States stature and preparedness will not be up to the high demands of its victory. When one tries to discover what Americans see as their responsibility in such a situation, one finds that extremely little thought is given to the subject. Typically, the most frequently cited study of the post-nuclear-war state, Kahn's *On Thermonuclear War*, depicts the United States busily building up its population and standard of living

[1] This outcome of an all-out nuclear war seems to be less likely than the opposite one, at least according to one rather reliable source: "Air Force planners put the strategic alternatives to their computers. All-out nuclear war was fought mathematically again and again on the machines—in terms of population distribution, bomb sizes, and defenses—each time with a different set of assumptions. And each time, no matter who struck first, with how much, against whatever possible preparations, the calculations showed that as long as cities were the targets, fifty-five to ninety per cent of Americans would die as against only twenty to thirty-five per cent of Russians." *The Reporter*, August 17, 1961, p. 21.

262

after such a war—it even suggests various preparations which ought to be made today to facilitate such activities—but offers no provisions to prevent new destruction once recuperation is completed.

The United States has no philosophy or image of a world government established by and under Western-American leadership. It is quite possible that after imposing some punishments on Russian "war criminals," demanding the disintegration of the Red Army (to free the "satellites"), insisting that all Communist countries conduct free elections and allow the sale of *Time* magazine and Coca-Cola, the American government will send the boys home, will dismantle the Western military machinery, and will retire to leave the forces of free enterprise and *laissez faire* to run their course. This would actually mean that armed nations would continue to populate the globe. Such a course could only lead sooner or later to a new arms race and war. While the Communist military bloc would be eliminated, and with it the immediate threat, the sociological conditions that created Communism and supported its expansion would remain. It is not far-fetched to expect a communist type of bloc to emerge again in less than a generation.

In the past, the United States, reluctantly and to a large degree despite itself, "became involved" (some American newspapers say "entangled") in commitments over half the world, which, we have seen, it is neither able nor willing to back with the necessary funds and intervention to insure development, democratization, and intrabloc peace. Moreover, these commitments are often viewed as temporary, as limited to the need to counter one particular threat—Communism—until it is somehow overcome. The necessity of establishing world order is not recognized.

But each bloc has only one power that commands the resources and manpower sufficient to establish a world order—a process that will require coercing of some nations. The superpower that survives Nuclear War I as a viable force will have a realistic chance to establish a world order. It will betray its historical mission, as well as its most elementary security interests, if it does not enforce global disarmament and establish a world government. I see no sign that the United States or the West will either recognize this need or live up to it.

Therefore *a nuclear war will not only wreak an unprecedented amount of destruction and death, but will, at the same time, be futile* (at least from a Western viewpoint). Nuclear war will either end in a draw (widely considered the most likely event), leaving both sides to prepare for the next round, or with Communist world domination (in which case we will be both Dead and Red), or the United States will come out victorious but unprepared to establish the kind of global security system that will prevent Nuclear War II and, for that matter, Nuclear Wars III, IV, and V—until either Communism wins or the radioactive clouds blanket everything. In other words, *whatever* the outcome of a nuclear war—a stalemate, Communist world government, or American victory—the war will have been futile or worse.

I cannot close these pages without expressing the hope that each man realizes in due time both the magnitude of mass murder and the futility of nuclear war, and that each does whatever he can to prevent it, by actively supporting a strategy that advocates that the West should:

—reduce unilaterally the cold war hysteria to see if the East and West cannot meet in fruitful negotiations;

—negotiate multilateral arms reduction (conventional first) with due inspection and safeguards;

—engage in focused development of a selected number of countries, starting with neighbors first and extending the development frontier as the amount and efficacy of available resources grows;

—encourage political freedoms everywhere in the West, in the "uncommitted" countries, and in the East, through nonviolent means;

—withdraw support from antidevelopment elites, tyrants, and colonial powers;

—work toward the long-run aim of global community through regional supranationalism, interbloc organizations, and the removal of barriers to interbloc shifting of countries, plus a change of both the United Nations organization and our attitude to it.

It is hard, but it can be done. No nation should be declared *prima facie* guilty of neglecting its historic mission, and drifting into nuclear hell just when the far-off gates of peace are becoming barely visible. The test of the free world, and in particular of the United States as its leading power, still lies ahead of us.

We are standing with one foot in a grave that is a hundred megatons deep; if we continue to dig, we will tumble in as surely as the bigger bombs follow the smaller ones. A last chance has been given; while we cannot leap out, we might gradually work our way up. We are not allowed to go on living on an earth populated with megaton bombs. We must choose between a new life—one of peace, freedom, and social justice—and the hard labor attaining it, or sooner or later our folly will lay us in the megaton grave.

# APPENDIX

## What the Bombs Can Do

by Leiba Brown and Ruth Leeds*

ADEQUATE and meaningful information about the effects of nuclear bombs is difficult to come by. Not only is much of it classified as military secrets, but such facts as are known are also given quite different interpretations. For example, Edward Teller's and Albert Latter's discussion of the effects of fall-out on life expectancy is such that our expectations of how long we might live remain unaltered:

> To see fallout radiation in proper perspective it should be compared not only with other kinds of radiation but also with other dangers to health. Some estimates are, for example, that being 10% overweight seems to reduce a person's life expectancy by 1.5 years, that the life-long habit of smoking one package of cigarettes a day cuts it by seven years, that living in the city instead of in the country reduces life expectancy by five years and so on. On this statistical scale the reduction in life expectancy from worldwide fallout at present levels is less than two days. Or . . . the worldwide fallout is as dangerous to human health as being one ounce overweight or smoking one cigarette every two months.[1]

At the other end of the emotional spectrum, Linus Pauling creates a tragedy out of this sanguinary view of the effects of fallout from nuclear testing:

> A decrease of two days in life expectancy might not be a serious matter if it meant that every person would die two days earlier than otherwise. But let us consider what death by leukemia or bone cancer or other disease means.

* Graduate students, Department of Sociology, Columbia University.
[1] Edward Teller and Albert Latter, "The Compelling Need for Nuclear Tests," *Life*, February 10, 1958.

One of the people of a group of 2500 may happen to have . . . one of his molecules damaged by fallout radiation in such a way as to cause him to die of leukemia or other disease, and the other 2499 might not be harmed at all by the fallout radiation. The first man may die 5000 days before he would have died if the bomb tests had not been made; his life expectancy will have been shortened by 14 years, and of the other 2499 not at all.

This amounts to an average decrease in life expectancy of two days per person. There are 2500 million people in the world, and if testing is continued, it may cause 1 million people . . . to die 10 or 15 or 20 years earlier than they would have if the bomb tests had not been carried out. We may say that we would be sacrificing 1 million people of the present generation to the bomb tests, if they were to be continued for another 24 years, and about 200,000 to the tests already made.[2]

The picture is further clouded by the difficulty of obtaining precise data on damage to be wrought by radiation. Laboratory experiments have enabled scientists to make precise calculations of the effects of varying amounts of radiation on rats. But these calculations yield only very gross estimates when applied to man, for man and rat differ in size, metabolism rate, life expectancy, and so on.

Finally, some of the clear, unambiguous facts are presented to make us chuckle at the foibles of man rather than sit up and take note of their portent. Thus, the *New Yorker*'s fever chart of the planet Earth, showing man's ups and downs in contaminating the air, the sea, and the soil informs us that crab grass has a very high resistance to radiation, being able to survive dosages as high as 6000 roentgens. (Pine trees, on the other hand, would die quickly under such adverse conditions.) A bloodsucker, politely referred to as a kissing bug and officially known as *Rhodinus prolixus,* is even tougher, being able to take up to 50,000 roentgens. But the survival trophy would have to be awarded to Speedwell or *Veronica officinalis:* to the genteel an herb, to the realist, a weed, which can sustain more than 100,000 units of radiation. Does this mean that following a

2 Linus Pauling, "Blessed Are the Peacemakers, But Not in Washington, D. C.," *I. F. Stone's Weekly,* February 24, 1958.

nuclear attack, once the processed food has been consumed, survivors will have to change their diet to weeds and bugs? Or does it mean that lower forms of life will once again inherit the earth?

Such factors as the foregoing might tempt us to hide from the reality of nuclear destruction because a sharp, serious portrait of the facts eludes us. But we cannot afford to ignore the issue until precise estimates and thoroughly tested, relevant facts come into focus. Detectives often make use of composite sketches to identify a suspect without a photograph. We, too, can benefit from a composite of gross estimates and partially validated data until such time as a clear picture becomes available.

## A Hypothetical Attack

The day is Friday, October 17, 1958. The target is your home, whether you live in New York, Seattle, San Diego, Peoria, or New Orleans. At 7:00 A.M., EST, about 1500 megatons of nuclear weapons, both A-bombs and H-bombs, were dropped on seventy-one urban areas and 153 other strategic targets scattered throughout the continental United States.[3]

We don't know what happened to you specifically when the payload was dropped, but we do know that approximately *twenty-three million Americans were killed on the day of the attack. About forty-seven million were injured. Less than nineteen million of the injured survived.*

Knowledge of the number of casualties answers only the immediate question. One might also ask how these seventy million persons met their deaths or sustained their injuries. What was the scope of the physical damage? What happened to the orderliness of society following the explosion? How far away must one have been from ground zero—the spot where the bomb exploded—to be safe? What happens to future generations? Is there any effective protection for the population? In short, what is the country like once the blinding flash has faded, the intense heat has cooled, the raging winds have blown themselves out, and the mushroom clouds have drifted to sea?

To consider just such questions, the Joint Committee on

[3] Joint Committee on Atomic Energy, Congress of the United States, *Biological and Environmental Effects of Nuclear War* (Washington, Government Printing Office, 1959).

Atomic Energy—better known as the Holifield committee—held Congressional hearings in June, 1959. The effects of a 1500-megaton payload described by military and scientific experts at these hearings form the basis for our account of the hypothetical attack.

## The Explosion and Its Effects

Instants after the bombs exploded at the earth's surface at each of the 224 target locations, balls of fire formed, emitting highly destructive thermal radiation. Nuclear reactions causing the explosions were accompanied by damaging radiation, much of which remained as part of the fall-out. Minutes after the explosion, a destructive shock wave formed in the air, moving rapidly away from the fireballs and leveling everything in its path. The fireballs excavated highly radioactive craters where they came to rest, and, as if they possessed a magic wand, all they touched vaporized.

### Effects on Physical Structures

*Blast Damage.* Throughout the country, a quarter of the homes—11,800,000 dwelling units—were completely demolished. Another eight million were badly damaged but could be made habitable again with major repairs. Still another 500,000 buildings sustained light damage. In buildings where total destruction had not reaped its toll, the shock wave broke gas lines and fuel tanks, upset stoves and furnaces, and short-circuited wiring, so that severe fire damage also resulted from the blast.

Thriving cities were reduced to rubble within seconds. When a ten-megaton bomb exploded in New York at Rockefeller Center, all buildings without steel supports, within a radius of seven and a half miles collapsed completely. Multistory brick apartment houses were mowed down. Wood-frame houses and stores within a nine-mile radius fell like the proverbial house of cards. Bridges within a three-and-a-half-mile zone were destroyed and, within ten miles, telephone and power lines were out of commission. In short, most buildings and communication and transportation networks, so vital for survival and evacuation, were demolished.

*Effects of Thermal Radiation.* The heat emitted by the fire

270

ball ignited most combustible materials within the destruction zone (up to twenty-five miles for a ten-megaton bomb). Any accessible paper, trash, window curtains, awnings and leaves caught fire immediately. Flames spread rapidly through the crowded wholesale districts and the slums. In some areas, depending on local weather and terrain, "fire storms" raged with unconquerable fury through woods and towns.

*Effects of the Crater.* Where the fireball touched the earth, it sucked up all beneath it, leaving a cavernous hole. All underground shelters, subways and other subterranean installations within the quarter-mile radius of the crater were destroyed, for the crater at its deepest was 240 feet.

*Effects of Fall-out.* Many buildings that were left standing were contaminated by radiation and thereby rendered temporarily useless for human purposes. The radioactive fall-out affected about thirteen million homes, making them uninhabitable for at least two months.

The physical damage caused by the attack, although far-reaching in its impact, did not turn the United States into the utter wasteland it became in Nevil Shute's *On the Beach.* Roughly one-third of the homes were still intact, and many of the roads could be used for travel. But our economic, political, cultural, religious, and medical centers, as well as our communications system, were ruined.

## EFFECTS ON MAN

Casualties caused by the impact of the air shock waves could not be isolated from deaths and injuries by fire and radiation. The blast directly hit persons close to ground zero, inflicting serious injury to lungs, stomach, intestines, eardrums, and the central nervous system. These same persons were also the most likely to be hit by flying debris, trapped by fire, or buried by collapsing buildings. Within a seven-mile radius of a ten-megaton burst, the secondary effects of blast accounted for many deaths.

*Thermal Effects.* Within a twenty-five mile radius of ground zero, any survivor who was out of doors when the bomb exploded sustained second-degree flash burns on his exposed skin. The thermal radiation ignited his clothing as well, causing severe flame burns. While the fire storms raged, many were trapped in burning buildings, suffocating from the inhalation of acrid fumes.

*Radiation Effects.* Nuclear radiation is measured in rems. A rem is that amount of radiation required to produce a biological effect equivalent to that of one roentgen of x-ray. A single dosage of up to 220 rems will cause nausea and vomiting for about a day, but it is not fatal. If a population is exposed to a dosage of 270 to 330 rems, about 20 per cent of the group will die within two to six weeks following exposure. The remaining 80 per cent will recover, following a three-month bout with radiation sickness. With a dosage of 550 rems or more, chances of survival are very slim, and recovery takes about six months for those few who do survive. A dosage of 1000 rems is virtually lethal.

The number of rems released in a nuclear explosion is determined by its location (air, surface, or underground) its tonnage, and its "cleanliness." The so-called clean nuclear warheads do not release enough energy to explode the highly destructive element, Uranium 238, but they do explode other elements that yield radioactive particles of Carbon 14 and Strontium 90. The "dirty" bombs, on the other hand, have the capacity to unleash Uranium 238. Once exploded, U-238 releases additional energy and an immense quantity of exceedingly poisonous fall-out. Thus, a "dirty" ten-megaton bomb gives off enough rems to kill a man within 140 miles of ground zero if he remains outside for thirty-six hours. The fifteen-megaton "superbomb" tested at Bikini in 1954 contained U-238, and its fall-out was responsible for the radiation sickness of the Japanese fishermen eighty miles from the test site. (Although the Congressional report on which our account is based did not state explicitly whether clean or dirty bombs were used, the weight of current reputable information suggests that most of the weapons tested, if not all, were dirty bombs. The report's fall-out statistics hold only for dirty bombs.)

The bombs the United States is likely to be bombed with will probably not be "clean," because Russia—as far as we know—does not know how to produce "clean" bombs, and the West refused to tell her how to "clean" them.

INITIAL NUCLEAR RADIATION EFFECTS. Each ten-megaton ex-

272

plosion instantaneously released 700 rem, covering a two-mile radius from ground zero. All unsheltered and unshielded persons within this area received a lethal dose of radiation. But anyone this close to ground zero was equally likely to succumb to blast or fire.

LOCAL FALL-OUT EFFECTS. Local fall-out is caused by those radioactive particles which descend to earth within several hundred miles of ground zero and within a few days of the explosion. Its damaging effects are greatly influenced by local weather, altitude, and terrain, and must be calculated separately for each region of the country.

Regardless of local conditions, the effects of fall-out were not felt immediately. The unsheltered and unshielded persons within 150 miles downwind from ground zero and within twenty-five miles of the crosswinds around the crater received at least 450 rems within forty-eight hours. These were the persons most likely to die or to be seriously ill for many months. But those who were able to spend the few days following the explosion indoors or could leave the areas vulnerable to fall-out had a good chance for survival, and, if taken ill, had a relatively quick recovery.

WORLDWIDE FALL-OUT. The effect of worldwide fall-out cannot be calculated precisely even for a specific set of conditions, with place, time, weather, altitude, terrain, density of buildings, and the like held constant. We do know that worldwide fall out leads to additional deaths by increasing a person's long-term susceptibility to such diseases as cancer. Long after the nuclear attack, then, the survivors continue to be exposed to additional radiation, which would eventually shorten the lives of some of them.

GENETIC EFFECTS. Approximately four out of 100 babies presently are born with defects, some of which were caused by damaged genes. To prevent an increase in the present 4 per cent rate of defective births, each person's gonads should sustain less than ten roentgens of radiation during his first thirty years of life, and no more than ten roentgens during each succeeding decade. Should radiation dosages increase on a mass scale, so that every American receives the ten-roentgen limit, the rate of defective births would increase by four per thousand in the first generation and by four per hundred in future generations.

The amount of cumulative radiation experienced by each of the survivors of the October 17 nuclear attack was about 250 to 500 roentgens. If we assume that genetically defective births increase at the same rate as the increase in exposure to radiation, then the rate of defective births would increase by at least 25 per cent. Furthermore, the genes damaged by fall-out would continue to be inherited by the next twenty to forty generations, carrying the curse of fall-out from generation to generation until we all are remembered only as the children-torturer generation.

## How Far Away Is "Safe"?

When we played hide-and-seek as children, the closer to base we hid, the easier it was to come home safely. But in a nuclear bombardment, as the figures in Table 1 indicate, "safe" is relatively far from ground zero.

Table 1

THE DISTANCE TO SAFE TERRITORY

Figures are estimates, calculated on the basis
of weather conditions for October 17, 1958

| Effect | Distance from Ground Zero | |
| --- | --- | --- |
| | One Megaton | Ten Megatons |
| *Inanimate objects* | | |
| Crater (dry soil) | Radius 650 feet Depth 140 feet | Radius 1250 feet Depth 240 feet |
| Brick apartment houses collapse | Radius 3 miles | Radius 7 miles |
| Ignition of light kindling materials | Radius 9 miles | Radius 25 miles |
| *Man* | | |
| Blast injury (flying debris) | Radius 3 miles Area 28 square miles | Radius 7 miles Area 150 square miles |
| Second degree burns on bare skin | Radius 9 miles Area 250 square miles | Radius 25 miles Area 2000 square miles |
| Initial nuclear radiation (700 rem) | Radius 1½ miles Area 7 square miles | Radius 2 miles Area 12½ square miles |
| Fallout: 15 knot winds (450 rem in 48 hours), no shielding | 40 miles downwind 5 miles crosswinds Area 200 square miles | 150 miles downwind 25 miles crosswinds Area 2500 square miles |

Let us suppose Rockefeller Center was ground zero for a ten-megaton bomb. To be safe from initial nuclear radiation, one would have to be at least as far downtown as the garment district, or as far uptown as the Museum of Natural History, or as far across town as the other side of the East River. To escape falling buildings and flying debris, one would have to be at least as far as the Bronx Zoo, the Statue of Liberty, or Forest Hills. To be spared second-degree burns, one would have to be as distant as Jones Beach or Greenwich, Connecticut. For safety from local fall-out, one would have to be in Rutland, Vermont, or Fort Ticonderoga, New York, to the north, or Lewistown, Pennsylvania, to the west, or the Atlantic Ocean to the east. One would not be safe south of New York, for then one would suffer the effects of the bombs dropped on Philadelphia, Baltimore, and Washington, D. C.

If one were in Rutland, Lewistown, or Ticonderoga, one would probably escape direct personal injury. The likelihood of getting radiation sickness from local fall-out is comparatively slight. Moreover, if one's home is in one of these towns, it will be untouched by blast or fire. But a "safe" distance from ground zero by no means assures immunity from the effects of nuclear war. The lucky people live in one of those towns not hit, out of the blow of the fall-out-carrying winds, and are not on a business trip or vacation in a target area when the bombs come. That is, such persons' bone structure and tissues will not suffer, but they will still never be the same again. Less fortunate relatives—perhaps brothers, sisters, parents—will have perished in a thermonuclear cloud; many millions of one's fellow citizens will have vanished; America will be lying in ruins. Actually, a survivor might not consider himself lucky at all.

## Recent Development

The Atomic Energy Committee account of the hypothetical attack, based on the technology and stockpiles of 1959, is already obsolescent. Today the talk is of neutron bombs and superbombs rather than of the ten-megaton bombs that figured in our hypothetical attack. With the recent resumption of nuclear testing by the Soviet Union and the United States, these monstrous bombs are more likely to become an ominous reality in the near future. So all the estimates of 1959—how many people will be killed? How many injured? The scope of physical damage? The distance to "safety"?—are far too optimistic.

## THE NEUTRON BOMB

The neutron bomb produces a hydrogen explosion by a fusion reaction which is not triggered by an antecedent fission reaction. The fusion process results in a lethal burst of fast neutrons, *which destroys all life in the target area.* Blast, heat, and fall-out, on the other hand, are by-products of the fission-fusion reaction, and thus would be minimal in a neutron-bomb explosion. People will die rather than burn, and most property will remain intact.

To build such a fissionless hydrogen bomb, extremely high temperatures are required. The techniques for achieving these temperatures have not been mastered at this writing, although most scientists agree that the bomb is feasible in principle, and we might expect to have it soon enough.

## SUPERBOMBS

The term "superbomb" specifically refers to a payload of 100 megatons, or one million tons of TNT, although the term has been used at times to designate any bomb of megaton range. Experts are not all agreed on the strategic merits of a 100-megaton bomb. Arguments have been put forth that five twenty-megton bombs can work more damage than one superbomb, that neither side has a target large enough to justify the use of 100 megatons, and that the means of delivering such a large bomb have not yet been developed.

Atomic scientists in the Pentagon estimate that a 100-megaton bomb would work total destruction within twelve miles of ground zero. *Half the population within the twelve- to twenty-mile zone from ground zero would be annihilated immediately.* The fall-out danger area would encompass approximately 20,000 square miles. Table 2 summarizes the destructive capabilities of bombs with varying megatonnage.

Table 2 shows that an increase in megatonnage does not lead to corresponding increases in blast and in thermal and radiation effects. But this should not lead to an underestimation of the superbomb, for its incendiary capabilities more than rival the

Table 2

| Megatons | Total Destruction Zone | Partial Destruction Zone | Fall-out Zone |
|---|---|---|---|
| 10 | 3-mile radius | 3- 7 miles | 2,500 square miles |
| 20 | 6 miles | 6-12 miles | 5,000 square miles |
| 100 | 12 miles | 12-20 miles | 20,000 square miles |

proverbial hellfires. The Atomic Energy Commission predicts that a 100-megaton bomb could unleash a firestorm which would cover 11,300 square miles, or an area which is larger than the state of Vermont.[4]

The Russians have only said that they could build super-bombs shortly before they resumed testing in 1961; Americans countered that they could do the trick too. How many super-bombs there are by now, or on order, and when delivered, is not public knowledge.

One thing is clear. The bombs constantly grow more powerful and more devastating. The chances of surviving nuclear attack grow slimmer. Weapons development might finally reach a point where there is no longer any "safe" distance from ground zero, and where no segment of the population will be able to escape destruction. There has already been mention of multigigaton bombs, dubbed by Russell Baker of *The New York Times* as "Doomsday in the big economy package." Little appears to be known to the public about this gigantic bomb, capable of an explosive force comparable to billions of tons of TNT, except that both the Soviet Union and the United States could build them if they so desire by 1968.

## Postscript, December, 1961: New Superbombs

The first part of this account was written in April, 1961. By the time it was set in type it needed to be revised. New facts made public and the development of weapons made earlier estimates of devastation both obsolete and overoptimistic. Then came the Russian tests that turned the horror story of 50-megaton bombs into part of our report about facts. When we saw the galley proofs from the press in December, 1961, we found that our report was again lagging; a whole new generation of super-bombs is reported in the making. Surely by the time these pages

[4] *New York Times*, October 2, 1961.

reach you, larger means of destruction will have been produced, though clearly we have not far to go. Almost-Doomsday-bombs, bombs that can wipe the globe clean, are already proceeding from the blueprint to the production stage.

## EFFECTS OF A 50-MEGATON PAYLOAD[5]

A 50-megaton explosion would wipe out entire regions and their populations through massive fire damage far exceeding the heavy destruction wreaked by blast alone. Blast would obliterate the central target area. If the bomb were exploded in the air, the blast would level all but the very heaviest concrete buildings within a radius of 2.75 miles and destroy most homes within a 14-mile zone. Suppose Manhattan were the target. The borough would be demolished in an instant, and the rest of New York City and Newark would be damaged beyond repair. Houses would be toppled by the pressure wave as far away as Passaic, New Jersey.

Thermal damage, however, would not only be more extensive, but could spread very widely. Houses would be ignited within a 35-mile zone, and for an additional ten miles out the thermal radiation would start spontaneous fires in dried leaves, trash, and other combustible materials. The simultaneous fires might well be swept up in a massive firestorm, leaving the entire zone and the areas far beyond it in ashes. This means that small suburban centers—White Plains, New York, or Lakewood, New Jersey, for example—would be engulfed in flames, and outlying towns such as West Point, New York, would be the seat of multiple fires at the least.

Persons exposed to the thermal radiation within a 49-mile radius would suffer fatal third-degree burns. The initial radiation dosage would average 700 roentgens—enough to kill nearly all exposed individuals.

Different effects would be maximized if the bomb were exploded at the earth's surface. The fireball would scoop out a crater one mile wide and several hundred feet deep. Within this area all life and all physical structures would be vaporized, including hardened deep underground installations and their inhabitants. The burst would create intense fall-out covering

[5] Based on a report in the *New York Times,* October 31, 1961.

278

more than 10,000 square miles downwind from the target, and the area would remain contaminated for years.

## NEW SUPERBOMBS[6]

The 50-megaton bomb represents only a small step in the direction of building bombs that could destroy regions and nations in one nuclear strike. Theoretically, there is no limitation on the size bomb that can be built. By wrapping a blanket of uranium around a fission-fusion bomb, for example, the total force of a superbomb explosion can be greatly multiplied. Less expensive bombs might use a blanket of sodium oxide or cobalt around a detonator set at one end of a pipe of heavy water. The new superbombs include the following:

*Nuclear Mines.* Heavy-water bombs with a boron blanket could be used as sea mines to raise a tidal wave 100 feet high and 200 miles from the point where the mine was buried at a depth of two miles. The wave would then engulf and destroy a large coastal region.

*Sodium-oxide Bomb.* A bomb containing 1,000 tons of heavy water could contaminate an area of 200,000 square miles with radiation. If only one-tenth of the sodium fall-out returned to earth in the stricken area, the average radiation dose would be a million roentgens. Any person receiving this dosage would collapse within 10 minutes. Animal and plant life would be destroyed, and the scene of the devastated country would be as bleak as the surface of the moon. In practically all forms of shelter no protection would be possible. The effects of remote fall-out for neighboring continents would be negligible, since radioactive sodium-24 decays relatively quickly.

*Cobalt-60 Bomb.* A superbomb with a blanket of Cobalt-60 and containing a large amount of U-238 could result in a close-range lethal fall-out covering an area as large as the continental United States. It is estimated that the neutrons obtainable from 2,500 tons of heavy water could produce enough Cobalt-60 to give a dose of 10,000 roentgens over the whole earth. Over a long period of time, only half this dosage would be required to kill all exposed persons who did not have access to a shelter over several years.

[6] Based on W. H. Clark, "Chemical and Thermonuclear Explosives," *Bulletin of the Atomic Scientists,* November, 1961, pp. 356–360.

Doomsday bombs are still in the realm of theory and estimates at this writing, but the 50-megaton bomb is a stark, terrifying reality. The much discussed 100-megaton bomb represents the next step, and it, too, may already be a reality. If even bigger bombs emerge from blueprints to the operational stage, we face the grim prospect that the existence of mankind will depend on this condition: that all those who have access to the Doomsday trigger will refrain from pulling it.

# INDEX

281